SpringerBriefs in Information Systems

Series Editor

Jörg Becker

For further volumes:
http://www.springer.com/series/10189

Tim A. Majchrzak

Improving Software Testing

Technical and Organizational Developments

 Springer

Tim A. Majchrzak
Institut für Wirtschaftsinformatik
Westfälische Wilhelms-Universität
Leonardo Campus 3
48149 Münster
Germany

ISSN 2192-4929   e-ISSN 2192-4937
ISBN 978-3-642-27463-3   e-ISBN 978-3-642-27464-0
DOI 10.1007/978-3-642-27464-0
Springer Heidelberg New York Dordrecht London

Library of Congress Control Number: 2011946088

Printed on acid-free paper

Springer is part of Springer Science+Business Media (www.springer.com)

For Imke

Foreword

We are delighted to announce a new series of the SpringerBriefs: SpringerBriefs in Information Systems. SpringerBriefs is a well-established series that contains concise summaries of up-to-date research with a practical relevance across a wide spectrum of topics with a fast turnaround time to publication. The series publishes small but impactful volumes with a clearly defined focus. Therefore, readers of the new series are able to get a quick overview on a specific topic in the field. This might cover case studies, contextual literature reviews, state-of-the art modeling techniques, news in software development or a snapshot on an emerging topic in the field.

SpringerBriefs in Information Systems present research from a global author community and allow authors to present their ideas in a compact way and readers to gain insights into a specific topic with minimal time investment. With succinct volumes of 50–125 pages, SpringerBriefs are shorter than a conventional book but longer than an average journal article. Thus, publishing research in the Springer-Briefs series provides the opportunity to bridge the gap between research results already published in journal articles or presented on conferences and brand new research results.

Information Systems research is concerned with the design, development and implementation of information and communication systems in various domains. Thus, SpringerBriefs in Information Systems give attention to the publication of core concepts as well as concrete implementations in different application contexts. Furthermore, as the boundary between fundamental research and applied research is more and more dissolving, this series is particularly open to interdisciplinary topics.

SpringerBriefs are an integral part of the Springer Complexitiy publishing program and we are looking forward to establishing the SpringerBriefs in Information Systems series as a reference guide for Information Systems professionals in academia and practice as well as students interested in latest research results.

The volume at hand is the first SpringerBriefs in Information Systems. It presents the work of Tim A. Majchrzak on software testing. The outline is exemplary for the intended scope: Not only a literature-driven introduction to software testing is given but also results from three current research topics are summarized and their future implications sketched.

Münster, January 2012   Jörg Becker

Preface

In spite of the increasing complexity of software, clients expect improvements in its quality. In order to enable high-quality software in this context, the tools and approaches for testing have to be reconsidered. This Brief summarizes technical as well as organizational aspects of testing. For the latter, an empirical study of best practices for testing has been conducted. As a result, a set of recommendations has been formulated, which help to organize the testing process in a company while taking into account parameters such as its size. It turns out that companies test very differently. While some (typically larger) companies have installed well established testing procedures and use state of the art tools e.g. in order to automate testing as far as possible, other (often smaller) companies test on an ad-hoc basis without predefined processes and with little tool support. In particular, the latter can benefit from the best practices formulated in this book. This part is particularly interesting for practitioners.

From a technical perspective, this Brief presents a new way for generating so-called glass-box test cases automatically. The approach is based on a symbolic execution of Java bytecode by a symbolic Java Virtual Machine (JVM). The latter is an extension of the usual JVM by components known from abstract machines for logic programming languages such as the Warren Abstract Machine. In particular, it contains a trail, choice points, and logic variables and it uses a system of constraint solvers. The symbolic JVM systematically follows all relevant computation paths and generates a set of test cases ensuring a predefined coverage of the control and data flow of the tested software. This part of the Brief is particularly interesting for researchers working on testing.

A third part shows how the mentioned test-case generator can be profitably used in an E-assessment system which automatically corrects Java classes uploaded by students. The test cases are generated from an example solution and serve as a measure for evaluating the correctness of the uploaded solutions to programming exercises. This approach has been successfully applied in a practical programming course. Corresponding experimental results are given.

This Brief is an extract of the PhD thesis of the author. It gives a concise overview of the mentioned aspects with many references to the relevant literature. It is interesting for practitioners as well as researchers. For studying the most interesting aspects in depth, a look into the mentioned literature is recommended.

Münster, December 2011   Herbert Kuchen

Acknowledgments

This book is based on my PhD thesis. In fact, it contains the revised first part of the thesis, which introduces the research topics that I dealt with, sketches its background, and thereby summarizes the body of knowledge of software testing. Therefore, I would like to thank again those people that supported me in the preparation of the thesis.

In particular, I am grateful for support by Prof. Dr. Herbert Kuchen, Prof. Dr. Jörg Becker, and Prof. Dr. Ulrich Müller-Funk who were the members of my doctoral committee. As my advisor, Herbert Kuchen also provided invaluable support that contributes to the quality of the content provided in this book. Moreover, he and Jörg Becker kindly wrote the foreword and the preface.

Feedback on the thesis manuscript was provided by Dr. Philipp Ciechanowicz, Prof. Dr.-Ing. Marco K. Koch, Thomas Majchrzak, Martin Matzner, Claus Alexander Usener, and Imke Wasner. Imke, my wife, also soothed me when ludicrous LaTeX package incompatibilities decelerated my progress. In the end, feedback and support are also reflected in this book. Thank you!

With regard to this Briefs volume I would like to thank Christian Rauscher from Springer-Verlag who comprehensively answered all my questions concerning the manuscript preparation and the publication process.

Münster, December 2011   Tim A. Majchrzak

Contents

Abbreviations

.NET	Microsoft .NET framework
ABS	Anti-lock braking system
ACM	Association for Computing Machinery
AI	Artificial intelligence
Ajax	Asynchronous JavaScript and XML
APA	American Psychological Association
API	Application programming interface
B2B	Business-to-business
B2G	Business-to-government
CASE	Computer aided software engineering
CAST	Computer aided software testing
CF	Control flow
CFG	Control flow graph
CLI	Common Language Infrastructure
CMMI	Capability Maturity Model Integration
CobiT	Control Objectives for Information and Related Technology
CPU	Central processing unit
CS	Computer science
CSTE	Certified software tester
DU	Def-use
EASy	E-Assessment System
ERCIS	European Research Center for Information Systems
ESC	Electronic stability control
FMEA	Failure mode and effects analysis
FMECA	Failure mode and effects and criticality analysis
FPP	Fredge Program Prover
GTB	German Testing Board
GUI	Graphical user interface
HCI	Human–computer interaction
I/O	Input/output
IAI	Institut für Angewandte Informatik

IDE	Integrated development environment
IEEE	Institute of Electrical and Electronics Engineers
IHK	Industrie- und Handelskammer
IoC	Inversion of control
IS	Information system
ISO	International Organization for Standardization
ISTQB	International Software Testing Qualifications Board
IT	Information technology
ITIL	IT infrastructure library
JIST	Journal of Information Science and Technology
JJ-path	Jump-to-jump path
JNI	Java native interface
JRE	Java Runtime Environment
JSR	Java Specification Request
JVM	Java virtual machine
LCSAJ	Linear code sequence and jump
LOC	Lines of code
MiB	Mebibyte, i.e. 2^{20} bytes
Muggl	Muenster generator of glass-box test cases
MVC	Model-view-controller
RE	Requirements engineering
ROI	Return on investment
RUP	Rational Unified Process
SE	Software engineering
SI	International system of units (Système international d'unités)
SJVM	Symbolic Java virtual machine
SMT	Satisfiability modulo theory
STQC	Standardisation Testing and Quality Certification
SWEBOK	Software Engineering Body of Knowledge
TCG	Test case generation
TDD	Test driven development
TMap	Test Management Approach
TPI	Test Process Improvement
TQM	Total Quality Management
UML	Unified Modeling Language
VM	Virtual machine
vs.	Versus
w.r.t.	With respect to
W3C	World Wide Web Consortium
XML	Extensible Markup Language
XP	Extreme Programming

Chapter 1
Introduction

In the following sections, this book's topic is introduced, objectives and research questions are discussed, and the course of action is sketched. First of all, the setting for software testing is described.

1.1 The Software Crisis

Since the advent of computers, the available computational power and the capacity of memory and storage systems have grown exponentially [1, 2]. At the same time, computer systems decreased in size and their prices plummeted. But it was software that made the vast computational power operational. Software enables humans to take advantage of general purpose computers for distinct applications in business, science, communications, specialized fields such as healthcare, and entertainment.

In the 1960s, the costs of developing software for the first time became higher than the costs of developing the corresponding hardware. As a consequence, the discipline *software engineering* was installed [3]. In 1972, Dijkstra eventually coined the term *software crisis* [4] which summarizes the observed phenomena. Software grows in size and complexity. This development is exacerbated by the fact that the increase in computational power demands more complex software in order to be utilized. Furthermore, the introduction of the Internet added more complexity. While programmers formerly had to care for local resources and how a program ran on a single computer, nowadays its embedding into a network and possible connections to a myriad of services have to be kept in mind.

Unfortunately, it can be observed that the software crisis is lasting as impressively demonstrated by the shift to *multicore* (or even *manycore* [5]) computer architectures [6]. In theory, the computational power of a central processing unit (CPU) (almost) doubles when doubling the number of cores. While there are hardware limitations for this rate and some overhead has to be taken into account, most software today is written sequentially. Despite some attempts, such as the release

T. A. Majchrzak, *Improving Software Testing*, SpringerBriefs in Information Systems,
DOI: 10.1007/978-3-642-27464-0_1, © The Author(s) 2012

of conveniently usable libraries (e.g. [7]), programming for multicore systems is not common; means to convert existing software in order to allow effective utilization of multiple cores are not yet satisfying. As a consequence, the misalignment between computational power and easy means of using it deteriorates. Until better ways have been found, programming for multicore computers will be burdensome. Programs that entirely utilize more than one core remain to be costly. It is unlikely that many programmers will use adequate programming techniques; in fact, it will stay a domain for experts and researchers [8].[1]

The software crisis has two main consequences. Firstly, software development projects exceed the calculated costs, the developed software lacks specified functionality and has inferior quality, or projects fail completely [9]. Secondly, possible amenities are not realized. It is either not feasible to write software for a desired task due to the inherent complexity of it, or the effort of development and the possibility of failure is avoided since the risks are considered to be too high. Both consequences result in increased costs and less welfare in an economic sense. Therefore, finding ways of effectively using software is very important.

Whereas it is impossible to quantitatively assess the missed welfare, studies document project failure. These studies underline that there were not only some large projects that failed but that irregularities seem to be inherent to software development. Reports of problems of varying severity can be found for any kind of project, for any industrial sector it has been conducted in, and for any project size [10]. Stories of failure easily fill up full books [11–13]. Some (almost) failed projects have extensively been studied by the literature (cf. [14, Chap. 1] [15, Chap. 2]). A prominent example is the software for the modernization of US taxing authorities (Internal Revenue Service). With a delay of 8 years and a loss of (at least) 1.6 billion USD it can be seen as one of the worst failures in the history of software development [15, p. 140ff.] [16, p. 1].

There are many more examples of projects that failed. Unfortunately, some failures endangered the live of humans or even lead to fatalities. The introduction of a new system for registering and dispatching emergency calls in London has been thoroughly studied. When the system was activated in October 1992, it did not properly work. Emergency calls were delayed and ambulances reached patients too late. The problems with the new system have been attributed for up to 30 fatalities [17, 18]. Despite administrative failures that caused the problems [19], it also was a technical disaster. Whereas it is good to know that lessons have been learned from such incidents [20], it has to be asked why they cannot be avoided beforehand. In retrospective, it seems like "good engineering practice had been ignored, every guideline of software engineering disregarded" and "basic management principles neglected" [21]. With a closer look, however, it has to be said that it apparently was a systematic

---

[1] Of course, there is much progress and the number of programs that effectively and efficiently use multicores increases. However, research often is fundamental and there is no programming paradigm that would allow to program for multicore computers as convenient as it is to write sequential programs.

problem "common to many software development projects" and it happened in a context that is "far from atypical" [21].

Even quantitative studies report high rates of projects that exceeded the budget or the assigned time, or that were aborted. Mayr has compiled an overview of seven studies from 1994 to 2009. The highest rate of successful projects is reported just as 32% (with the lowest finding being 16%); budget or time exceeding projects make up 44–63% of all projects; 18–31% of all projects fail [22].

Some of the cited studies have been target of criticism [23–25]. Nevertheless, the overall results could not be falsified [25]. In spite of the variety of the results, the general conclusion of the studies is that at least 2/3 of all software development projects encounter at least less severe problems. This number might be much too high [26] [15, p. 6f.],[2] but it remains without question that not meeting a development project's aims is an expectation rather than a rare occurrence. Even among authors that have a positive view and acknowledge that software quality in general has improved over the last years, it is agreed that no satisfying level has been reached, yet [28]. It is hence not surprising to find recent studies that examine why software development companies fail [29].

1.2 Why Test Software?

Even though software development projects fail on a daily basis, problems that arise in specific projects are primarily noticed by the public. Most failed projects are business-to-business (B2B) projects and, therefore, just noticed by people who work for the affected businesses, who are working as business analysts, or are employed in the software industry. Projects, however, that are governmentally driven, or receive a high scientific interest, are likely to be observed by the public and to receive media attention. If problems occur, the public gets a negative impression because it fears the "waste" of taxpayer money [in case of business-to-government (B2G) projects], because it feels deceived about the risks, or because a project is seen emotionally (such as space missions).

Prominent and well-studied examples of projects that nurture the public's image of unreliable software are the crash of the *Ariane 5* rocket on its first flight [30], and the loss of *NASA Mars Climate Orbiter* [31]. Examples from Germany are the long-delayed road charge-project *Toll Collect* [32–35] and the electronic health insurance card ("Elektronische Gesundheitskarte") [36–38].

Project failure often is a consequence of mismanagement. In general, software development is prone to underestimating the required effort. Having a closer look at projects however reveals that neglecting software testing or ill-conducted tests are part of the problems or even the main cause; especially it has to be noted that some

---

[2] More "systematic approaches to assessing and aggregating research outcomes in order to provide a balanced and objective summary of research evidence" have been demanded to address empirical studies in software engineering [27].

failures could have been prevented if the software had been *tested* more thoroughly. This argument can be supported with the two examples mentioned below:

- The first flight of Ariane-5 (flight number V88) ended after only 40 s. The rocket changed its course due to software malfunction. Shortly after leaving its course, it was automatically destroyed. The problem was tracked down to reusing software from its predecessor. It had worked smoothly in Ariane 4 but was transferred to Ariane 5 without re-assessing it, without simulating its functions with predicted data from Ariane 5, and without testing it. Due to different flight characteristics, the software encountered data which it did not expect, malfunctioned, and caused the rocket to leave its course. This activated self-destruction which avoided an uncontrolled flight and crash [39, 40].
- Mars Climate Orbiter's mission was to inspect climatic conditions in the atmosphere of Mars. In September 1999 it was destroyed due to atmospheric stresses and friction after its attempt to orbit the planet. Climate Lander should enter the orbit at about an altitude of 150 km; however, it tried to orbit at 57 km which is far too near. The problem was caused by a simple software problem: Lockheed Martin, a supplier for the systems of Climate Lander, used imperial units instead of the units from the international system of units (SI). Since no conversion was intended, the imperial units were taken as SI units and consequent calculations lead to course corrections that eventually brought the Climate Lander into the fatal position [41, 42].

The deficits that lead to both problems could have been detected by software testing. In particular, they would not even have required sophisticated analysis but merely the execution of test cases with realistic data. Finding the defects could have saved an immense amount of money—but testing is worth the effort even if failure does not mean a nine-digit loss of money (in USD or EUR) as typically found in space travel projects. This also has been observed by the technicians responsible for Ariane 5; the aftermath of the incident included the static code analysis of 90,000 lines of code (LOC) of Ada that constitutes the systems [43].

Many complex systems fail due to not exhaustingly tested software [44]. Software testing as a main part of the development process is, therefore, essential for the successful production of high quality software. It is by no means a subordinate task but intellectually challenging [14, p. 84]. Improving the quality of software is very important [45] and is the underlying aim of all research compiled in this book. When researching software testing, (at least) two particularities should be kept in mind:

1. Despite decades of research spent on software testing,[3] no definite solutions have been found. No silver bullet has yet been found [49]. Therefore, new and unusual approaches should be tried while learning from the existing ones.
2. Similar to *Wirth's Law* [50] it can be argued that software systems grow faster in size and complexity than methods to handle complexity are invented [51].

---

[3] Besides some previous works, testing has been recognized since the 1970s [46]. The first book on software testing was arguably written by Hetzel [47]. Testing formerly meant to check whether software matches its requirements; it then became the search for defects [48].

Testing software is no mere economic obligation. Several cases describe software problems that caused harm to humans [52], and "risks to the public" have continuously reported by the Association for Computing Machinery (ACM) [53–56]. This is very tragic and underlines the need to increase software quality and to align it with the criticality a system has. It has been found that system failure has a serious impact on society [57]. Testing can help to avoid such failure. It even is argued that preventing software from harming humans is an ethical obligation [58].

Software development projects that encounter troubles are not doomed to fail [59, 60]; in the remainder of this book it will be shown that software testing is one way to prevent failure and to counter problems. A *culture of testing* [51, 61] will contribute to strategies that lower the risk of development projects.

1.3 Objectives and Research Questions

This book aims at fulfilling several objectives. It

- illustrates the importance of software testing,
- gives an overview of software testing that is comprehensive in scope yet concise in description,
- summarizes a recent research thread on technical aspects of software testing, in particular on the development of the tool Muggl,
- summarizes a recent research thread on organizational aspects of software testing, in particular the project "Softwaretests" with the Institut für Angewandte Informatik (IAI) and the Industrie—und Handelskammer (IHK) Nord Westfalen (shortly named IHK project),
- summarizes a recent research thread on the combination of e-learning, in particular e-assessment, and testing,
- draws a conclusion, and
- describes open research questions.

From these objectives, a number of research questions can be drawn:

1. By which technical means is the automated creation of test cases possible?
2. How can the state space explosion encountered in tools for the automated test case generation be controlled?
3. Is it possible to support software developers and testers in working with automatically generated test cases?
4. How do companies test software and how successful are they in doing so?
5. Is it possible to explicate the implicit knowledge that companies have of optimizing software testing processes and setting up a suitable technical background for testing?
6. How can explicated knowledge be prepared in a form that makes it accessible for practitioners?
7. Can theoretical knowledge be derived from this explicated knowledge?

8. How can lectures in computer science be supported by e-assessment?
9. Is it possible to combine technical work on software testing with other subjects of information system (IS) research?
10. How can such combinations look like and what are the experiences with them?

Questions 1–3 are addressed in the research on technical aspects of software testing in Chap. 4 (p. 71ff.); questions 4–7 are answered in the work on organizational aspects of software testing in Chap. 5 (p. 95ff.); questions 8–10 are exemplarily answered for the field of e-assessment in Chap. 6 (p. 111ff.).

1.4 Structure of the Book

Chapter 2 introduces software testing; key notions and key concepts are explained. Moreover, different kinds of testing are highlighted, and it is suggested how to classify the field of testing. A rough introduction of the underlying research design is given in Chap. 3.

Chapters 4, 5, and 6 describe the results of the research on technical and organizational aspects of testing as well as on testing and e-assessment. The three chapters are structured in the same way. First, the background is explained and related work by other authors is highlighted. Then, a recent research thread that contributed to the field is discussed. Eventually, an overview of published work of this thread is given.

In Chap. 7 a conclusion is drawn by first summarizing the book, then compiling the lessons learned, and by finally discussing the findings in consideration of the limitations and boundaries of the included work. Future work both with regard to the author's activities and to open research questions is described in Chap. 8.

The citation style in this book follows the computer science style with numbered labels. Where applicable and helpful, page numbers or chapters of citations are given for book and book-like publications. Page numbers are given if direct citations are used or a statement is found on a specific page; chapters are preferred if a statement is embedded into a broader context.

For style and uniformity the first-person singular personal pronoun (I) is avoided in the remainder of this work. The same applies to its objective and possessive forms. In most applicable cases, passive forms or the first-person plural (we) are used. This is used to honor that scientific progress is a *joint effort*.

References

1. Moore, G.E.: Cramming more components onto integrated circuits. Electronics **38**(8), 114–117 (1965)
2. Schaller, R.R.: Moore's law: past, present, and future. IEEE Spectr. **34**(6), 52–59 (1997)
3. Naur, P., Randell, B.: Software Engineering: Report of a Conference Sponsored by the NATO Science Committee, Garmisch, Germany. Scientific Affairs Division, NATO (1969)

4. Dijkstra, E.W.: The humble programmer. Commun. ACM **15**, 859–866 (1972)
5. Held, J.: Foreword. Intel Technol. J. **13**(4) (2009)
6. Held, J., Bautista, J., Koehl, S.: From a Few Cores to Many: a Tera-scale Computing Research Overview. White paper, Intel (2006)
7. Ciechanowicz, P., Kuchen, H.: Enhancing Muesli's data parallel skeletons for multi-core computer architectures. In: 12th IEEE International Conference on High Performance Computing and Communications (HPCC), pp. 108–113. IEEE, Washington, DC (2010)
8. Fuller, S.H., Millett, L.I.: Computing performance: Game over or next level? Computer **44**(1), 31–38 (2011)
9. Charette, R.N.: Why software fails. IEEE Spectr. **42**(9), 42–49 (2005)
10. Flowers, S.: Software Failure: Management Failure: Amazing Stories and Cautionary Tales. Wiley, New York (1996)
11. Glass, R.L.: In the Beginning: Recollections of Software Pioneers. IEEE Computer Society Press, Los Alamitos (1997)
12. Glass, R.L.: Computing Calamities: Lessons Learned From Products, Projects, and Companies That Failed. Prentice Hall, Upper Saddle River (1999)
13. Glass, R.L.: Computingfailure.com: War Stories from the Electronic Revolution. Prentice Hall, Upper Saddle River (2001)
14. Thaller, G.E.: Software-Test, 2nd edn. Heise, Hannover (2002)
15. Glass, R.L.: Software Runaways: Lessons Learned from Massive Software Project Failures. Prentice Hall, Upper Saddle River (1998)
16. Wallmüller, E.: Risikomanagement für IT–und Software-Projekte. Hanser Fachbuchverlag, München (2004)
17. Page, D., Williams, P., Boyd, D.: Report of the Inquiry into the London Ambulance Service. South West Thames Regional Health Authority, London (1993)
18. Beynon-Davies, P.: Information systems 'failure': the case of the London ambulance service's computer aided despatch project. Eur. J. Inf. Syst. **4**(3), 171–184 (1995)
19. Landry, J.R.: Analyzing the London ambulance service's computer aided despatch (LASCAD) failure as a case of administrative evil. In: Proceedings of the Special Interest Group on Management information system's 47th Annual Conference on Computer Personnel Research, SIGMISCPR'09, pp. 167–174. ACM, New York (2009)
20. Fitzgerald, G., Russo, N.L.: The turnaround of the London ambulance service computer-aided despatch system (LASCAD). Eur. J. Inf. Syst. **14**(3), 244–257 (2005)
21. Finkelstein, A., Dowell, J.: A comedy of errors: the London ambulance service case study. In: Proceedings of the Eighth International Workshop on Software Specification and Design, pp. 2–4. IEEE Computer Society, Washington, DC (1996)
22. Mayr, H.: Projekt Engineering: Ingenieurmäßige Softwareentwicklung in Projektgruppen, 2nd edn. Hanser Fachbuchverlag, München (2005)
23. Glass, R.L.: The Standish report: does it really describe a software crisis? Commun. ACM **49**(8), 15–16 (2006)
24. Jørgensen, M., Moløkken-Østvold, K.: How large are software costoverruns? a reviewof the 1994 CHAOS report. Inf. Softw. Technol. **48**(4), 297–301 (2006)
25. Laurenz Eveleens, J., Verhoef, C.: The rise and fall of the chaos report figures. IEEE Softw. **27**(1), 30–36 (2010)
26. Glass, R.L.: IT failure rates—70% or 10–15%? IEEE Softw. **22**(3), 111–112 (2005)
27. Brereton, P., Kitchenham, B.A., Budgen, D., Turner, M., Khalil, M.: Lessons from applying the systematic literature review process within the software engineering domain. J. Syst. Softw. **80**(4), 571–583 (2007)
28. Balzert, H.: Lehrbuch der Softwaretechnik: Softwaremanagement, 2nd edn. Spektrum Akademischer Verlag, Heidelberg (2008)
29. Li, S., Shang, J., Slaughter, S.A.: Why do software firms fail? capabilities, competitive actions, and firm survival in the software industry from 1995 to 2007. Inf. Syst. Res. **21**(3), 631–654 (2010)

30. Ariane 5 Inquiry Board: ARIANE 5—Flight 501 Failure. Ariane 5 Inquiry Board (1997). http://
    esamultimedia.esa.int/docs/esa-x-1819eng.pdf
31. NASA: Mars Climate Orbiter Mishap Investigation Board Phase I Report (1999)
32. http://www.spiegel.de/wirtschaft/0,1518,268635,00.html
33. http://www.spiegel.de/wirtschaft/0,1518,341851,00.html
34. http://www.handelsblatt.com/politik/deutschland/regierung-kontra-toll-collect-
    mautmilliarden-verzweifelt-gesucht;2518634
35. http://www.computerwoche.de/schwerpunkt/t/Toll-Collect.html
36. http://www.heise.de/newsticker/meldung/Ministerium-laesst-neue-Kosten-Analyse-
    fuerGesundheitskarte-erstellen-164110.html
37. http://www.heise.de/newsticker/meldung/Diskussion-um-Kosten-fuer-die-
    elektronischeGesundheitskarte-209256.html
38. http://archiv.sueddeutsche.de/j5e38a/2952628/Gesundheitskarte-teurer.html
39. Nuseibeh, B.: Ariane 5: who dunnit? IEEE Softw. **14**(3), 15–16 (1997)
40. Le Lann, G.: An analysis of the Ariane 5 flight 501 failure—a system engineering perspective.
    In: Proceedings Conference Engineering of Computer-Based Systems, pp. 339–346 (1997)
41. Oberg, J.: Why the Mars probe went off course. IEEE Spectr. **36**(12), 34–39 (1999)
42. Euler, E., Jolly, S., Curtis, H.: The failures of the Mars climate orbiter and Mars polar lander:
    a perspective from the people involved. In: Proceedings of Guidance and Control, vol. AAS
    01-074. American Astronautical Society, Escondido (2001)
43. Lacan, P., Monfort, J.N., Ribal, L.V.Q., Deutsch, A., Gonthier, G.: ARIANE 5—The soft-
    ware reliability verification process. In: Kaldeich-Schürmann, B. (ed.) Proceedings of the Data
    Systems in Aerospace (DASIA), pp. 201–205. European Space Agency, Paris (1998)
44. Kopec, D., Tamang, S.: Failures in complex systems: case studies, causes, and possible reme-
    dies. SIGCSE Bull. **39**(2), 180–184 (2007)
45. Jones, C.: Software Quality: Analysis and Guidelines for Success. Thomson Learning, Farm-
    ington Hills (1997)
46. Sneed, H.M., Winter, M.: Objektorientierter Software. Hanser, München (2002)
47. Hetzel, W. (ed.): Program Test Methods. Prentice Hall, Englewood Cliffs (1973)
48. Gelperin, D., Hetzel, B.: The growth of software testing. Commun. ACM **31**(6), 687–695
    (1988)
49. Brooks, F.P., Jr.: No silver bullet—essence and accident in software engineering. In: Proceed-
    ings of the IFIP Tenth World Computing Conference, pp. 1069–1076 (1986)
50. Wirth, N.: A plea for lean software. Computer **28**(2), 64–68 (1995). http://doi.ieee
    computersociety.org/10.1109/2.348001
51. Majchrzak, T.A.: Best practices for the organizational implementation of software testing. In:
    Proceedings of the 43rd Annual Hawaii International Conference on System Sciences (HICSS-
    43), pp. 1–10. IEEE Computer Society, Washington, DC (2010)
52. Gotterbarn, D., Miller, K.W.: The public is the priority: making decisions using the software
    engineering code of ethics. Computer **42**(6), 58–65 (2009)
53. Neumann, P.G.: Risks to the public in computer systems. SIGSOFT Softw. Eng. Notes **11**(1),
    2–14 (1986)
54. Neumann, P.G.: Illustrative risks to the public in the use of computer systems and related
    technology. SIGSOFT Softw. Eng. Notes **21**(1), 16–30 (1996)
55. Neumann, P.G.: Risks to the public in computers and related systems. SIGSOFT Softw. Eng.
    Notes **24**(4), 26–29 (1999)
56. Neumann, P.G.: Risks to the public. SIGSOFT Softw. Eng. Notes **35**(3), 24–32 (2010)
57. Tamai, T.: Social impact of information system failures. Computer **42**(6), 58–65 (2009)
58. Gotterbarn, D., Miller, K.W.: The public is the priority: making decisions using the soft-
    ware engineering code of ethics. Computer **42**(6), 66–73 (2009). http://dx.doi.org/10.1109/
    MC.2009.204
59. Keil, M., Cule, P.E., Lyytinen, K., Schmidt, R.C.: A framework for identifying software project
    risks. Commun. ACM **41**(11), 76–83 (1998)

60. Keil, M., Robey, D.: Turning around troubled software projects: an exploratory study of the deescalation of commitment to failing courses of action. J. Manag. Inf. Syst. **15**(4), 63–87 (1999)

61. Majchrzak, T.A., Kuchen, H.: IHK-projekt softwaretests: Auswertung. In: Working Papers, vol. 2. Förderkreis der Angewandten Informatik an der Westfälischen Wilhelms-Universität, Münster e.V. (2010)

Chapter 2
Software Testing

Software testing as a part of software development is a very diverse topic—or even seen as an *art* [1]. Therefore, an introduction into software testing is given. This chapter summarizes why software is tested, which terms are important, what software testing is, how software testing can be done, and how it is organized. Furthermore, basics of test automatization, management, and documentation are described. Additionally, testing standards are mentioned.

The structure of the chapter is aligned with standard literature on software testing [2–7]. In the literature there is no common order in which topics are introduced but the intersection of various sources helps to arrange an adequate synopsis. While the chapter draws a holistic picture of testing, aspects that are important for the topics of this book are given special attention.

Besides giving the background for the following chapters, this chapter can be used as a brief introduction to software testing and as a reference for testing techniques.

2.1 Testing Basics

First of all, the term *defect* is introduced. Then, the aims of testing can be sketched. Finally, a classification for testing is proposed and important standards are named.

2.1.1 Defects

A variety of terms is used to describe the fact that software is flawed. The seemingly arbitrary or even synonymous usage of terms such as *bug, defect, error, failure, fault, mistake,* or *problem* is confusing.[1] Not all of these are (directly) related

---

[1] Switching to German does not help. There are less terms commonly used, but *Fehler* can be used as a translation for all of the above mentioned terms besides *mistake*.

T. A. Majchrzak, *Improving Software Testing*, SpringerBriefs in Information Systems, DOI: 10.1007/978-3-642-27464-0_2, © The Author(s) 2012

to software testing, and some of them even have contradicting definitions in the literature. Moreover, it has to be discussed what the actual meaning of terms is and which kind of states of a program or components of it have to be distinguished in the domain of software testing. It e.g. can be asked whether software is flawed if it does not work *at all*, does not work as *intended*, or does not work as *specified*.

Terms are not formally defined but their meaning with regard to software testing is presented. If possible, a consensus of explanations found in the most prevalent sources is given. All terms introduced in this section are also listed in the glossary in the backmost part of this work (p. 137ff.). Since it is the most important term, *defect* is introduced first and the other terms' relations to it are explained.

According to Cleff, there are two definitions for *defects* [5, p. 10ff.]:

- The *property based definition* addresses the absence of a guaranteed property of a software. Usually, properties are based on the specification and have been contracted between principal and agent. A defect in this sense is characterized by not fulfilling a specified performance [6, p. 28f.]. It has to be distinguished from a case in which software does not perform as expected. A property based defect is statically bound to the program code [2, p. 5ff.]—this does not mean that it will deterministically occur, though.
- The *risk based definition* can be derived from product liability judicature. It addresses risks that arise from defective software. Defects could potentially cause harm and pose the unauthorized or misappropriate usage of software.

Defects may also be called *faults*; in this work, the term *defect* will be used. It has been suggested to include occurrences in which software does not behave as intended by its users as defects [6, p. 28f.]. While software should be intuitive in order to avoid wrong usage and make it ergonomic, this definition is problematic. Software that does not behave as expected might be deficient in terms of jurisdiction (w.r.t. product liability), and requirements engineering (RE) could have failed, but including such cases as defects is prone to arbitrariness. Testing has to be done based on a specification or following general norms and best practices. This could include *usability* checks if usability is part of the specification [8]. However, general assessment of a program's usability is concerned by the fields of *usability engineering* [9, 10] and human-computer interaction (HCI) [11–13].

The term *bug* can be used to subsume defects and unexpected behavior of programs which do not violate the specification. Therefore, it can be used in a rather informal way to describe any characteristic of a program that is undesired from a user's view [14, p. 19f.]. Bugs thus can be signs of defects. However, one bug might be caused by multiple defects or other way around.

Terms that can be defined more precisely are *failure* and *error*. Errors describe a mistake in the life cycle of a software that leads to an incorrect result [3, p. 354ff.]. They (at least indirectly) are caused by mistakes humans make or their misunderstanding of a program's specification, the programming language used, or other vital parts of the development process [2, p. 7]. If the consequence is identified when executing a program, a failure has been found; this failure hints to the existence of a defect.

While a defect is static, failures occur *dynamically* [2, p. 6f.]. Even though some defects will cause failures regardless of the way a program is used, failures can only be identified when executing a program and are often bound to the input given to it.

The relationship of error, defect and failure can be illustrated with an example (cf. [3, p. 354f.]). A simple program expects two parameters a and b and prints the sum of a and two times b. Consider the main statement of the program to be[2]:

```
print a + b * 2;
```

If the programmer typed too fast or did not work carefully, he could type a wrong number. In other words: an error occurred. The actual statement would then e.g. be:

```
print a + b * 3;
```

This is the defect. If the program is tested, a failure might be observed. If the tester knows that the program was specified to calculate $a + 2b$ and he tested it with parameters $(2, 5)$, he would notice that the output was 17 instead of 12 as expected. Ideally, this would lead to the discovery of the defect. At the same time it becomes clear that testing does not necessarily reveal defects. If the (only) input would have been $(2, 0)$, there would not have been a failure—despite the defect.

When testing software, each condition that violates a program's specification is called an *incident* [5, p. 10]. Incidents can be failures. However, their cause can be external. A malfunctioning testing environment, an erroneous test tool, mistakes while performing the test, or insufficient user rights of the tester might be the reason for a condition that would also be expected if the tested program contained defects [5, p. 10]. Only failures should be reported to software developers in order to fix them [5, p. 10] because external effects are beyond their responsibility. Reporting them should include documenting them, preferably following a standard such as IEEE 1044 [15].

It is suggested to classify defects as well as failures. From a tester's perspective, even each incident should be categorized in order to decide how to proceed with it. Typically, classification is done by specifying a level of *severity*, a *priority*, incident related information, and optionally comments [14, p. 34f.].

In general, no other terms to describe the cause or signs of malfunction of software will be used in this work. Additionally, the term *test case* has to be defined. A test case is the description of an atomic test. It consists of input parameters, execution conditions, and the expected result [4, p. 171]. Execution conditions are required to set up the program for testing, e.g. if the test case requires it to be in a defined state. Test cases not necessarily are literal descriptions of tests; they also can be on hand as executable code or in a format specified by a test tool. Test cases that are stored in

---

[2] No actual programming language is used. A file header and a function or method definition have been omitted. The statement would look similar in many common object orientation programming languages, though. Some languages would require a *cast* from the numeric type to a literal type or a parameter for formatting.

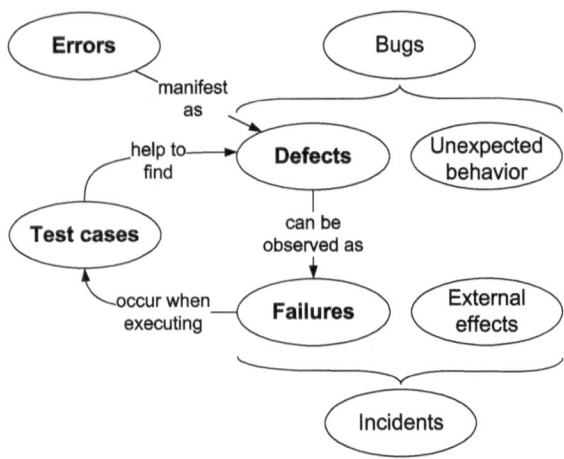

executable form, i.e. that are small programs by themselves, can also be called *test
drivers* [16, p. 132].

The most important terms and their relations are summarized in Fig. 2.1. Of course,
there are many more terms in the domain of software testing. Some of them are
explained in the following sections; many more are explained in the glossary.

2.1.2 Aims of Testing

"To test a program is to try to make it fail" [17]. Thus, finding failures is the main
aim of testing [5, Chap. 3, p. 59f.]. This aim aligns with the question *Why test software?* asked at the beginning of this book (Sect. 1.2). Despite its charming simplicity,
subordinate aims can be identified in definitions on software testing. Testing *without*
aims can be seen as a waste of time and money [18, p. 223].

According to the IEEE Standard 610.12-1990 (IEEE Standard Glossary of Software Engineering Terminology)[3] testing can be defined as follows [19, 20]:

1. "The process of operating a system or component under specified conditions,
   observing or recording the results, and making an evaluation of some aspect of
   the system or component."
2. "The process of analyzing a software item to detect the differences between
   existing and required conditions (that is, bugs) and to evaluate the features of
   the software items."

---

[3] The standard lists further definitions for testing. This includes acceptance testing, component
testing, functional testing, integration testing, loopback testing, mutation testing, performance
testing, regression testing, stress testing, structural testing, system testing, and unit testing.

The first definition suggests that finding failures can be accompanied with an evaluation. This, for example, applies to testing a program's performance. Strictly speaking, identifying an unsatisfactory performance also is a failure since the system does not perform as specified. Thinking of performance testing when trying to find failures is not obvious, though. The second definition is somewhat fuzzy but aligns with the above mentioned considerations.

Omitting superfluous arguments and aims that are almost equal to finding failures, literature hardly mentions subordinate aims. In fact, many authors do not explicitly define the aims of testing at all but either take them as given (for instance [6]) or embed testing in a context of organizational optimization (e.g. [21]). Other authors describe aims of tasks that testing is embedded into (such as *quality management* [18]), or aims derived from roles in the testing process (for instance *test analyst* [3]). Furthermore, it is common to discuss aims for quality which should be reached using software testing [2, 4]. These aims include security, applicability, continuity, controllability, functionality, usability, integrability, performance, and efficiency [22, Chap. 12].

If subordinate aims are discussed, they are found in the context of test execution rather than in the context of motivating why testing is pursued. Typically, these aims are general aims of software development; software testing can be used to reach them or to close the gap between the current status and fulfilling the objectives. Such aims are

- decreasing costs to remove defects,
- decreasing costs defects cause (due to system failure),
- assessing software quality,
- meeting norms and laws,
- avoiding lawsuits and customer related problems,
- increasing the trust into the software developed or into a company that develops software products [5, p. 59ff.], and
- supporting *debugging* as good as possible [14, p. 54f.].

These aims have an economic background. They either try to decrease costs or increase revenue both directly and with keeping long-term effects (such as a company's image) in mind.

From the testing perspective, all aims can be subsumed to finding failures. However, it can be argued that the aim of testing is to increase the value of software. Eliminating defects (and, to be able to do so, finding failures) is the instrument to reach higher quality and, therefore, value [23]. Increasing value has to be kept in relation with testing effort to keep the aim operational.

Besides the aims of testing from the external perspective, testing as seen as a task in developing software also should have aims. These aims should be "objectively measurable" [18, p. 245] and usually try to achieve quantitative criteria such as coverage or a modification of complexity figures.

2.1.3 Classification and Categorization

Due to its diversity, software testing has a variety of facets. A basic categorization was carried out by structuring this chapter. In addition, testing can be ordered by *phases*. While testing is part of an overall development process, it can be split into several subprocesses. Test processes ought to strive for quality improvements [4, Chap. 20]. A framework of testing processes is explained in Sect. 2.3.1.

   Testing techniques—also referred to as *methods*—can be classified by their characteristics. Hence, possibilities for classification are presented which will be used for the methods introduced in Sect. 2.2.

   Common classification schemes are by main characteristic of a test (cf. [2, p. 37f.]), by the target of testing (e.g. GUI or integration, cf. [5]), and by the available information (see below). It is also possible to resign from using a classification of techniques in favor of defining adequate techniques for each phase of testing [6, Chaps. 6–17]. For this book, a scheme based on main characteristics is used since it poses least ambiguity—especially in combination with splitting the test process into phases.

   There are three main classes of testing techniques: *static* and *dynamic* techniques [2, p. 37ff.], as well as complete enumeration (*exhaustive testing*). The latter will not be considered further because it almost is without relevance and is only possible for the most simple programs [5, p. 54] [18, p. 224]. Consider a tiny program that takes two integer numbers as parameters and returns their sum. Assuming that the underlying functionality (basic I/O) has been *proven* correct, there are still $2^{32} * 2^{32} = 2^{64}$ possible combinations of the input parameters for 32 bit data types—for 64 bit integers it would even be 2^{128} ($\approx 3.4 * 10^{38}$) possibilities. A (structure oriented) dynamic test would show that one test case is enough.

   Static testing does not create test cases since there is no execution of the program to be tested [2, p. 43ff.]. Static tests can be subdivided into techniques for *verification* and *analysis*. Verification is done *formally* or *symbolically*. It theoretically is possible to prove that a program behaves in the way it is intended to. The effort to do so is immense and static testing usually is done for small modules of programs in areas where correctness is crucial (such as the central control of a nuclear power plant). *Static code analysis* is a technique that checks the source code or some form of intermediary code (for instance *bytecode*) for the assertion of properties. Techniques are *style analysis*, *slicing*, *control flow analysis*, *data flow (anomaly) analysis*, and *code reviews* [2, Chap. 8]. Furthermore, the calculation of *metrics* allows to draw quantitative conclusions about the status of development and testing [24, p. 283ff.].

   The main categorization of *dynamic techniques* is to divide techniques by their orientation on a program's *structure* or *functions*. Over 50 different dynamic techniques are known [25, p. 328], but only some of them are widely used. Structure oriented tests can be subdivided into techniques based on the *control flow* and based on the *data flow*. Structure based techniques assess a program's behavior by monitoring how it is executed, and how data is processed. This is done on a low technical level. Functional tests abstract from the low level execution but create test cases based on the functionality a program should provide. Since the functionality is specified, they can also be called *specification oriented* tests. [3, p. 31].

Besides these two categories, four further classes of dynamic techniques can be identified. *Dynamic analysis* is used to detect *memory leaks* and *performance bottlenecks* [3, p. 128ff.], and for dynamic symbolic execution. Symbolic execution takes a special role. It can be seen a static verification technique and even be used to draw complete conclusions [2, p. 44f.]. However, it may also be combined with dynamic testing and thereby becomes an approach for creating test cases. The tool Muggl, which will be introduced in Chap. 4, uses this technique. Due to its character, symbolic execution can be seen as a technique of dynamic analysis.

In contrast to Liggesmeyer [2], *performance tests*, such as *load tests* and *stress tests*, are categorized as dynamic tests, too. They require the execution of a program but due to their focus on a program's performance can be seen as an own category. Defining them as other dynamic (e.g. functional) testing techniques being constantly repeated would be ambiguous and would neglect their importance.

Experience based tests can be subdivided into *intuitive testing* (*error guessing* [2, Chap. 5]), and *explorative testing* [3, p. 108f.]. Both techniques are completely manual. They are based on a tester's skill and discretion.

Finally, there is a number of further techniques which do not fall into the above described categories: *back-to-back tests* [25, p. 376], *mutation testing* [4, p. 548], *statistic testing* [25, p. 368], *random testing* [2, p. 208], and *using original data* for testing [26, p. 97].

The categorization proposed in this section is summed up in Fig. 2.2. It has to be noted that this categorization may be inadequate if techniques are categorized from a business angle. *Integration*, *system*, *acceptance*, *beta*, and likewise tests usually are more or less manually conducted dynamic tests. From a business perspective, it is more important that an acceptance test is done in cooperation with customers than which particular technique is used. However, for categorization purposes the above suggestion is adequate.

In many situations it also helpful to distinguish test techniques based on the information available when creating test cases. Dynamic tests can be classified as black-box tests, glass-box tests (also known as white-box tests), and gray-box tests. This classification is very useful when a less granular categorization than sketched above is needed. Such a lack of granularity can be criticized, though [2, p. 40]. Black-Box tests abstract from the source code. Most functional tests are Black-Box tests. Glass-Box tests utilize knowledge of the code; control flow oriented and data flow oriented techniques are Glass-Box tests. Gray-Box tests fall in between; they do not focus on utilizing the source code but are at least conducted by persons that have knowledge of it [7, p. 119].

A completely different method to classify testing techniques is proposed by Pezzè and Young. They suggest to define basic principles of testing which techniques should follow. These principles are *sensitivity*, *redundancy*, *restriction*, *partitioning*, *visibility*, and *feedback characteristic*. With regard to the chapters in their book, Pezzè and Young however follow a common classification scheme [4].

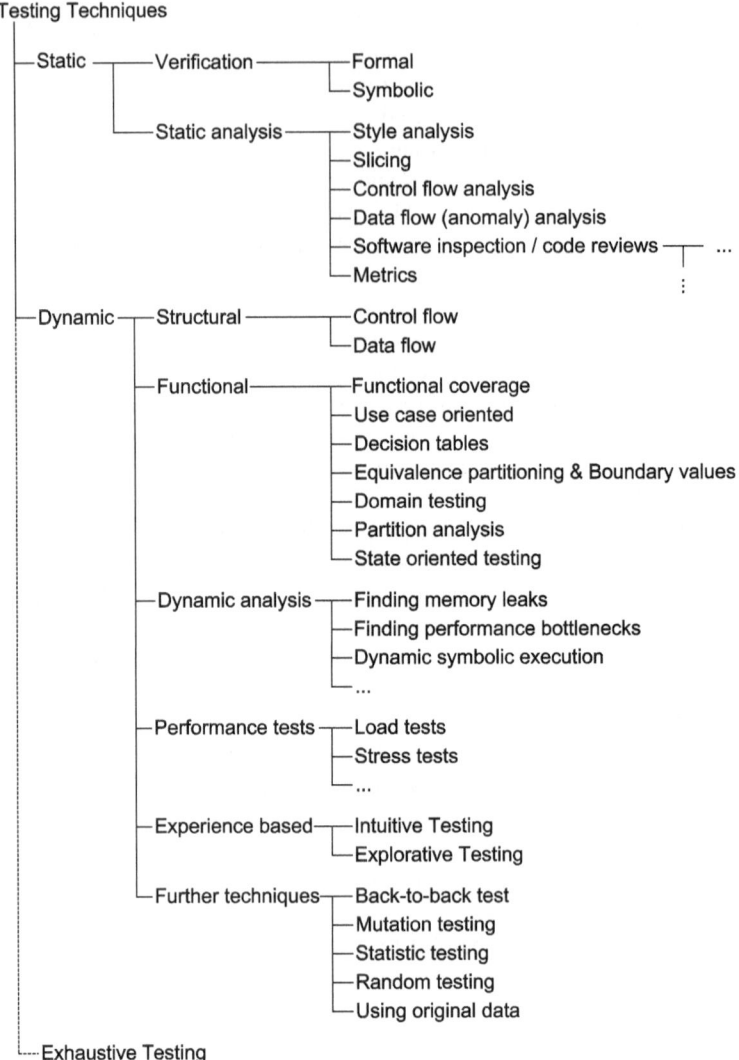

Fig. 2.2 Categorization of testing techniques (inspired by [2, p. 38])

It was decided to exclude *model checking* and *model based testing* from the categorization scheme. Model checking has gained much popularity in the last years, but despite being a verification technique, it usually is not seen as a testing technique. Model based testing is either based on model checking or subsumed by other techniques mentioned above. Examples for such techniques are the analysis of control flow and data flow or combinatorial techniques [4, p. 277]. Please refer to [27–29] for an introduction into model checking and to [30] for a survey on recent progress. Pezzè and Young introduce model-based techniques [4, Chap. 14]. It can be noted that some techniques are similar to testing techniques introduced in Sect. 2.2. However, as the name suggests, model checking deals with *checking* a model with regard to the assertion of properties, and not with *testing* it.

2.1.4 Standards

As a consequence of the business criticality of testing and the usage of software in fields where failure endangers humans, standards have been developed. They describe what testing is, how subdisciplines of it ought to be organized, or which testing aims have to be met for distinct purposes of using software. This book roughly follows the categorization proposed by Spillner et al. [24, Chap. 13].

An elaborate discussion of standards and their application is out of scope of this work. A comprehensive introduction is given by Spillner et al. [24, Chap. 13]. They also name a myriad of standards that apply to different phases of testing and in the areas of processes, products, documentation, and methods. A list of applicable standards is also given in [18, p. 426ff.].

2.1.4.1 Terminology and Positioning

First of all, there are general standards that define terminology such as IEEE 610.12-1990 [19, 20] already mentioned in Sect. 2.1.2. These standards are complemented by more specific ones, for instance the ISO/IEC 12119:1994 Standard on *Information technology—Software packages—Quality requirements and testing* [31].

Besides these very general standards, testing organizations try to standardize the body of knowledge on software testing. Organizations such as the ISTQB [32] or their national associations such as the German Testing Board (GTB) [33] publish curricula. There are both general curricula and curricula that address advanced testing management or technical roles of testing. Commonly, curricula are available free of charge (e.g. from the GTB [34]) while literature that delivers the actual knowledge or is used to prepare for certifications (cf. Sect. 2.3.5) is published in books (such as [3, 24, 35]).

2.1.4.2 De facto Standards and Technical Specifications

A number of documents and best practices became de facto standards for testing without being published or without being denominated a standard. In particular, technical specifications can be seen as preliminary stages of standards [24, p. 360f.].

Technical standards are released by large software vendors and by consortia (both industry based and non-profit consortia). Typical examples are the standards for Web development released by the World Wide Web Consortium (W3C) [36]. Some technical standards specify aims for testing or quality criteria.

So called *bodies of knowledge*, which sum up best practices from a particular field, can also be regarded as de facto standards. An examples is the Software Engineering Body of Knowledge (SWEBOK) [37], which also comprises a chapter on software testing. Process models that evolved to be used in many projects also take a role as de facto standards. For example, the *V-ModelXT* [38, 39] evolved from the V-Model 97 [40] and is widely used in development projects led by the German Government or German authorities. It also contains testing-related advices.

2.1.4.3 Company, Sector, or Application Related Standards

International enterprises, in particular multi-national software development companies, employ norms and standards for their development processes [24, p. 359f.]. In general, they are not officially published but used internally and in collaboration with key customers. They are especially used to provide templates, establish general terms and procedures, and to align processes.

Sector specific standards define requirements that have to be met in order to ensure the fail-safe or failure-tolerant operation of systems. Typically, requirements are very special or software is similar in design (e.g. it has to do a high number of physical calculations) [24, p. 361f.]. This applies to areas such as astronautics, aviation, healthcare, infrastructure, military, and telecommunication [24, p. 361]. The aviation norm *DO-178B* [41] (*Software Considerations in Airborne Systems and Equipment Certification*) defines testing techniques to be used and testing aims to be met with regard to aviation systems' levels of criticality. A similar norm is DIN EN 50128 (*Railway applications. Communications, signalling and processing systems*) which applies to railroad transportation systems [42]. For the healthcare sector, IEC 62304 regulates properties medical device software has to fulfill [43]. Testing can be used to check whether the requirements defined by standards are met [5, p. 71f.].

Application related standards address requirements of software that is tailored to a distinct domain of usage. This e.g. applies to *embedded systems* which often are used in sensitive areas. For instance, embedded systems control the anti-lock braking system (ABS) and the electronic stability control (ESC) that increase the safety of cars. While company and sector related standards are likely to apply in distinct fields, there are some standards that apply to application domains. In the above case, IEC 61508 (*Functional safety of electrical/electronic/programmable electronic safety-related systems*) [44] applies. It defines levels of security and boundaries for the expected probability of breakdowns.

2.1.4.4 General Standards

Spillner et al. [24, p. 365] identified almost 90 International Organization for Standardization (ISO) standards that concern software development and over 40 IEEE documents on software engineering. Without focusing on software testing directly, applying these standards influences the way software is tested. They comprise terminology guidelines, process suggestions, documentation templates, and method advise [24, p. 365]. Thus, they especially regard the organizational implementation of testing and the interfaces to other software development processes.

Further standards that influence software testing are IT frameworks such as the IT infrastructure library (ITIL) [45] or Control Objectives for Information and Related Technology (CobiT) [46]. Some of them directly propose guidelines for testing (for instance CobiT) while others change the framing conditions for software development in general (for instance ITIL). Despite different aims, reference models and evaluation frameworks such as Capability Maturity Model Integration (CMMI) [47] influence software development and thereby testing in a similar way as IT frameworks.[4]

Testing related process models are no *de jure* standards but might be standards in companies. The most notable process models are Test Management Approach (TMap) [50, 51] and Test Process Improvement (TPI) [52, 53]. A detailed introduction is e.g. given by Pol et al. [22, Chap. 8].

Finally, even more general standards have relevance for software testing. This considers all standards and norms that deal with product quality, product and process security, liability, and other product or production related details. The most prominent example is a Total Quality Management (TQM) approach based on the DIN EN ISO 9000 [54], DIN EN ISO 9001 [55], and DIN EN ISO 9004 [56] norms. TQM is an continuous improvement process that aims at improving product quality and at involving the customer [57, p. 1].

2.2 Testing Techniques

Even with an classification scheme at hand (cf. Sect. 2.1.3, Fig. 2.2) it is almost impossible to exhaustively describe the available testing methods. Not only is their number high but particularly less used methods are not uniquely named. Moreover, the discriminatory power between several techniques is not always given. While one author might describe a couple of techniques as distinct ones, they could be subsumed by another one and seen as mere variations.

On this account, the (quite) brief compilation of techniques in this section serves three purposes:

- Firstly, to give an overview by introducing at least one technique per proposed category.
- Secondly, to be comprehensive in that the most widely used methods are explained.
- Thirdly, to be the foundation for later chapters of this book.

---

[4] It has to be noted that not all computer scientists are convinced of the usefulness of such models or at least the way they are applied. Proposing a "software process immaturity model" [48, 49] is not only humorous but also hints to skepticism.

2.2.1 Static Techniques

Static techniques consider the program at a given point, usually without executing it. They can be subdivided into *verification* and *static analysis*. Static techniques give direct hints to defects rather then identifying failures [25, p. 251].

2.2.1.1 Verification

Verification techniques aim at formally checking a program against its specification. Some of them can even prove the correctness of a program. This cannot be done with other testing techniques [5, p. 56].

Formal techniques pursue this in the literal sense. Based on the specification of the program, consistency of the program and its specification is proven [2, p. 321ff.]. Consequently, an exhaustive specification is required and it has to be transferred to a formal specification. It is not possible to validate [58] a program using formal techniques—in fact, they are not suitable to detect problems in the specification. Formal verification techniques are only used for programs in fields such as power plant control, aviation, or military [25, p. 285]. A prominent example is the application for the metro transportation system of Paris [59] based on B models [60].

Proving the correctness of a program can for instance be done using the axioms of the *(Floyd-)Hoare Logic* [61, 62] and by following *inductive assertions* [63]. A concise introduction is given by Roitzsch [25, p. 287ff.]. Hoare Logic also is an important part of Formal Specification methods; therefore, it is part of the research on e-assessment included in this book. More details are given in Chap. 6. According to Wallmüller [18, p. 218] an alternative to Hoare Logic are approaches based on *abstract data types* (e.g. [64], also cf. [65]).

An extension is *symbolic model checking* which utilizes automata theory [2, p. 45]. Formal techniques are very powerful. However, the effort is tremendous and often impractical even for small programs. Thus, they are rarely used by practitioners [2, p. 45].

Symbolic tests can be seen as a bridge between dynamic techniques and formal ones. In contrast to dynamic techniques they do not rely on samples but can draw full conclusions. The source code or an intermediary code of the program under consideration is executed symbolically. This means that variables in the program are treated as logic variables instead of parameterizing them with constant values. Commonly, an environment programmed for this purpose is used. With the given statements or instructions of a program, a *symbolic execution tree* can be built [25, p. 309f.], which is similar to a control graph. In the next step, paths trough this tree are determined (*path-sensitivity* [4, p. 404]), and the parameters required for program execution to take this path are described. Combinations of input parameters and expected output can be used as test cases.

For some programs, symbolic testing can prove correctness [2, p. 44]. In general, it is capable of detecting a very high number of defects [25, p. 315f.].

2.2.1.2 Static Analysis

Static analysis does not execute the program under consideration and does not necessarily require tool support [2, p. 43f.]. The code is analyzed and interpreted [66, p. 6]. However, tool usage is strongly suggested as static analysis techniques are suitable for automatization. In general, being static is both the blessing and the curse of the techniques described below [3, p. 115ff.]. Initiating static analyses is possible at an early point of development. However, in general no defects are found but only hints to them.

Style analysis (also informally known as *checking programming guidelines* [3, p. 122f.]) is a technique that checks source code for its compliance with predefined conventions. These conventions can be corporation-wide guidelines as well as best practices for programming languages [2, p. 271ff.]. Due to the availability of plug-ins, style analysis can seamlessly be integrated into an integrated development environment (IDE) [67]. Style analysis is particularly recommended for embedded systems but also advisable in general [2, p. 275]; moreover, it can be a good choice to maintain so called *legacy* systems [18, p. 217]. It can be expected that programmers get used to the mandatory programming style after a while. Besides establishing a corporate programming guideline that harmonizes programming styles [67], styles provided by programming language vendors (for instance [68]) and in practitioner textbooks (for instance [69]) should be followed. A comprehensive introduction is given by Kellerwessel [70]. It has been noted that style analysis should be combined with using a modern programming language, which—if correctly used—reduces the risk of programming in a *bad* style [18, p. 217].

Despite the fact that *slicing* can be done both statically [71, 72] and dynamically [73], it is attributed to the static analysis techniques [2, p. 285]. Slicing is used to automatically discover interrelations within programs, for examples with regard to the influence of statements on variables. This helps to conclude which part or even which statement of a program causes an undesired action. Patterns of defects can be identified [14, p. 178]. Whereas static slicing does not require the execution of a program, dynamic slicing takes into account information that become available during execution only [2, p. 289ff.]. Slicing can be used to better understand a program and to support finding defects [2, p. 285ff.]. Various slicing strategies exist [14, p. 179ff.]; an overview of past and current research threads is given in [74].

Control flow analysis statically checks code in order to detect anomalies. The goal is to detect code that cannot be executed for semantic reasons (*dead code*) and loops that cannot be left once entered [3, p. 118ff.]. *Call graphs* take this concept to a higher level. They document how modules are linked to each other and help to plan tests [3, p. 126ff.].

Data flow (anomaly) analysis—or *dataflow anomaly detection*—is used to detect parts of programs that deviate from the expectation. Similarly to the work of a compiler it tries to detect peculiar parts of programs; in theory, these parts could also be identified by carefully working humans [2, p. 292ff.]. The typical attempt is to check variables for being defined, referenced (i.e. read), and dereferenced (i.e. set to be undefined). After checking the program, anomalies such as redefining variables without reading them, defining and immediately dereferencing them, or dereferencing and then trying to read a variable can be detected [2, p. 293ff.]. Compiler support for this kind of analysis is strongly recommended; explicit invocation of data flow analysis is reported to be rather uncommon [2, p. 302f.].

Control flow and data flow analysis can be combined with tools that automatically scan the code for anomalies. They can be based on various assessment techniques and might also offer visual support [14, Chap. 11].

Software inspections and *code reviews* are an extensive field with a number of techniques. It is known since the early days of testing [75]. The general idea is to manually assess the source code. Not only defects are searched for, but reviewers assess whether the desired level of quality has been reached and whether conventions are fulfilled [18, p. 201]. Well conducted reviews are very cost-effective and significantly contribute to the overall assurance of software quality [3, p. 303ff.]. Liggesmeyer distinguishes between three main techniques [2, Chap. 9]: *commenting reviews*, *informal reviewing sessions*, and *formal inspections*. Commenting reviews are the simplest technique; programs, modules or documentation is assigned to reviewers who check and comment it. Informal reviewing sessions are commonly organized as a structured walkthrough. Developers show their work to reviewers who directly comment on them. Formal inspections are the most sophisticated technique. They are not mere walkthroughs but have formally defined phases and roles. They are highly structured, which increases the effort required to conduct them but greatly increases the outcome.

A review's success is based on the participants and their interplay [18, p. 216f.]. Typically, the number of participants per review is between four and ten; participants take different roles and usually one of them is the *moderator* [25, p. 251ff.]. It can be argued that reviews are beneficial for the working atmosphere and contribute to the employees' education [4, p. 384]. The corporate culture has to be adequate for reviews, though [76, p. 119].

More detailed subclasses for reviews are e.g. suggested by Bath and McKay who (among others) mention *technical reviews*, *management reviews*, *audits*, and *design reviews* [3, p. 310]. Audits are typically less technically driven than reviews [18, p. 198ff.]. It has been noted that reviews can be more effective in removing defects than (dynamic) testing [77, p. 108] and lead to immediate improvements of the code [18, p. 201]. According to Liggesmeyer, code reviews are widely used by practitioners [2, p. 305].

A technique that is similar to reviews and that can be combined with reviews is the identification of so called *anti patterns* [78]. Whereas *design patterns* describe proven strategies to implement recurring functionality of software [79], anti patterns describe how *not* to implement functionality [80]. Anti patterns are also referred to as *code smells*, i.e. parts of source code that have a "bad smell" due to potential problems [81]. Corresponding constructs can be found both manually and with tool support. The code should then be *refactored*, i.e. changed to a better style while preserving its functionality [82]. It is recommended to use refactoring to change the code to adhere to patterns [83]. Some code smells are also found by the above described techniques. For instance, dead code can be identified by control flow analysis.

Metrics describe key figures that are generated from source code, intermediary code, programs, program documentation, or systems that manage testing related data. Metrics aggregate data and allow to draw conclusions, or to estimate duration or time requirements. They are used to assess a program's quality, to handle complexity, to control the development process, and to check if standards are met [2, p. 232f.]. Furthermore, they are useful to estimate effort, costs, and duration, to proactively identify problems, for reasons of comparison, and to judge the effectivity of newly introduced tools and methods [2, p. 232f.]. They can also help to find *problematic* areas in the code [3, p. 362ff.]. Code that becomes too complex due to nested statements, methods that are very long, and similar criteria hint to potential problems.

Some metrics are also important for the operation of testing tools. For example, the percentage of covered control flow graph edges and def-use chains can be calculated [84]. However, metrics in general only take a subordinate (or rather auxiliary) role in testing. Therefore, no introduction into different kinds of metrics and their usage is given. Please refer to either [2, Chap. 7] or [24, Chap. 11].

In addition to the above mentioned techniques, manual inspection of diagrams can be seen as a static technique [2, p. 276ff.]. This e.g. applies to control flow graphs, Nassi–Shneidermann diagrams [85], and structure diagrams.

2.2.2 Dynamic Techniques

Dynamic techniques are based on executing the code in order to detect failures. They comprise a high number of techniques which can be put into six categories. Descriptions are given in the following sections.

2.2.2.1 Structure Oriented

Structure orientation means that a program is tested against its own code [66, p. 8ff.]. It forces testers to check the code in detail. The effort and the required skill of employees for structure oriented techniques are high but it is possible to effectively find defects [3, p. 77ff.]. The main criticism is that the structure itself might be incorrect, for example as a result of incorrect requirements. While other techniques might at least help to reveal this, it cannot be detected based on the structure [3, p. 81]. Advice on choosing functional oriented techniques is provided by Bath and McKay [3, p. 94ff.].

There is a number of structure oriented techniques that are very simple. Since they are inferior in results to control flow testing, they will not be discussed in detail. For *statement tests*, as many test cases are created as are needed to cover each (source code) statement at least once. *Branch tests* require each branch—i.e. each transition from a statement that involves a decision—to be covered at least once. Various kinds of *condition tests* require atomic conditions or combinations of them to be covered [3, Chap. 5]. Condition tests that are derived from source code can also take the evaluation of statements by compilers into consideration to reduce the number of test cases [5, p. 161ff.]. For example, in most object oriented programming languages *bitwise or* (the | operator) is evaluated completely, whereas *logic or* (the || operator) does not require complete evaluation if the first operand is true.

Control flow testing tries to cover each path through a program. For this purpose, a control flow graph (CFG) is built [2, p. 85]. It is set up by checking each program statement in the source code or instruction in the machine or bytecode. Each statement/instruction forms a node in the graph, whereas transitions make up edges. Simple statement such as $x = 2$ just have a transition to the next statement; conditions have two (e.g. if (...)) or more (e.g. switch (...)) transitions. A technique to create CFGs for Java is described in [84]. With the given CFG, test cases are created that cover each transition at least once. The set of test cases is tried to be kept as small as possible. Alternatively, a threshold for the desired coverage rate can be defined [3, p. 92]. A reasonable threshold can often be reached with a much smaller number of test cases than were needed for full coverage. This is caused by test cases that cover multiple paths trough the program whereas some transitions require tailored test cases to cover them. Selecting a threshold might even be a necessity. Due to semantic restrictions not all edges might be coverable [4, p. 259f.].

It is possible to subdivide control flow testing, e.g. into *path testing* and *loop testing*. The latter is also known as linear code sequence and jump (LCSAJ) [86] or jump-to-jump path (JJ-path) [87] [88, Chap. 10]. This is not done in the recent literature, though. Some lesser known techniques are explained in [25, p. 408ff.]; different coverage criteria are discussed in [7, p. 73]. A comparison of control flow based techniques is presented in [4, p. 258f.]. Sometimes, path testing also is used as a synonym for control flow testing (e.g. in [3, p. 92]).

Data flow testing uses information on how data is processed by a program. For this purpose, it is checked when variables are read and written [2, p. 142]. This can be done on a source code level but also for intermediary code or machine code. For intermediary or machine code that is run on a stack machine, it becomes more complex because loading a variable onto the stack does not imply that it is read.

A very effective way to test the data flow is to check the coverage of full definition-usage chains (*def-use (DU) chains*, sometimes referred to as *set-use pairs* [77, p. 293ff.] or *all DU-paths* [2, p. 148f.]). They can be defined as follows [84]:

X: variable, S, S', S'': statement or instructions
$def(S):=\{X|S \text{ writes to } X\}$
$use(S):= \{X|S \text{ reads from } X\}$

If $X \in def(S) \bigcup use(S')$ and $X \notin def(S'')$ for each S'' on a path from S to S', (X, S, S') forms a def-use chain. In other words: there is a def-use chain between two statements/instructions if the first one defines (i.e. writes) a variable and the second one reads (i.e. uses) it without another statements/instructions changing the variable in the meantime. Similarly to control flow tests, data flow tests try to find test cases that cover all or a threshold of all DU chains. For semantic reasons, covering all chains is impossible for some programs. Data flow testing can reveal defects that are not detectable with control flow testing. However, it can become much more complex. In particular, intraprocedural DU chains can be created (e.g. to cope with *aliases* [4, p. 109]). Whereas intraprocedural CFGs are built by simply connecting graphs at the statements/instructions that invoke and leave methods, chains that reach among methods have to be generated explicitly [84]. For the intricacy of interprocedural data flow testing also cf. [4, p. 109ff.]; special attention also has to be given to arrays and pointers [4, p. 106ff.].

Besides full DU chains [4, Chap. 6], many weaker criteria for data flow testing are known. Examples are *all defs* and *all uses* (if desired limited to some kinds of usage) [2, Chap. 4] [25, p. 433]. In general, they base upon weaker assumptions and are more convenient to find and to cover. However, the stricter the criterion is the more likely are defects to be found. How criteria subsume each other is given in a graphical overview by Roitzsch [25, p. 447f.]. Liggesmeyer also describes two additional techniques, the *required k-tuples test* [2, p. 163ff.] and *data context coverage* [2, p. 171]. An approach of testing based on coverage has been suggested for testing with only a very limited amount of available time [16, p. 227f.].

2.2.2.2 Function Oriented

To test a program's functions, cause and effects of it are taken into considerations. While structure oriented techniques focus on the program itself, function oriented techniques have a higher level view [66, p. 234]. Testers read the specification documents and design corresponding test cases [2, p. 50]. Therefore, function orientation can also be called *specification orientation* [3, p. 31]. Test cases are derived in a systematic way rather than choosing a *brute force* approach [4, p. 189].

Testing with function oriented techniques does not necessarily lead to full testing coverage but helps to ensure that specifications are met [3, Chap. 4]. Despite not being the primary aim, function oriented techniques can also reveal inconsistencies or even mistakes in the specification [5, p. 47f.]. In general, function oriented tests of modules should not be conducted by the developers that implemented them [7, p. 83]. Advice on choosing function oriented techniques and a discussion of their practical relevance is provided by Bath and McKay [3, p. 60ff.].

The most simple function oriented technique besides random testing (see Sect. 2.2.2.6) is testing for *functional coverage*. It is tried to cover each function with one test case [25, p. 334ff.]. Function coverage is not only inefficient but also faces severe limitations when testing object orientation programs [25, p. 337].

So called *use cases* depict scenarios in which a program is actually used [3, p. 59]. They are used in requirements analysis and specification. Some specifications already contain prepared use cases [5, p. 141]. The Unified Modeling Language (UML) provides *use case diagrams* for visualization [89]. Each use case is made up of a number of paths through the program. For each use case, as many test cases have to be created as are required to cover each corresponding path at least once [3, p. 59f.]. It can also be organized as *thread testing* where testers assess functionality in an order that end-users would typically chose [90, p. 22]. Use case testing is customer oriented, but it is very likely that tests are left out [3, p. 59f.]. Functionality will be untested if the usage of a program differs from the developers' intention.

Decision tables are special forms of combinatorial tests. They are useful to describe business rules [77, p. 174]. Decision tables summarize rules in clearly arranged tables. Each rule is made up of *conditions* and *actions*. Each combination of conditions triggers a number of actions. Typically, conditions take the values "applies", "applies not", or "irrelevant" [26, p. 94ff.]. Actions might occur (or not). One test per table column is needed [77, p. 176]. However, full coverage of the rules is possible. Consequently, it is easy to test with a given decision table and the technique is very popular; however, creating the table is challenging or even almost impossible if only imprecise requirements for a program are available [3, p. 44f.]. Besides, tables grow exponentially in the number of conditions [2, p. 79]. Decision tables are used for *cause effect analyses* that try to decrease the number of required test cases [5, p. 125ff.]. It also helps to graphically depict a cause and effects graph [25, p. 352f.], which is built based on a program's specification [18, p. 232].

Equivalence partitioning (in older literature also called *input testing* [88, p. 57]) is a very common approach. It is almost universally usable [2, p. 289ff.]. Instead of testing randomly, test cases align with classes that are to be tested. This is done both in a macro and in a micro perspective [77, p. 144]. For example, parts of a program are chosen for being tested based on their characteristic. In a module of the program, equivalence classes are created that directly address its elements. There are two kinds of equivalence classes: *valid* and *invalid* ones. Think of a text field that takes values for full hours of a 24 h clock. −1 and 31 are examples for invalid classes. 0−23 is the class of valid values. For testing, *one* representative value from each class is taken [5, p. 123f.]. Testing could be done by having three test cases for −1, 5, and 28. Of course, other values are possible. Equivalence partitioning is an efficient technique but prone to leave out tests [3, p. 35ff.]. This usually is caused by accidentally creating classes that subsume more than one class. It also has to be noted that equivalence classes in general are not disjunct [4, p. 188].

Using numeric values (in particular intervals) is sometimes described to be *boundary values analysis* whereas equivalence partitioning only uses textual or property values [77, p. 144ff.]. Boundary values have been found to be related to failures [7, p. 90]. To set up boundary values, classes have to be partitioned beforehand [3, p. 38]. Equivalence partitioning with alphanumerical values can also be called *syntax testing* [88, p. 85].

It is recommended to test *special values* along with a boundary value analysis [25, p. 346]. Values such as zero, the maximum value for a variable, empty data structures, null references, so called *magic numbers*, and reserved statements might trigger special routines or lead to other problems. A list of typical special values is for instance given in [25, p. 347].

Due to the high number of combinations in large tables, approaches have been found that increase efficiency. *Domain testing* is used to check equivalence classes' boundaries and reduce the number of test cases required to test all (remaining) classes. They not only use functional equivalence classes that were derived from the specification but also structural equivalence classes [25, p. 392]. Several examples for domain testing are given by Black [77, Chap. 16] and Roitzsch [25]; examples are *path domain tests* and *tests of code that hints to defects*. Additional techniques for the same purpose are *orthogonal arrays* (cf. [91]) and *all-pair tables* [77, Chap. 18]. Both mean to reduce the numbers of test cases required to satisfyingly test with equivalence classes. In general, this can be done with success but there is the risk to omit required test cases [3, p. 48f.]. Graphical support for this task is provided by drawing *classification trees*. They visualize the pairing which can increase lucidity— or alternatively lead to immense trees with the opposing effect [3, p. 58].

Another approach towards combinatorial testing is to take equivalence partitioning as the basic idea and to derive concrete techniques from it. *Category partitioning* as described by Pezzè and Young [4, p. 204ff.] basically resembles the above description of equivalence partitioning. They also propose techniques for optimization such as *pair-wise testing* (also known as *all pairs* [92]) [4, p. 215ff.] and *catalog based testing* [4, p. 219ff.]. Therefore, it has to be noted with regard to the literature that combinatorial techniques are introduced in a variety of distinctions and with a variety of names.

Partition Analysis is an approach that combines different ideas, namely verification and testing [93]. It can be attributed to various categories [2, p. 206]. Partition analysis uses symbolic execution and defines three criteria for comparing specification and implementation of a program: compatibility, equivalence, and isomorphism [2, p. 206f.]. If verification of these partly fails, additional tests are conducted [2, p. 207f.]. More information is given in [94]; a newer approach is described in [95].

A technique that takes the idea of structured testing to black-box tests is *state oriented testing*. It sometimes is attributed to the model based techniques [4, p. 129]. Without knowing a program's code its possible states are figured out. The aim of testing is to cover each transition between states at least once. This is easy and efficient for programs that have known states and a small number of transitions [3, p. 48]. In contrast to other functional tests, a program's memory (i.e. its state) is taken into account [2, p. 58]. If a program can be described as a finite state machine, tool support is available [5, p. 135]. Nevertheless, manual effort cannot be completely circumvented [4, p. 130].

State oriented testing is not applicable if the number of states is unknown or if a high number (say, at least a couple of 100) of transitions has to be covered. The *state space explosion* quickly becomes problematic for human testers, but even machines cannot keep control of the states that generally grows exponentially with the size of a program [2, p. 64]. Therefore, it is mainly used to test software for embedded systems [3, p. 49]. Based on tests with state machines, *statistic state oriented tests* have been developed. They take into account the probability that a function is used and try to find those defects first that are more likely to be encountered during an actual usage of a program [25, p. 363ff.].

It is not only possible to test function *oriented*, but to test the functions of a program. This is called *functional testing*; however, the term is potentially misleading. The technique aims to check whether the software adheres to its specification [3, p. 141]; this task is conducted completely manual. Besides, it can be argued that a program is rather *checked* in order to determine if it complies with the requirements instead of being *tested*. Typical techniques are *checking for correctness, checking of commensurability*, and *interoperability testing*; a detailed introduction is given in [3, Chap. 10].

2.2.2.3 Dynamic Analysis

Dynamic analysis techniques can reveal defects that are almost impossible to find with other techniques [3, p. 128]. The kind of failures encountered can be critical and at the same time hard to reproduce. Resource problems are likely to occur after a software has been finished. Such defects are very expensive to fix [3, p. 128f.]. Besides finding defects, dynamic analysis can be used to visualize a program's performance and to deduce runtime information. Dynamic analysis might slow down execution, and it is dependent on the programming language used [3, p. 129f.].

Memory leaks describe a conditions in which programs continuously allocate more memory than they need. In most cases, memory is correctly allocated but not completely deallocated after not being needed any more [96, p. 254]. Subject to the program, memory leaks can be annoying to fatal. In some cases they are not noticed, in others they slow down execution or even lead to a crash of the executed program. They are hard to reproduce since it can take a long time (in extreme cases months) before they have consequences, and they are usually hard to fix. They are more common in programs that have been developed with programming languages that do not use garbage collection[5] [4, p. 406ff.]. Tool support is highly recommended for detecting memory leaks [3, p. 131].

Software that consists of multiple large modules or that has sophisticated algorithms might be subject to *performance bottlenecks*. They either occur if a program heavily uses distinct parts of the hardware (for example the mass storage system) or if single components of it have a by far inferior performance compared to others. In both cases, analysis tools can help. They supply information collected during execution and can also depict them graphically [3, p. 135]. A *resource monitor* could for example show that the mass storage system is often accessed randomly or that a program uses many CPU cycles at certain times of execution. Both might be countered with adequate strategies. Also, slow algorithms (e.g. for data structure access) can be detected. Other tools can reveal communication deficits. An example would be synchronous messages that block execution due to high latency. Once detected, it can be checked whether replacing them with asynchronous messages is possible.

Dynamic symbolic execution sometimes is attributed to symbolic tests (see Sect. 2.2.1.1). The basic principles are the same: variables are treated as logic variables (also referred to as *logic expressions* [18, p. 219]) instead of parameterizing them with constant values. However, in place of statically checking the code, it is executed—hence dynamic symbolic execution. Since information that is only

---

[5] Garbage collection automatically frees memory and deallocates data structured not used anymore [97, 98].

available dynamically can be used, results are more precise. For example, *dynamic binding* and *virtual invocation* can be taken into account. This can be extremely complex, though [4, p. 405]. Besides, techniques known from logic programming can be utilized since the symbolic execution tree is used as a *search tree*. An example is *backtracking* [99, p. 90]. The test case generation (TCG) tool presented in this book, Muggl (see Chap. 4), is based on dynamic symbolic execution.

There are further dynamic analysis techniques that try to discover programming problems that cannot be detected statically. An example for a rather often described technique is the detection of *wild pointers* [3, p. 132ff.]. They are also called *dangling pointers* (cf. [100]). Pointers hint to memory addresses that are used to read or store data, or as jump addresses. Incorrect pointer usage and pointer arithmetic can cause various problems. Finding (and removing) wild pointers can avoid some of them. Another example is *lockset analysis* which tries to discover *race conditions* [4, p. 409]. Race conditions can occur when multi-threaded programs use shared variables; they are hard to detect and tend to be nondeterministic.

2.2.2.4 Performance Tests

Performance tests can also be called *efficiency tests* [3, p. 171]. They are used to assess the runtime behavior with regard to resource utilization and response times. Adequate performance is not only a factor for usability but important for the overall quality of a program. Performance tests are also conducted to ensure that a program will work under unforeseeable future conditions [3, p. 171f.]. There are two main testing techniques and a number of additional techniques that rather measure than test.

Load tests are used to assess a program's behavior under load. The load, i.e. the sum of inputs to the program, resembles the typical workload that is estimated for the program. Aims of load tests include

- to check how programs handle parallel requests and how many requests they can process in parallel,
- to find out how the session management of a program works, i.e. how seamless parallel usage is handled,
- to assess the response times of the system under varying conditions, and
- to monitor resource usage in relation to the program's load [3, p. 172ff.].

Load tests can also be called *volume tests* [7, p. 124f.]. In general, load tests should be distinguished from *benchmarks* which measure a program's performance and try to generate key figures [7, p. 131ff.].

Stress tests have a different aim. Rather than using typical workloads, programs are tested with loads that are beyond the expected workload. In fact, loads are even beyond the maximum noted in the specification in order to fathom how the program behaves under such workloads. In general, programs should behave *graceful*. Instead of an abrupt crash, a program should be able to save opened files, persist sessions, and ensure that no data is corrupted. Ideally, a program should switch to a mode of minimal resource usage. For example, if it is flooded with requests, a program could try to accept them as long as possible and answer them once the number of incoming requests decreases. In a Web environment this strategy might however be fatal; requests not immediately answered will—due to short *timeouts*—not be received anyway and clients will send more requests. Therefore, in this case unanswerable requests should be discarded until the load decreases. In contrast to this, a crash is undesired since it would take a while to reboot the program. If a crash is unavoidable, it should be a *graceful degradation* [3, p. 174], i.e. an emergency shutdown and not a halt at a random point.

Furthermore, stress tests can be used to locate bottlenecks in programs [3, p. 174]. This especially applies to programs that are part of larger systems. For example, a system that provides data from files on request is likely to hardly utilize CPU and memory but to create heavy I/O load on the mass storage systems. If a number of requests arrives that is hard to handle, it should not try to deliver all files at once which would degrade the mass storage's performance and eventually lead to a throughput near to zero. Instead, it should use the bountiful amount of memory and store requests. They can be processed once I/O load is lower. In addition to this, stress tests might hint to implement a memory cache for frequently requested files.

Stress tests can adhere to various strategies. *Bounce tests* vary between nominal and extraordinary loads to check whether a program adapts its resource usage [3, p. 175]. It has been argued that stress tests can also be tests that do not induce a high load but just violate the quantitative specification of a program. An example is to test a program that should accept 16 parallel users with 17 users [7, p. 128f.]. However, this rather is a functional test than a stress test.

A number of further techniques mean to assess a program's performance rather than to test it. *Scalability tests* are called tests but aim at finding out whether systems scale. Scaling means the adaption to changed patterns of usage [3, p. 176f.]. A scalable program could simply adapt to an increased workload, could perform more requests on upgraded hardware, or be prepared to spawn multiple instances on different machines. This is checked with regard to the estimated future requirement. Checks of the *resource utilization* and *efficiency measurement* are used to monitor a program's performance and to derive key figures from its execution. Key figures can be response times as well as throughput figures and similar data [3, p. 178ff.]. They help to learn how a program works and which parts of it might need improvement. One challenge that particularly concerns monitoring of programs is to avoid a bias induced by actually monitoring them [3, p. 180]. Measurement results can considerably be altered by the very act of measuring.

All performance tests should be done with tool support [3, p. 188ff.] [101, p. 195f.]. Measurements require tools or at least specialized routines within programs in order to receive the data needed to calculate the key figures or to monitor resources. Load and stress tests could theoretically be done with a (very) high number of testers but having specialized employees simply generate load by e.g. clicking buttons or continuously reloading Web pages is extremely inefficient (and, by the way, frustrating).

Besides testing its performance, a program can be checked for its reliability. Such *reliability tests* incorporate elements from load tests and manual assessment. They are used to fathom whether a program will fulfill its intended tasks without the risk of outages or undesired behavior [3, p. 233f.]. While performance tests address the actual performance, reliability tests e.g. check whether *failover* routines work correctly, backups are created as planned, and restoring data is possible [3, Chap. 14]. The latter can also be called a *recovery test* [7, p. 129f.]. Reliability can be assessed both with regard to functionality and time figures. Concerning failover functionality, it can be checked whether a program is tolerant towards failures. Ideally, failures should not disrupt the core functionality but be handled by the program as good as possible. Methods commonly used are *failure mode and effects analysis* (FMEA) [102, 103] and *failure mode and effects and criticality analysis* (FMECA) [104].

2.2.2.5 Experience Based

Experience based techniques do not rely on a structured approach but utilize a tester's experience. Thus, they are also called *free* testing techniques [5, p. 169f.]. Testers need to have a lot of experience and high testing skills in order to test effectively [25, p. 366]. The reproducibility of the tests is low.

Intuitive testing is an almost random approach where testers test whichever functions they think should be tested [3, p. 106]. It is also called *error guessing* [5, p. 170ff.]. Testers have in mind where defects might be or what might cause failures (*error hypotheses*). Thaller calls this their "sixth sense" [7, p. 93]. With the created test cases they check whether the guessed errors actually exist. To steer this technique, *checklists* can be used [3, p. 108]. Additionally, testers can rely on so called *bug taxonomies* which classify defects [5, p. 171f.]. Knowing typical defects helps to derive error hypotheses.

Explorative techniques are characterized by the fact that testers do not know the program they test but rather explore it. Finally, *attacks* are used to check whether a program is prone to common problems. It often is used for security testing (cf. with the following section). If qualified testers are available and testing has to be done in a short time, experience based techniques can be very effective. With a greater number of testers it can become inefficient, though, and some defects are likely to stay hidden. [3, p. 108f.]

2.2.2.6 Further Techniques

Dynamic testing is heuristic and accepts that test case generation is fuzzy to some degree [25, p. 375]. *Diversifying* techniques try to overcome this fuzziness. The two main methods are back-to-back tests and mutation tests.

For *back-to-back tests*, two or more programs are independently built by multiple development teams based on the same specification. They are intended to be semantically equal [25, p. 376] (i.e. redundant [2, p. 180]). For testing, the programs are run and their outputs are compared. In general, divergences are reported to all development teams in order to check for their cause. Testing is iterated until all programs behave equally. Back-to-back testing can dramatically reduce the number of defects but is costly [25, p. 383]. Nevertheless, it can be cost-effective [105]. Back-to-back testing is especially used for embedded systems [2, p. 184].

Mutation tests do not mean to test a program but the tests written for this program [7, p. 130]. They are attributed to *fault based* testing [4, p. 353ff.]. So called *mutants* are derived from the original program. Mutants are marginally changed and then tested with the original test cases [106]. It can be said that errors are "injected" [101, p. 197f.]. The quality of test cases is reflected by their ability to identify mutants [25, p. 384]. Good test cases are likely to reveal new defects [7, p. 85]—and the mutants. The changes in mutants follow typical programming mistakes such as typos, wrong usage of brackets, and inverted operators [25, p. 384]. *Strong mutation* tests cover the whole program while *weak mutation* tests [107] cover only some components. To increase testing efficiency, mutation tests can be parametrized. However, mutation tests are only applicable with tool support [25, p. 390]. It is estimated that a program of n lines of code requires n^2 strong mutation tests [108].

It is possible to test completely *random*. The difference to error guessing is that there is no intuition that a tester follows, but test cases contain random parameters. This usually is done by using so called test data generators [25, p. 194f.]. The surprising effectiveness of this technique has been demonstrated with Quickcheck, a tool originally developed in Haskell [109–111]. Ports or tools inspired by it exist for the most common programming languages such as Java [112, 113] and C++ [114].

Statistic Testing is based on probability distributions of the usage of classes, methods, or other program components. Tests are generated and their contribution to covering classes, methods, or other program components is assessed. It is specifically used for system tests in which the reliability of a program is checked [25, p. 368]. If statistic testing is done with uniformly distributed tests, test generation equals random testing. This also can be called *stochastic testing* [2, p. 517].

Instead of specifying test cases, programs can be tested with *original data*. This can only be done if very similar programs exist or the tested program is an upgraded version of an older program. The idea is to record data formerly fed to a program and to use it as input for the program to test [26, p. 97ff.]. This kind of testing seems effective because it uses realistic input data. The code coverage of such tests is reported to be low, though [25, p. 195]. This might be improved by carefully selecting the data. Additionally, old datasets might be used as input data for load tests and stress tests [26, p. 97ff.].

2.2.3 Testing of Web based Programs

In recent years, *testing of Web based programs* has become important. Not only has the number of such applications increased but the numbers of them in comparison to classical *rich client* applications has also become much greater. With the emergence of the so called Web 2.0, Web based programs have gained complexity. They are expected to be as comfortable to use as rich client programs. The interaction of client-side scripts such as JavaScript and server-run application parts add further complexity.

In general, most of the techniques that have been described also apply to software that is used on the Internet or accessed via Internet based protocols. Some particularities have to be taken into consideration that arise from the architecture. Often, the model-view-controller (MVC) design pattern [115] is used. Consequently, programs consist of a number of layers that take distinct tasks and encapsulate functionality. Testing the *presentation layer* might for examples reveal failures that are caused by the *business logic layer*, but it will be very hard to locate them. These particularities apply to other multi-layered applications, too. The same applies to load and stress tests. There are some particularities, but they are not only found in Web based software.

Fields of testing that only apply to Web based programs address the interaction of client and server side. For example, programs can be tested with regard to their output (e.g. Web browser compatibility [6, p. 820]) or the interaction of client side and server side code. In particular, partly loading Web pages using asynchronous JavaScript and XML (Ajax) is a challenge. Some tests require specialized tools to perform them with Web based programs (cf. Sect. 2.4).

Especially Web based programs that can be accessed via the Internet can be target of attempts to compromise them. Hence, testing of Web based programs includes security tests (see Sect. 2.2.2.6). Many security tests can be parameterized for Web applications.

2.2.4 Additional Techniques

Not all techniques fit into the chosen categories. Above all, some techniques cannot be categorized because they apply to all or most categories, or amend techniques with context related additions. Such techniques are discussed in this section. Additionally, some techniques are mentioned that might be categorized as non-functional testing techniques; however, in contrast to e.g. performance tests they are rather *checks* than tests by their character.[6]

Object orientation and testing has gained increasing attention in the last ten years. Most testing techniques either originate from the era of imperative programming or are independent of a programming paradigm. Thus, trying to optimize them for testing object oriented programs and to reconsider their applicability is advisable [2, p. 408]. Apparently, object orientation has not simplified testing [116] but rather risen the level of complexity [66, 117, 118]. The most notable differences of

---

[6] A comparison of tests and checks is given in [5, Chap. 7]. Unfortunately, classifying techniques as tests and checks is ambiguous.

object oriented testing concern the phases of module and system testing [4, p. 306ff.] [66, p. 21ff.]:

- Due to modularization, there are more interprocedural interdependencies. This does not only rise complexity but also means that defects might arise due to the interplay of modules developed by several developers.
- Sharing of class members (*fields*) might couple methods of classes that are not meant to or at least do not appear to share data. Method results might be subject to a class' state.
- Programming for reusability and a more generalized functionality of classes introduces more possibilities to test them. In particular, testing has to go beyond the currently required functionality of a program. As a consequence, paradigms such as *test first* demand only explicitly specified functionality to be implemented.
- There is no linear growth between the size of the class and its complexity. In fact, its complexity rises faster.
- Code instrumentation (i.e. the usage of code for a given analytic purpose) is more complex. Dynamic binding complicates static testing methods [7, p. 166].
- Modularization, inheritance, and polymorphism have to be given special care. Manual inspection becomes burdensome [2, p. 409].

Techniques to overcome the above mentioned challenges are diverse and numerous. Detailed remarks on using testing techniques for object oriented programs are given by Sneed and Winter [66], and by Vigenschow [101, Chap. 9]. Liggesmeyer [2, Chap. 13] gives advice how to modify existing techniques; Pezzè and Young present novel approaches [4, Chap. 15].

Particularities apply when programs are tested that do not follow the imperative paradigm. Examples are programs that have been built using *functional* (e.g. [119]) and *logic programming* languages (e.g. [120]). Despite the effort to write such programs, testing might be easier due to the mathematical foundation of the paradigms (cf. [76, p. 135ff.]). While the coverage in textbooks is low, testing of functional and logic programs is an active field of research (cf. e.g. [121, 122]. Details, however, are out of scope.

Embedded software requires special attention for testing. Embedded systems are not only prevalent but also used in many critical contexts such as safety technology and healthcare [2, p. 439]. In general, many of the above described methods can be applied. In particular, static methods are feasible since most embedded systems have a limited number of states and do not consist of a lot of code. It might be possible to simulate them as state machines. Extensive embedded systems often are split into separate subsystems. Ideally, testing should prove correctness [2, p. 440]. Many embedded systems are also *real-time systems*. As a consequence, parts of the software need to comply with real-time requirements in particular with regard to their response characteristics. Embedded systems are used for a variety of purposes [101, p. 222f.]. Their criticality follows their real-time behavior [101, p. 223]: in *hard real-time* systems, time violation has fatal consequences; in *soft real-time* systems, time violations are annoying but not fatal; *stable real-time* systems act *soft* until a deadline is reached. Testing thus needs to take time criticality into account. Embedded systems have to be failure-tolerant [101, p. 224]. Even if failures occur, the system should continue its work. Testing thus has to include this functionality—embedded software has to be checked for reliability and availability [2, p. 441f.]. Besides, in many cases quantitative figures on a system's reliability are expected [2, p. 439] (for instance by the contractual partner). Due to their specialty, distinct techniques will not be discussed in this book. Introductions are given in [101, p. 226ff.] and [2, Chap. 14].

Security tests subsume techniques from various other techniques and some special methods. Typically, so called *penetration tests* are *attacks* that try to compromise a program [3, Chap. 13]. Attacks could aim at *crashing* the system, at gaining unauthorized rights for using it, on altering or deleting data, on retrieving classified data, and generally at using a system in a way it is not intended to or the user is not allowed to. Typically used testing techniques are stress tests, static analysis, and function oriented tests. The latter can be used to find program statements prone to so called *buffer overflows* [123] which can be used to insert malicious code into a program. Security testing is a field of its own and not further discussed here. An introduction is e.g. given in [124, 125]. First and foremost, security of web applications and test methods for them have gained increased attention in the last years (cf. [126, 127]). Security testing should follow checklists and guidelines (e.g. [6, Chap. 24] or [128]).

Regression testing is not a technique of its own but has to be mentioned along the other techniques. It describes the repetition of tests after the tested program has been changed [2, p. 192f.]. Regression testing should show that defects of past versions have been fixed and that no new defects have entered the program as side effects [25, p. 242ff.]. It is of no importance whether a program was changed as part of development, to add functionality, or to fix defects. Regression testing should either aim for efficiency or automatization. Automatization is a mean to increase efficiency. Regression testing relies on an adequate documentation [4, p. 483f.]. Ideally, only those tests are repeated that would find failures in changed components [66, p. 14f.]. Alternatively, all tests are repeated if this is possible without human intervention. Advice for choosing which tests are to be repeated is e.g. given in [4, p. 484ff.].

Companies often buy software instead of developing it on their own. Large companies nevertheless employ developers and testers; software these companies buy uses to be customized or at least adapted to the existing system landscape. Therefore, *testing of standard software* is seen as a technique of its own. It, however, follows many of the techniques described earlier. In most cases, no glass-box tests can be done because the source code is not (fully) available. Failures need to be documented with much care in order to report them to the company that develops the program. Testing should not only find defects but make sure that a program meets the expected reliability. At the same time, the effort should be kept low [6, p. 841]. An introduction and checklists are provided by Perry [6, Chap. 22].

Testing *usability* and *accessibility* has some characteristics of testing but could also be categorized as a *check*. It ascertains how usable a program is, how effective it works, how satisfied its users are, and how easy users adapt to it [3, Chap. 11]. Inspection and review techniques similar to those of static analysis can be used although testing is dynamic in this case.

Similar considerations apply to tests for *maintainability* and *portability* [3, Chaps. 15, 16]. It is without questions that it is vital for most programs to be maintainable and that some programs need to be portable. Nevertheless, judging the portability of a program with regard to its adaptability, installability, replaceability, ability to coexist with other programs, and its conformity with standards (*portability compliance*) [129] is not really a test. Testing for maintainability should be accompanied with an *impact analysis* that shows which part of a program would be affected by e.g. a migration to another platform [5, p. 103ff.]—this analysis is *not* a test. Consequently, for this work these kinds of tests are seen as checks despite their naming as *tests*. An exception are portability tests in multi-platform environments. They assess whether programs that exist in versions for multiple platforms behave in the same way [6, p. 876f.]. This is done by using techniques as described earlier and comparing the results.

Another testing-related activity that not really is a test is examining a program's documentation [6, Chap. 20]. Checking the documentation is vital; creating and maintaining it accounts for 10–25% of the total development costs of standard software [6, p. 797]. Writing a documentation cannot be compared to writing a computer program, though. Incorrect specification will be reflected in the documentation and there are typical mistakes that are done when writing it; nevertheless, it does not have the technical character of programming and programming related activities.

Finally, quality assurance of the specification and of requirements rather is a management activity than a check. Nevertheless, it often is mentioned in textbooks about testing. An introduction is for instance given by Roitzsch [25, p. 258ff.].

2.2.5 Techniques with Regard to Phases

While the above discussed techniques can be used in all phases of testing, they especially apply to the first phases. Technically speaking, tests conducted in different phases of testing are no techniques of their own. However, some techniques are rather used in one phase than in others. Besides, some particularities apply to some phases. Therefore, it for instance is spoken of *integration tests* as if it was a technique. More details are e.g. given in [4, Chap. 22].

For integration tests it has to be decided whether all components are integrated at once ("big bang integration" [77, p. 309]) or if components are added (and tested) successively. The latter can be done in a bottom up, top down, or backbone (simplest functions first) approach [88, p. 113f.]. A distinction is also possible by *incremental* vs. *not incremental* and *dependency oriented* vs. *function oriented* strategies [5, p. 23ff.]. Integration tests are done when distinct components have been sufficiently tested [5, p. 23] but should not be postponed too long [96, p. 267]. They can follow the same techniques that are applied to a broader set of by then integrated components. In general, integration tests are less technically driven than component tests [26, p. 53ff.]. Consequently, rather manual testing methods are chosen.

System tests are integration tests on a broader level. They use the same methods, but the focus is even less technical. They consist of a high number of distinct tests [25, p. 75]. Sometimes, advanced system tests that try to fathom whether a system can be considered to be *finished*, are called *smoke tests* [130, Chap. 17].

Similar to integration testing, *acceptance tests* are rather a phase than a method. Their particularity is a focus on black-box tests and the involvement of customers or other non-technical personnel that is hoped to accept the program. The aim *should* be to highlight the program's quality and to get user feedback instead of finding defects.

2.3 Organization of Testing

Testing is based on technical methods but it also has an organizational dimension. Successful testing is bound to preconditions that have to be met in companies that conduct software tests. Test organization comprises of seeing testing as a process and dividing it into phases, of documenting tests, of test management, and of certifications for testers. The first two tasks are even important for academic software development, or software development by single users.

2.3.1 Phases of Testing

If testing is meant to be effective and efficient, it is not just done at one fixed point in the development process. It neither is static but the testing techniques should adapt to the status of the program under development. By no means, software development and testing should follow a "code and fix" approach [77, p. 28f.].

Therefore, testing is done in phases. This partitioning is called *staging* by practitioners [26, p. 13]. There is no definite scheme for the phases used; but there is a typical layout which can superficially be followed or become a corporation-wide standard. The partitioning proposed roughly resembles the classical V-Model [40, 131] and has been described in [132] and subsequentially in [133].

1. *Component test* (also known as *module test* or *unit test*)
   Developers test modules they coded. They work both incremental and iterative. Testing responsibility remains with the developers even though there can be guidelines on how to test. Usually, the level of documentation is low. Since developers know their own code, they conduct Glass-Box tests and probably also Gray-Box tests. Black even distinguishes between component and unit tests: unit tests concern "an individual piece of code" whereas component tests already deal with "pieces of the system" [21, p. 5f.].

2. *Central component test*
   In contrast to the first phase, this optional test is usually not done on the developers' working stations. Components are tested on a system which is similar

to the target system for the finished software product. Developers are usually supported by testers.

3. *Integration test* (also known as *product test* [21, p. 6f.])
   This test usually is not done on developers' working stations but on a testing system. Components developed by multiple developers are integrated and their interplay is checked. In general, developers are still responsible for this test [18, p. 224] and it is finished with a formal approval. Developers assure interoperability; if integration related problems are found in a later phase, interoperability has to be fixed and the integration test repeated.

4. *Performance test*
   A first, optional performance test can be conducted whilst or shortly after the system test. It aims at getting a first idea of the system's performance and at finding possible performance bottlenecks.

5. *System test*
   The system test is a large-scale integration test which is less technically focused. No more Glass-Box but only Black-Box tests are used. *Test stubs* [101, p. 180f.] and so called *mock objects* [134], which simulate behavior of missing components in earlier phases, are successively removed. Testing commonly is done by dedicated testers who do not know the source code. Testing should be documented with much effort and the phase be finished with a formal approval that assures the program's quality to be at a level that satisfies the customer. System tests are regarded as particularly important—there even are textbooks that solely deal with them [135].

6. *Performance test*
   As soon as all main components are integrated, another optional measurement can be done. It is driven functionally and not done by developers. Whereas the first performance test could reveal algorithmic limitations and general misconceptions, the system performance measures the program under realistic conditions.

7. *Acceptance test*
   The customer, an internal department, or an academic principal tests the almost finished program. The system is checked for compliance with the specification. Thus, it can be part of the development contract [21, p. 7f.]. In certain software development projects this phase can be omitted. If development follows an agile paradigm, acceptance tests are regarded as the *key* test [136].

8. *Pilot test*
   A pilot test can be done with internal departments or with key customers. The almost finished product is installed on a number of systems. It is first tested and eventually can be used productively. Beta tests put the concept of pilot tests to a larger number of testers. They can be conducted in a closed community or public.

9. *Productive usage*
   Software is put into regular operation.

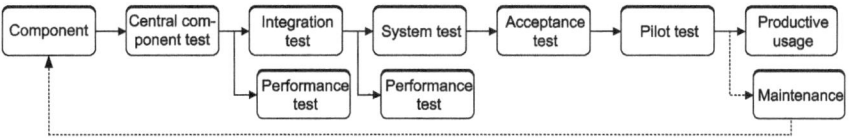

Fig. 2.3 Schematic model of testing phases

10. *Maintenance*

Optionally, the system is maintained. This is particularly important if development is a periodic process that leads to new releases of the program.

Of course, the above phases can only be realized by companies of sufficient size. Smaller companies and academic developers will not have distinct testers, probably no reserved systems for testing, and a less sophisticated organizational background. In this case, the model gets much simpler and will rely on a skeleton of component, integration, and system test with an optional acceptance test [18, p. 225]. In the opposite direction, a large company could add subphases and even more organizational embedding.

The above model does not behave like the waterfall model [137]. While the order of the phases is fixed—there simply is no reason to do a system test before doing an integration test—there can be feedback in the testing process, it can partly be parallelized, and it can be iterative. This is also reflected in the so called *W-Model*, an extension of the V-Model [138, 139].

The phases are shown in Fig. 2.3. From the left to the right the program under development becomes more mature. At the same time, the technical focus of testing gets lower; acceptance testing is purely functional. If testing is successful, the number of defects found should shrink with each phase. At the same time the severity and with it the costs for removing a defect increases from left to right [133]. Fixing a defect in a finished program could be more than 100 times as costly as avoiding it during specification [6, p. 91f.]. Staging thus rises testing efficiency [21, p. 8f.].

If a software development process model is used, phases might look differently. This applies less to rather formal frameworks such as the Rational Unified Process (RUP) [140] but even more to *agile* models such as Extreme Programming (XP) [136]. Overviews of some widely used models are given by Spillner et al. [24, Chap. 3] and Wallmüller [18, p. 127ff.]. There are ample possibilities for extension. For example, requirements engineering [141] can be combined with testing [142, 143]. This helps to identify requirements, test software based on its specification, and can even help to find defects. Furthermore, it is possible to subdivide phases (e.g. there is the "phase model for low level tests" [22, Chap. 10]). Additions to the phases and their embedding into the overall development process are clearly out of scope of this work.

Agile software development [144, 145] has become increasingly popular. It originates in XP [136], which it is still attributed to [146]. Agile development includes agile testing [147]. It refrains from structuring and formal processes in favor of *agility*. However, agile testing requires management support since it has to be embedded into a fitting organizational background. Using some agile techniques in combination with formal processes is possible, but in general agile testing is done in alignment with flexible project management approaches such as *Scrum* [148, 149].

2.3.2 Test Driven Development

Usually, testing phases follow development phases. Even if testing and development are parallelized, testing follows coding of a module. Test driven development (TDD) is an approach that changes this basic order. It is also named *test first development* [150, p. 203], which explains its principle. First of all, a test case is written, and then code is implemented. The code's aim is to enable the successful execution of the test case [5, p. 20f.]. Typically, unit testing tools are used [151, p. 36f.]. In general, testing phases still exist and many tests (e.g. static analyses) are done the same way and at the same time as in classical development. However, development always follows the implementation of unit tests.

With test driven development, the implemented functionality tends to be simple. It *only* has to fulfill the tests' requirements. Nevertheless, TDD is said to improve maintainability and to even increase code reusage [150, p. 195]. To work test driven, developers need to write code with much discipline [151, p. 8]. TDD can also decrease development costs because defects are discovered at a very early stage of development [150, p. 202]. They are also likely to be found shortly after they were introduced [151, p. 9] which supports to locate them. However, similar to XP (which it relates to [150, p. 204f.]), TDD is no definite solution. In order to be successfully applied, it has to be in alignment with the philosophy met in a company.

Test driven development has become a field of its own; more detail on it is e.g. given in [150–152].

2.3.3 Documentation

Documenting the testing effort is essential. It is no exaggeration to say that tests that have not been documented are worthless. Only if developer and tester are the same person and defects are fixed immediately, this claim does not hold. Even in this case, testing efficiency is reduced. Companies tend to neglect documenting, though [18, p. 149].

A software test documentation typically tracks the kind of tests conducted, the parameters and conditions that are applied to them, the involved employees, and the outcome. It also varies with the testing phases to reflect changing aims. Thus, a *test plan* could also be attributed to the documentation [4, p. 522]. A universal documentation helps to learn from former test runs. It greatly increases the reusability of test cases and hence improves regression testing [4, p. 517f.]. Moreover, it helps to control testing [18, p. 258ff.]. Data (e.g. on the success) can be aggregated and checked. This can be extended to become a *test controlling* which helps to proactively avoid testing related problems [153]. With a growing database, the test documentation can also be a resource of knowledge on testing related problems [26, p. 56ff.].

The starting level for a test documentation usually is characterized by the usage of spreadsheets. Preparing such spreadsheets can be seen as a managerial task [21, Chap. 5]; this is especially true if templates become mandatory. Tool support increases efficiency [18, p. 155]. If a dedicated system is employed, it can greatly reduce the manual effort for documenting tests [67]. Aligning this system with a *test case management* system enables automatic reporting of test cases [67]. Testers merely need to check whether the automated data import was successful and whether documented test cases should be annotated with additional information.

Documenting tests can be seen as a strategic decision. It has to be aligned with the preconditions met and the chosen management approach towards testing. Documents can make up a hierarchy that deals with varying levels of technical details [24, Chap. 4]. Documenting tests can become part of a *test concept*. It is even possible to set up test documentation phases.

The test documentation can be used to install a *test reporting*. Reporting helps to learn about a project's status and the already implemented functionality. Furthermore, it can help to determine how the developed program's functionality will look like [6, p. 17]. It might also be used to determine when the project will be finished.

Besides being discussed in the literature on testing, there also is the IEEE Standard 829 (*IEEE Standard for Software Test Documentation*) [154, 155] which gives detailed advice on how to maintain a test documentation. Documentation obligations are also becoming part of IT related business frameworks such as the earlier mentioned CobiT [26, p. 58].

It has also been suggested that the documentation of the software under development should be tested [6, Chap. 20]. However, it is questionable whether this procedure satisfies the characteristics of being a test. In addition, technical details are less important for software documentation papers such as handbooks or manuals. Checking the documentation will require the collaboration of software developers, GUI designers, and writers or editors that prepare comprehensible texts. In conclusion, it is agreed with those authors who distinguish between testing and checking (cf. e.g. [5, Chap. 6]) and who regard an assessment of program documentations as *checking*. Nevertheless, documenting is essential in any phase of a software development process that strives for software quality [18, p. 149f.].

2.3.4 Test Management

If testing is done in teams, software developing companies employ an at least high two-digit number of employees, or companies emphasize a controlled testing process, test management becomes important. Test management therefore can be seen as a *management discipline* with strategic impact. Of course, even for single developers it is important to *manage* their testing effort and for example work phase oriented (see Sect. 2.3.1); this section deals with the management of testing in companies.

Test management is particularly advisable due to the high level of specialization among testers [18, p. 240]. There is a number of roles that need knowledge of test management:

- Testers need to understand how to work in teams and in alignment with software developers. In general, developers should not test the program they have implemented; testers should not try to fix defects they find [96, p. 258]. Thus, close cooperation is needed.
- For large projects, test managers can be installed that take similar functions like development project managers or senior software architects. In particular, they should set up *testing plans* [96, p. 273].
- For projects with a three-digit number of involved employees, a central testing manager might coordinate teams of testers.
- Project managers and controllers need to understand how testing is done.
- Executives should understand the impact of testing as well as its preconditions. Otherwise, testing is likely to be neglected instead of being seen as an important task (cf. "culture of testing" [153]).

Traditionally, test management has been neglected or even been seen as superfluous [18, p. 242f.]. It, however, can contribute to improved software development processes [18, p. 240ff.]. Thus, it supports to decrease costs while increasing software quality. Consequently, modern textbooks on testing often have at least one chapter on test management. In can be aligned with a holistic quality management approach (cf. Sect. 2.1.4.4 on the DIN EN ISO 9001 standard).

According to Wallmüller, software quality management should follow a set of principles [18, p. 17ff.]:

- It should define operational properties to measure quality. Furthermore, it should support to survey and to analyze them. In this context, it is particularly important to generate *metrics* and infer advisable actions from them. Metrics are key figures that measure technical or individual performance [24, p. 283ff.].
- It should provide product oriented and project oriented quality planning.
- Feedback from quality assessment should be used to improve processes. Ideally, this would lead to a process of continuous refinements [26, p. 33].
- Quality assessment should always be conducted by at least two employees.
- It should develop a proactive quality control. The maxim is to avoid defects in software products rather than to find failures and fix the corresponding defects.
- It should support testing and development with the aim of finding failures in early phases of development.
- Integrated quality management should be provided. This means that test management must not be a task of its own but interwoven with the development process.
- It should support independent quality assessments. In particular, it should ensure that software is not only tested by its developers to prevent conflict of aims.
- It should examine the effort for quality management and seek to improve it.

At the same time, unsuccessful strategies should be avoided. In the style of anti patterns in software development (Sect. 2.2.1.2, p. 45) they are called *software project management anti-patterns* and collected in the literature [156, 157].

In contrast to other disciplines that have a technical background and require management, test managers require profound knowledge of the technology [21]. Therefore, test management does not only consist of tasks that can be derived from the above mentioned principles. Besides this focus on supporting the strive for high quality software and continuous process improvements, it should also provide technical support. This can be done in the form of infrastructure support. A *test lab*— also known as a *test center* [26, p. 47ff.]—provides the technical infrastructure for timely tests under realistic conditions [21, p. 293ff.]. Test centers can be part of a sophisticated *testing organization* [18, p. 255f.]. Furthermore, test management deals with staffing a test team, test outsourcing, test project management, test planning [18, p. 242ff.], and the economics of testing [21, Chaps. 8, 10, 12]. Finally, test managers are also responsible for the education of the testing staff and personnel that does preparatory work for testers [24, Chap. 10].

A detailed overview of test management and software quality management is given by Black [21], Spillner et al. [24] and Wallmüller [18].

2.3.5 Certification

Certificates in the context of the IT industry attest humans that they have a certain level of knowledge or skill in an IT related field. They are very common in IT jobs and are seen as an additional form of education [158, 159]. Apparently, certificates have been used in the industry for more than three decades [160]. Certification is particularly common in the fields of enterprise applications (cf. [161–163]) and programming languages (cf. [164–166]). In addition to certification for humans, it also is possible to certify companies' adherence to standards.

After scanning the literature, it can be said that testing is particularly popular for certifications. There is a myriad of textbooks on testing related certifications (for instance [167]) and especially on certifications by the International Software Testing Qualifications Board (ISTQB) (such as [168, 169]). There are not only basic, but also advanced courses that usually require a basic course as their foundation [170]. A Google web search [171] shows a great number of courses to prepare for certificates on testing. It also shows that the ISTQB certification seems to be the most popular one; nevertheless, there are several other courses such as the certified software tester (CSTE) [172] or the Standardisation Testing and Quality Certification (STQC) [173]. Unfortunately, there are no scientifically assessed numbers available on the total number of certified testers per program; numbers found on the Web vary widely.

Interestingly, general books on software testing such as [2, 4] do not cover certificates. It is however dealt with in newer literature on test management [21, p. 334ff.].

Certifications "might or might not" involve training, but each certified person has passed an exam [21, p. 334]. Thus, without importance whether the person has taken a course and expanded his knowledge or not, companies can rely on the certified knowledge. In other words: this person is very likely to master a predefined level of knowledge and has a set of testing skills. Nevertheless, it can be argued that certifications do not reflect experience and so called *soft skills*. Both can be seen as very important for testing [26, p. 48]. Besides, certifications are not free of charge. Typical courses cost a low four-digit sum plus a high three-digit sum for the exam (cf. [174]). If organized as on-the-job training and targeting employees that do not yet have testing skills, this fee should be acceptable for companies. However, it is rather high if payed by individuals before applying for a job. Notwithstanding, a discussion of pros and cons of testing certificates from a business or from an employee's perspective is out of scope of this work. A decision for or against certifications is particularly bound to a company's culture [26, p. 58ff.].

2.4 Tool Support and Automatization

Textbooks on software testing usually advise the use of test tools and test automatization. This is common sense: test tools promise to make testing much more effective by offering techniques humans are incapable of; automatization promises to relieve humans of repetitive tasks and make testing more economic [101, p. 159]. However, tools are much less commonly used than usually expected. Automatization is hardly used at all [26, p. 17f.]. These findings from the IHK project only seemingly do not align with the literature. None of the textbooks cited in this chapter suggest specific tools (besides very basic solutions) or give advice on automatization that is easy to implement.

Tool support for testing is a topic of its own. Therefore, the current status is introduced only briefly. Test automatization will be given more emphasis in Chap. 4, as the tool Muggl means to automate testing. It has to be noted that most tools not only extend the testing scope but also offer more or less sophisticated automatization. Therefore, this work distinguishes between automatizing some testing tasks which makes testing more convenient, and *true* automatization. The latter describes (almost) completely automated testing. This book does not follow an approach which treats *test tool usage* and *test automatization* as synonymous. This is e.g. assumed by Cleff [5, Chap. 8] and Thaller [7, Chap. 8].

2.4.1 Test Tools

Test tools—also known as computer aided software testing (CAST)—can serve a variety of purposes. In general, they are "vehicles" for test techniques [6, Chap. 5]. Spillner et al. propose the following distinction [24, p. 324ff.]:

- Tools for the management and control of testing have a less technical focus. They are used to plan testing, measure the testing effort and results, and manage the suite of test cases.
- Test case generators, as the name suggests, generate test cases. Generation strategies vary widely as does the level of automatization.
- Analytic tools automate static tests or enable static testing techniques that would not be feasible without tool support.
- Execution of tests is supported by a number of specialized tools. They can work on a low abstraction level and execute suits of test cases or on a high abstraction level and offer *Capture&Replay* capabilities. Examples for the first category are unit test tools such as JUnit [175] or CppUnit [176]. An introduction to unit test tools is given by Vigenschow [101, p. 160ff.]. The second category comprises of tools that particularly focus on GUI testing. They can monitor testers' actions and automatically repeat them at a later time. This can be even done in a script based manner to parameterize such tests [101, p. 191ff.].
- Specialized tools support particular situations. Examples are tools to tests Web applications such as HtmlUnit [177] or Selenium [178] and mutation test tools.

Much more detailed classifications on a more technical level have been suggested [179]. Computer aided software engineering (CASE) and similar tools can also be regarded as a way to improve testing [18, p. 169f.]. However, a very detailed view is unsuitable for an overview as given here. Another suggestion is to align the classification with that of testing techniques. Consequently, dynamic, static, formal, and analyzing tools can be distinguished [2, Chap. 12]. Bath and McKay use a combination of the latter and Spillner et al.'s approach [3].

Test tools are particularly useful if they are capable of taking over repetitive tasks [5, Chap. 8] [21, p. 81ff.], if a high level of precision is needed, if automated metric generation and documenting of tests is desired [2, p. 392], or if large amounts of data need to be processed. The main aim thus is a higher efficacy [3, p. 324f.]. A checklist to judge tools by usefulness is given by Liggesmeyer [2, p. 404f.]. While it is undisputed that test tools can highly increase testing effectiveness and efficiency, there are a number of risks. They arise from unrealistic expectations towards test tools, underestimating effort and time required to introduce tools, putting too little effort into continuous improvement and maintenance of tools, and unreflected trust in tools [5, p. 272ff.]. Another important decision is *make-or-buy*; merits, costs, and risks have to be taken into account [3, p. 349f.]. Standard solutions usually are powerful but costly and probably inflexible; implementing tools requires much time but allows to tailor them to processes [26, p. 30f.].

Evaluating test tools requires considerable effort. It is not merely a decision that weights price and performance but has to take into account the effect on processes as well as other organizational consequences, the target adequateness [6, p. 188ff.] of the tools, and other side-effects [24, p. 330ff.]. Ample time to install a tool and get into working with it should be considered [7, p. 233]. Tools should also be selected based on their integration capabilities [3, p. 340ff.] [180]. Introducing selected tools should be controlled and the merits of the introduction continuously checked

[5, p. 275ff.] [6, Chap. 5] [24, p. 330ff.]. A guideline for choosing and installing tools is e.g. provided by Perry [6, Chap. 5]. Initial experiences from improvements due to the usage of tests tools are presented by Thaller [7, p. 239ff.]. After all, choosing tools should be based on a process that evaluates the usefulness of test automatization [4, p. 497].

2.4.2 True Automatization

Defining the ideal testing technique is no challenge. Consider a tool that requires source code or a program file as input and that generates a suite of test cases that detects all possible failures. It furthermore helps to suggest which defects cause the failures and aids in fixing them. Unfortunately, no such tool exists. It is highly questionable whether it is possible to implement such a tool at all. As stated at the beginning of this chapter, it is only possible to test against a specification. Therefore, true automatization that does not require human intervention requires a computer-readable specification. This is for example done by model checking. However, the effort is high and impractical in many cases. Merely repeating steps does not qualify as automatization. It goes beyond what Capture and Replay tools do [181, p. 26]. Nevertheless, automatization is an important aim. The maxim is to relief humans of as much effort as possible.

Automatization is recommended for testing programs of considerable size [6, p. 72f.]. Regrettably, automatization becomes more complicated with a program's size. In the course of developing Muggl, we noticed that it is notably easier to generate test cases for single algorithms than for modules or even extensive programs.

It is important to note that automatization is no universal cure [3, p. 343ff.] unless it is *perfect* or reasonably intelligent. Self-verification of software could be impossible[7] and it is questionable whether computer systems will soon reach a level of artificial intelligence (AI) that would allow them to replace human testers in manual testing task (cf. with the discussion of the *AI winter* [182, 183]). Automatization is simple and feasible in some cases but desirable yet impossible in others [4, p. 497ff.]. It should be based on an analysis of usefulness and costs [184]. Automatization requires a highly structured approach and much discipline. Or, as Bath and McKay put it [3, Chap. 18]: "Automatizing chaos merely accelerates it."[8]

In general, four fields of testing are suitable for extended automatization:

- The generation of metrics [4, p. 502ff.]. Tools that analyze source code, bytecode or programs and calculate key figures are widely available [26, Appendix B].
- Automatically generating the test documentation while executing tests poses little technical challenge [67].

---

[7] As of today, it is seen as impossible due to the *halting problem*. Programs might verify themselves under certain conditions, but no universal approach is known.

[8] Translated from the German original by the author.

- Tools for static analysis and automated proofs are currently in development but very promising [4, p. 505ff.].
- TCG is possible in a variety of steps from manual to fully automated.

A problem of test automatization is that it is "more expensive to automate a test than to perform it once manually" [181, p. 5]. Consequently, it has to be well planned in order to avoid a waste of resources. Nevertheless, automatization offers a number of merits [181, p. 9f.]:

- It helps to run existing tests on new versions of a program. Also, the reuse of test cases can be improved.
- It enables to run regression tests more often—ideally, they are repeated continuously.
- Tests can be performed that would be impossible without (half-)automated tool support.
- Resources can be utilized more efficiently if tasks are automated while humans focus on techniques that require supervision.
- Economic and organizational targets such as an earlier time-to-market and a higher confidence in products can be met.
- Testing might become more reliable [22, p. 472].
- Testing of derivative programs, upgrades, etc. becomes easier [7, p. 228f.].

Automatization comes at a price; it is prone to cause problems if not implemented carefully. Despite its merits it has several limitations [181, p.10ff.]:

- Management expectations often are unrealistic. Automatizing takes much time and effort until satisfying results can be reached. At the same time it is almost impossible to introduce test automatization without management support.
- Automatization does not necessarily find additional defects. Automatization *might* find more defects, but the aim could also be to find defects more efficiently.
- Maintenance of automated tests and test automatization tools can require a considerable amount of time and tie up resources. Unfortunately, interoperability of commercial tools is a problem as well [26, p. 87ff.].
- Automatization does not replace manual testing. Despite progress in automatization, manual tests will be required for the foreseeable future. If an extreme level of reliability is required, manual testing with tremendous effort is likely to reveal more failures than automated testing (also cf. [26, p. 17f.]). In particular, tools neither have "imagination" [181, p. 24] nor intuition.

It is, nonetheless, refrained from supporting the argument that "test automatization does not improve effectiveness" [181, p. 24]. While in many cases manual testing with high effort is more effective and automated testing might "adversely affect the evolvability of testing" [181, p. 24], progress with Muggl is promising. Automated testing is not a "quick cure" [185, p. 350]. But under certain—admittedly still limited—conditions, automated test case generation is effective (also see Chaps. 7 and 8).

References

1. Myers, G.J., Sandler, C.: The Art of Software Testing, 2nd edn. Wiley, Chichester (2004)
2. Liggesmeyer, P.: Software-Qualität: Testen, Analysieren und Verifizieren von Software, 2nd edn. Spektrum-Akademischer Verlag, Berlin (2009)
3. Bath, G., McKay, J.: Praxiswissen Softwaretest—Test Analyst und Technical Test Analyst. Dpunkt, Heidelberg (2010)
4. Pezze, M., Young, M.: Software Testing and Analysis: Process, Principles and Techniques. Wiley, New York (2007)
5. Cleff, T.: Basiswissen Testen von Software. W3L GmbH (2010)
6. Perry, W.E.: Software Testen. mitp, Bonn (2003)
7. Thaller, G.E.: Software-Test, 2nd edn. Heise, Hannover (2002)
8. Rubin, J., Chisnell, D.: Handbook of Usability Testing: How to Plan, Design, and Conduct Effective Tests. Wiley, Hoboken (2008)
9. Nielsen, J.: Usability Engineering. Morgan Kaufmann Publishers, San Francisco (1994)
10. Leventhal, L., Barnes, J.: Usability Engineering: Process, Products and Examples. Prentice Hall, Upper Saddle River (2007)
11. Sears, A., Jacko, J.A. (eds.): The Human–Computer Interaction Handbook: Fundamentals, Evolving Technologies and Emerging Applications, 2nd edn. CRC Press, Boca Raton (2008)
12. Sharp, H., Rogers, Y., Preece, J.: Interaction Design: Beyond Human–Computer Interaction, 2nd edn. Wiley, Hoboken (2007)
13. Shneiderman, B., Plaisant, C., Cohen, M., Jacobs, S.: Designing the User Interface: Strategies for Effective Human–Computer Interaction, 5th edn. Addison Wesley, Reading (2009)
14. Zeller, A.: Why Programs Fail: A Guide to Systematic Debugging. Morgan Kaufmann, San Francisco (2006)
15. IEEE, The Institute of Electrical and Electronics Engineers, Inc.: IEEE Std 1044-2009: IEEE Standard Classification for Software Anomalies. New York (2010)
16. Marick, B.: The Craft of Software Testing: Subsystem Testing Including Object-Based and Object-Oriented Testing. Prentice-Hall, Upper Saddle River (1995)
17. Meyer, B.: Seven principles of software testing. Computer **41**(8), 99–101 (2008)
18. Wallmüller, E.: Software-Qualitätsmanagement in der Praxis, 2nd edn. Hanser, München (2001)
19. IEEE, The Institute of Electrical and Electronics Engineers, Inc.: IEEE Std 610.12-1990: IEEE Standard Glossary of Software Engineering Terminology. New York (1990)
20. IEEE, The Institute of Electrical and Electronics Engineers, Inc.: IEEE Std 610.12 (H)-1990: IEEE Standard Glossary of Software Engineering Terminology (HyperCard Stack). New York (1990)
21. Black, R.: Managing the Testing Process, 3rd edn. Wiley, Indianapolis (2009)
22. Pol, M., Koomen, T., Spillner, A.: Management und Optimierung des Testprozesses: Ein praktischer Leitfaden für erfolgreiches Testen von Software mit TPI und TMap, 2nd edn. dpunkt, Heidelberg (2002)
23. Myers, G.J., Sandler, C.: The Art of Software Testing. Wiley, Chichester (2004)
24. Spillner, A., Roßner, T., Winter, M., Linz, T.: Praxiswissen Software Test—Test Management. Dpunkt, Heidelberg (2008)
25. Roitzsch, E.H.P.: Analytische Softwarequalitätssicherung in Theorie und Praxis: Der Weg zur Software mit hoher Qualität durch statisches Prüfen, dynamisches Testen, formales Beweisen. Monsenstein und Vannerdat (2005)
26. Majchrzak, T.A., Kuchen, H.: IHK-Projekt Softwaretests: Auswertung. In: Working Papers, Vol. 2. Förderkreis der Angewandten Informatik an der Westfälischen Wilhelms-Universität, Münster e.V. (2010)
27. Clarke, E.M., Grumberg, O., Long, D.E.: Model checking. In: Proceedings of the NATO Advanced Study Institute on Deductive Program Design, pp. 305–349. Springer, Secaucus (1996)

28. Baier, C., Katoen, J.P.: Principles of Model Checking Representation and Mind Series. The MIT Press, Cambridge (2008)
29. Bérard, B., Bidoit, M., Finkel, A., Laroussinie, F., Petit, A., Petrucci, L., Schnoebelen, Ph., McKenzie, P.: Systems and Software Verification: Model-Checking Techniques and Tools. Springer, Heidelberg (2001)
30. Jhala, R., Majumdar, R.: Software model checking. ACM Comput. Surv. **41**(4), 21:1–21:54 (2008)
31. ISO: ISO/IEC 12119:1994 Information Technology—Software Packages—Quality Requirements and Testing. Geneva (1994)
32. http://www.istqb.org/
33. http://www.german-testing-board.info/
34. http://www.german-testing-board.info/de/lehrplaene.shtm
35. Spillner, A., Linz, T.: Basiswissen Softwaretest: Aus- und Weiterbildung zum Certified Tester—Foundation Level nach ISTQB-Standard. dpunkt (2010)
36. http://www.w3.org/
37. Abran, A., Bourque, P., Dupuis, R., Moore, J.W., Tripp, L.L. (eds.): Guide to the Software Engineering Body of Knowledge—SWEBOK. IEEE Press, Piscataway (2004)
38. Höhn, R., Höppner, S. (eds.): Das V-Modell XT: Grundlagen, Methodik und Anwendungen. Springer, Berlin (2008)
39. http://www.v-modell-xt.de/
40. Dröschel, W., Heuser, W., Midderhoff, R. (eds.): Inkrementelle und Objektorientierte Vorgehensweisen mit dem V-Modell 97. Oldenbourg, München (1998)
41. n. A.: DO-178B, Software Considerations in Airborne Systems and Equipment Certification. Radio Technical Commission for Aeronautics (RTCA) (1992)
42. CENELEC: DIN EN 50128, Railway applications. Communications, signalling and processing systems. Software for railway control and protection systems. European Committee for Electrotechnical Standardization (CENELEC) (2001)
43. IEC: IEC 62304:2006 Medical Device Software—Software Life Cycle Processes. Geneva (2006)
44. IEC: IEC 61508 Edition 2.0. International Electrotechnical Commission (IEC) (2010)
45. n. A.: The Official Introduction to the ITIL 3 Service Lifecycle: Office of Government Commerce. The Stationery Office (2007)
46. http://www.isaca.org/Knowledge-Center/cobit/Documents/CobiT-4.1-Brochure.pdf
47. n. A.: CMMI for Development, Version 1.2. Carnegie Mellon Software Engineering Institute (2006)
48. Finkelstein, A.: A software process immaturity model. SIGSOFT Softw. Eng. Notes **17**(4), 22–23 (1992)
49. http://www.grisha.ru/cmm/cimm.htm
50. Pol, M., Teunissen, R., van Veenendaal, E.: Gestructureerd testen: Een inroductie tot Tmap. Tutein Nolthenius (1998)
51. Pol, M., Teunissen, R., van Veenendaal, E.: Software Testing: A Guide to the TMap Approach. Addison-Wesley, Boston (2001)
52. Koomen, T., Pol, M.: Test Process Improvement: A Practical Step-by-Step Guide to Structured Testing. Addison-Wesley, Boston (1999)
53. Sogeti: TPI Next—Business Driven Test Process Improvement. UTN Publishers, The Netherlands (2009)
54. ISO: ISO 9000:2005 Quality Management Systems—Fundamentals and Vocabulary. Geneva (2005)
55. ISO: ISO 9001:2008 Quality Management Systems—Requirements. Geneva (2008)
56. ISO: ISO 9004:2009 Managing for the Sustained Success of an Organization—a Quality Management Approach. Geneva (2009)
57. Kanji, G.K., Asher, M.: 100 Methods for Total Quality Management. Sage Publications, London (1996)

58. Balzert, H.: Lehrbuch der Softwaretechnik: Softwaremanagement, 2nd edn. Spektrum Akademischer Verlag, Heidelberg (2008)
59. Behm, P., Benoit, P., Faivre, A., Meynadier, J.M.: Météor: a successful application of B in a large project. In: Wing, J., Woodcock, J., Davies, J. (eds.) FM'99—Formal Methods, Lecture Notes in Computer Science, vol. 1708, p. 712. Springer, Heidelberg (1999)
60. Leuschel, M., Falampin, J., Fritz, F., Plagge, D.: Automated property verification for large scale B models. In: Proceedings of the 2nd World Congress on Formal Methods, FM '09, pp. 708–723. Springer, Berlin (2009)
61. Hoare, C.A.R.: An axiomatic basis for computer programming. Commun. ACM **12**(10), 576–580 (1969)
62. Hoare, C.A.R.: Proof of correctness of data representations. Acta Informatica **1**, 271–281 (1972)
63. Floyd, R.W.: Assigning meanings to programs. Proc. Symp. Appl. Math. **19**, 19–32 (1967)
64. Zilles, S.N.: Algebraic Specification of Data Types. Project Mac Progress Report 11. Massachusetts Institute of Technology, Cambridge (1974)
65. Bergstra, J.A., Heering, J., Klint, P.: Algebraic Specification. ACM, New York (1989)
66. Sneed, H.M., Winter, M.: Testen Objektorientierter Software. Hanser, München (2002)
67. Majchrzak, T.A.: Improving the technical aspects of software testing in enterprises. Int. J. Adv. Comput. Sci. Appl. **1**(4), 1–10 (2010)
68. Oracle: How to write Doc comments for the Javadoc tool. http://www.oracle.com/technetwork/java/javase/documentation/index-137868.html (2004)
69. Sutter, H., Alexandrescu, A.: C++ Coding Standards: 101 Rules, Guidelines, and Best Practices. Addison-Wesley, Boston (2004)
70. Kellerwessel, H.: Programmierrichtlinien in der Praxis. mitp, Bonn (2002)
71. Weiser, M.: Program slicing. In: Proceedings of the 5th International Conference on Software Engineering, ICSE '81, pp. 439–449. IEEE Press, Piscataway (1981)
72. Weiser, M.: Program slicing. IEEE Trans. Softw. Eng. **10**(4), 352–357 (1984)
73. Korel, B., Laski, J.: Dynamic program slicing. Inf. Process. Lett. **29**(3), 155–163 (1988)
74. Xu, B., Qian, J., Zhang, X., Wu, Z., Chen, L.: A brief survey of program slicing. SIGSOFT Softw. Eng. Notes **30**(2), 1–36 (2005)
75. Fagan, M.E.: Design and code inspections to reduce errors in program development. IBM Syst. J. **15**(3), 182–211 (1976)
76. Frühauf, K., Ludewig, J., Sandmayr, H.: Software-Prüfung. vdf Hoschulverlag, Zürich (1991)
77. Black, R.: Pragmatic Software Testing. Wiley, Indianapolis (2007)
78. Koenig, A.: Patterns and antipatterns. JOOP **8**(1), 46–48 (1995)
79. Gamma, E., Helm, R., Johnson, R., Vlissides, J.: Design Patterns. Elements of Reusable Object-Oriented Software. Addision-Wesley, München (1995)
80. Brown, W.H., Malveau, R.C., McCormick, H.W., Mowbray, T.J.: Anti-Patterns: Refactoring Software, Architectures, and Projects in Crisis. Wiley, New York (1998)
81. Fowler, M.: Refactoring: Improving the Design of Existing Code. Addison-Wesley, Boston (1999)
82. Opdyke, W.F., Johnson, R.E.: Refactoring: an aid in designing application frameworks and evolving object-oriented systems. In: Proceedings of the Symposium on Object Oriented Programming Emphasizing Practical Applications (SOOPA) (1990)
83. Kerievsky, J.: Refactoring to Patterns. Pearson Higher Education, London (2004)
84. Majchrzak, T.A., Kuchen, H.: Automated test case generation based on coverage analysis. In: TASE '09: Proceedings of the 2009 3rd IEEE International Symposium on Theoretical Aspects of Software Engineering, pp. 259–266. IEEE Computer Society, Washington, DC (2009)
85. Nassi, I., Shneiderman, B.: Flowchart techniques for structured programming. SIGPLAN Notices **8**(8), 12–26 (1973)
86. Hennell, M.A., Woodward, M.R., Hedley, D.: On program analysis. Inf. Process. Lett. **5**(5), 136–140 (1976)

87. Woodward, M.R., Hennell, M.A.: On the relationship between two control-flow coverage criteria: all JJ-paths and MCDC. Inf. Softw. Technol. **48**(7), 433–440 (2006)
88. Alper, M.: Professionelle Softwaretests: Praxis der Qualitätsoptimierung Kommerzieller Software. Vieweg, Braunschweig (1994)
89. Booch, G., Rumbaugh, J., Jacobson, I.: The Unified Modeling Language User Guide, 2nd edn. Addison-Wesley, Boston (2005)
90. Watkins, J.: Testing IT: An Off-the-Shelf Software Testing Process. Cambridge University Press, New York (2001)
91. Lazic, L., Mastorakis, N.: Orthogonal array application for optimal combination of software defect detection techniques choices. W. Trans. Comp. **7**(8), 1319–1336 (2008)
92. Kuhn, D.R., Wallace, D.R., Gallo, A.M.: Software fault interactions and implications for software testing. IEEE Trans. Softw. Eng. **30**(6), 418–421 (2004)
93. Richardson, D.J., Clarke, L.A.: Partition analysis: a method combining testing and verification. IEEE Trans. Softw. Eng. **11**(12), 1477–1490 (1985)
94. Richardson, D.J., Clarke, L.A.: A partition analysis method to increase program reliability. In: Proceedings of the 5th International Conference on Software Engineering, ICSE '81, pp. 244–253. IEEE Press, Piscataway (1981)
95. Podgurski, A., Yang, C.: Partition testing, stratified sampling, and cluster analysis. SIGSOFT Softw. Eng. Notes **18**(5), 169–181 (1993)
96. Mayr, H.: Projekt Engineering: Ingenieurmäßige Softwareentwicklung in Projektgruppen, 2nd edn. Hanser, München (2005)
97. Jones, R., Lins, R.: Garbage Collection: Algorithms for Automatic Dynamic Memory Management. Wiley, New York (1996)
98. Sankaran, N.: A bibliography on garbage collection and related topics. SIGPLAN Notices **29**(9), 149–158 (1994)
99. Hofstedt, P., Wolf, A.: Einführung in die Constraint-Programmierung, Grundlagen, Methoden, Sprachen, Anwendungen. Springer, Heidelberg (2007)
100. Eyre-Todd, R.A.: The detection of dangling references in C++ programs. ACM Lett. Program. Lang. Syst. **2**(1–4), 127–134 (1993)
101. Vigenschow, U.: Objektorientiertes Testen und Testautomatisierung in der Praxis. Konzepte, Techniken und Verfahren. Dpunkt, Heidelberg (2005)
102. Georgieva, K.: Conducting FMEA over the software development process. SIGSOFT Softw. Eng. Notes **35**(3), 1–5 (2010)
103. Scientific N., Program T.I. (2000) Failure Modes and Effects Analysis (FMEA)—A Bibliography. Technical Report, NASA Langley Technical Report Server
104. Neufelder, A.M.: Ensuring Software Reliability. Marcel Dekker, New York (1992)
105. Vouk, M.A.: Back-to-back testing. Inf. Softw. Technol. **32**(1), 34–45 (1990)
106. DeMillo, R.A., Lipton, R.J., Sayward, F.G.: Program Mutation: A New Approach to Program Testing. Software Testing pp. 107–128 (1979)
107. Howden, W.E.: Weak mutation testing and completeness of test sets. IEEE Trans. Softw. Eng. **8**(4), 371–379 (1982)
108. Howden, W.E.: Completeness criteria for testing elementary program functions. In: Proceedings of the 5th International Conference on Software Engineering, ICSE '81, pp. 235–243. IEEE Press, Piscataway (1981)
109. Claessen, K., Hughes, J.: QuickCheck: a lightweight tool for random testing of haskell programs. In: SIGPLAN Notices, pp. 268–279. ACM Press (2000)
110. Paris, J., Arts, T.: Automatic testing of TCP/IP implementations using QuickCheck. In: ERLANG '09: Proceedings of the 8th ACM SIGPLAN Workshop on ERLANG, pp. 83–92. ACM, New York (2009). http://doi.acm.org/10.1145/1596600.1596612
111. Claessen, K., Palka, M., Smallbone, N., Hughes, J., Svensson, H., Arts, T., Wiger, U.: Finding race conditions in Erlang with QuickCheck and PULSE. In: ICFP '09: Proceedings of the 14th ACM SIGPLAN International Conference on Functional Programming, pp. 149–160. ACM, New York (2009)
112. http://quickcheck.dev.java.net/

113. http://www.jcheck.org/
114. http://software.legiasoft.com/quickcheck/
115. http://heim.ifi.uio.no/trygver/themes/mvc/mvc-index.html
116. Rumbaugh, J.E., Blaha, M.R., Premerlani, W.J., Eddy, F., Lorensen, W.E.: Object-Oriented Modeling and Design. Prentice-Hall, Englewood Cliffs (1991)
117. Jones, C.: The Economics of Object-Oriented Software. Technical Report, Software Productivity Research, Massachusetts (1997)
118. Beizer, B.: Software System Testing and Quality Assurance. Van Nostrand Reinhold, New York (1984)
119. Dybjer, P., Haiyan, Q., Takeyama, M.: Verifying Haskell programs by combining testing and proving. In: Proceedings of the Third International Conference on Quality Software, QSIC '03, pp. 272–279. IEEE Computer Society, Washington, DC (2003)
120. Lu, L., Greenfield, P.: Logic program testing based on abstract interpretation. In: Proceedings of the International Conference on Formal Methods in Programming and Their Applications, pp. 170–180. Springer, London (1993)
121. Silva, J., Vidal, G.: Forward slicing of functional logic programs by partial evaluation. Theory Pract. Log. Program. 7(1–2), 215–247 (2007)
122. Fischer, S., Kuchen, H.: Data-flow testing of declarative programs. In: Hook, J., Thiemann, P. (eds.) Proceeding of the 13th ACM SIGPLAN International Conference on Functional Programming (ICFP), pp. 201–212. ACM (2008)
123. Klein, T.: Buffer Overflows und Format-String-Schwachstellen. Dpunkt, Heidelberg (2004)
124. Poguntke, W.: Basiswissen IT-Sicherheit: Das wichtigste für den Schutz von Systemen & Daten. W3L GmbH (2007)
125. Wysopal, C., Nelson, L., Zovi, D.D., Dustin, E.: The Art of Software Security Testing: Identifying Software Security Flaws. Addison-Wesley, Boston (2006)
126. Hope, P., Walther, B.: Web Security Testing Cookbook: Systematic Techniques to Find Problems Fast. O'Reilly, Beijing (2008)
127. Andrews, M., Whittaker, J.A.: How to Break Web Software: Functional and Security Testing of Web Applications and Web Services. Addison-Wesley, Boston (2006)
128. https://www.bsi.bund.de/DE/Themen/ITGrundschutz/itgrundschutz_node.html
129. ISO: ISO/IEC 9126:2001 Software engineering—Product quality. Geneva (2001)
130. Grood, D.: Test Goal: Result-Driven Testing. Springer, Heidelberg (2008)
131. Forsberg, K., Mooz, H.: The relationship of systems engineering to the project cycle. Eng. Manag. J. 4(3), 36–38 (1992)
132. Majchrzak, T.A.: Status quo of software testing—regional findings and global inductions. In: Proceedings of the 9th ISOneWorld Conference. The Information Institute (2010)
133. Majchrzak, T.A.: Status quo of software testing—regional findings and global inductions. J. Inf. Sci. Technol. 7(2) (2010)
134. Thomas, D., Hunt, A.: Mock objects. IEEE Softw. 19(3), 22–24 (2002)
135. Sneed, H.M., Baumgartner, M., Seidl, R.: Der Systemtest, 2nd edn. Hanser, München (2009)
136. Beck, K.: Extreme Programming Explained: Embrace Change. Addison-Wesley, Boston (1999)
137. Royce, W.W.: Managing the development of large software systems: concepts and techniques. In: ICSE '87: Proceedings of the 9th International Conference on Software Engineering, pp. 328–338. IEEE Computer Society Press, Los Alamitos (1987)
138. Spillner, A.: Das W-Modell—Testen als paralleler Prozess zum Software-Entwicklungsprozess. Softwaretechnik-Trends 21(1), 4–5 (2001)
139. Spillner, A.: Management des Testprozesses von Anfang an—das W-Modell. Lect. Notes Inform. P-23, 65–76 (2002)
140. Kruchten, P.: The Rational Unified Process: An Introduction. Addison-Wesley, Boston (2003)
141. Sommerville, I., Kotonya, G.: Requirements Engineering: Processes and Techniques. Wiley, New York (1998)
142. Lim, M., Sadeghipour, S.: Werkzeugunterstützte Verknüpfung von anforderungen und tests—voraussetzung für eine systematische qualitätssicherung. Softwaretechnik-Trends 28(3), 32–33 (2008)

143. Tochtrop, G.: Testexperte als Anforderungsmanager—Ein Erfahrungsbericht. Softwaretechnik-Trends **28**(3), 34–37 (2008)
144. Martin, R.C.: Agile Software Development: Principles, Patterns, and Practices. Prentice Hall, Upper Saddle River (2003)
145. Shore, J., Warden, S.: The Art of Agile Development. O'Reilly, Beijing (2007)
146. Warden, S., Shore, J.: The Art of Agile Development: With Extreme Programming. O'Reilly Media, Beijing (2007)
147. Adzic, G.: Bridging the Communication Gap: Specification by Example and Agile Acceptance Testing. Neuri Limited, London (2009)
148. Cohn, M.: Succeeding with Agile: Software Development Using Scrum. Addison-Wesley, Boston (2009)
149. Schwaber, K.: Agile Project Management with Scrum. Microsoft Press, Redmond (2004)
150. Beck, K.: Test-Driven Development by Example. Addison-Wesley, Boston (2002)
151. Koskela, L.: Test driven: practical tdd and acceptance tdd for java developers. Manning Publications, Greenwich (2007)
152. Astels, D.: Test Driven Development: A Practical Guide. Prentice Hall, Upper Saddle River (2003)
153. Majchrzak, T.A.: Best practices for the organizational implementation of software testing. In: Proceedings of the 43rd Annual Hawaii International Conference on System Sciences (HICSS-43), pp. 1–10. IEEE Computer Society (2010)
154. IEEE, The Institute of Electrical and Electronics Engineers, Inc.: IEEE Std 829-1998: IEEE Standard for Software Test Documentation. New York (1998)
155. Konradt, U., Sarges, W. (eds.): E-Recruitment und E-Assessment: Rekrutierung, Auswahl und Beratung von Personal im Inter- und Intranet. Hogrefe, Göttingen (2003)
156. Stamelos, I.: Software project management anti-patterns. J. Syst. Softw. **83**(1), 52–59 (2010)
157. Brown, W.J., III, H.W.S.M., Thomas, S.W.: Anti Patterns in Project Management. Wiley, New York (2000)
158. Hitchcock, L.: Industry certification: value, validity, and a place for SoDIS. SIGCSE Bull. **37**(4), 59–63 (2005)
159. Hitchcock, L.: Industry certification and academic degrees: complementary, or poles apart? In: Proceedings of the 2007 ACM SIGMIS CPR Conference on Computer Personnel Research: The Global Information Technology Workforce, SIGMIS CPR '07, pp. 95–100. ACM, New York (2007)
160. Ketchel, J.S.: Certification for the computer professional—individual reparation strategies. In: Proceedings of the ACM '81 Conference, ACM '81, pp. 234–238. ACM, New York (1981)
161. Lawson, S.: DB2(R) for z/OS(R) Version 8 DBA Certification Guide. IBM Press (2004)
162. Stanek, W.: Microsoft Vista Certification Exams in a Nutshell. O'Reilly Media, Beijing (2007)
163. Redbooks, I.: IBM Tivoli Monitoring V 6.1. Vervante (2006)
164. Sybex Inc.: Java 2 Certification Virtual Test Center. SYBEX Inc., Alameda (2001)
165. Manning, W.: SCJP Sun Certified Programmer for Java 6 Exam. Emereo Pty Ltd, London (2009)
166. Coggeshall, J., Tabini, M.: The Zend PHP Certification Practice Test Book—Practice Questions for the Zend Certified Engineer Exam. Marco Tabini & Associates (2005)
167. Shuja, A., Krebs, J.: IBM Rational Unified Process Reference and Certification Guide: Solution Designer. IBM Press (2007)
168. Graham, D., Veenendaal, E.V., Evans, I., Black, R.: Foundations of Software Testing: ISTQB Certification. International Thomson Business Press (2008)
169. Bradtke, R.: ISTQB 100 success Secrets—ISTQB Foundation Certification Software Testing the ISTQB Certified Software Tester 100 Most Asked Questions. Emereo Pty Ltd, London (2008)
170. Black, R.: Advanced Software Testing—Vol. 1: Guide to the ISTQB Advanced Certification as an Advanced Test Analyst. Rocky Nook (2008)
171. http://www.google.de/search?q=testing+certification
172. http://www.softwarecertifications.org/qai_cste.htm

173. http://www.stqc.nic.in/
174. http://knowledge-department.de/seminare.html
175. http://www.junit.org/
176. http://sourceforge.net/projects/cppunit/
177. http://htmlunit.sourceforge.net/
178. http://seleniumhq.org/
179. Brössler, P., Siedersleben, J.: Softwaretechnik: Praxiswissen für Softwareingenieure. Hanser, München (2000)
180. Majchrzak T.A.: Technische aspekte des erfolgreichen testens von software in unternehmen. In: Knoop, J., Prantl, A. (eds.) Schriftenreihe des Instituts für Computersprachen, Bericht 2009-X-1: 15. Kolloquium Programmiersprachen und Grundlagen der Programmierung, pp. 193–207. Technische Universität Wien, Maria Taferl (2009)
181. Fewster, M., Graham, D.: Software Test Automation: Effective Use of Test Execution Tools. ACM Press, New York (1999)
182. Crevier, D.: AI: The Tumultuous History of the Search for Artificial Intelligence. Basic Books, New York (1994)
183. Hendler, J.: Avoiding another AI winter. IEEE Intell. Syst. **23**(2), 2–4 (2008)
184. Menzel, M.: Software-Testautomatisierung: Leitfaden für die effiziente Einführung. Vdm Verlag Dr. Müller (2006)
185. Bates, C.: Experiences with test automation. In: Fewster, M., Graham, D. (eds.) Software Test Automation: Effective Use of Test Execution Tools, ACM Press, New York (1999)

Chapter 3
Research Design

Scientific research usually is conducted based on a set of explicit or implicit assumptions and by pursuing one or more methods. Basic philosophical assumptions and the chosen methods constitute the *research design* [1, 2]. The method should be chosen wisely in advance to achieve one's aims. It is the only guarantee to obtain knowledge that is "valid, reliable and thus scientific" [3, p. 15]. The following sections explain the methods used, and sketch the research process. This research design "reflects decisions about the priority being given to a range of dimensions of the research" [4]. It also is important as it enables other to understand, validate, or—if desired—reproduce and possibly falsify [5] the research [6]. A much longer discussion of the research's philosophical underpinnings and the research design have been included in the author's dissertation thesis [7, Chap. 3].

3.1 General Considerations

Drawing the research design of the work included in this book has to take into account two particularities. Firstly, it contains three threads of research. The term *thread* has been chosen to characterize the partly parallel work on distinct research projects—all of them address software testing. The first thread is research on technical aspects of software testing, in particular on Muggl. It is the successor of the Java tool GlassTT for automated test case generation based on symbolic execution. Work on Muggl is described in Chap. 4. The second thread deals with organizational aspects of testing. In a joint project (*IHK project*) with industry partners, best practices for software testing in enterprises were compiled. It is described in Chap. 5. The third thread combines the test tool with the work of Dr. Susanne Gruttmann and Claus A. Usener on e-learning and in particular e-assessment (abbreviated to *testing and e-assessment* in the remainder). Research lead to the integration of Muggl with the e-assessment system EASy. Details are given in Chap. 6.

Secondly, the research conducted has some inherent differences. While the research philosophy and the basic method is the same for all research included in this

T. A. Majchrzak, *Improving Software Testing*, SpringerBriefs in Information Systems,   57
DOI: 10.1007/978-3-642-27464-0_3, © The Author(s) 2012

Table 3.1 Epistemological assumptions according to Becker and Niehaves

Category	Realizations		
Ontological aspect What is the object of cognition?	Ontological realism	Ontological idealism	**Kantianism**
Epistemological aspect What is the relationship between cognition and the object of cognition?	Epistemological realism	**Constructivism**	
Concept of truth What is true cognition?	**Correspondence theory of truth**	**Consensus theory of truth**	Semantic theory of truth
Source of cognition capability Where does cognition originate?	Empiricism	Rationalism	**Kantianism**
Methodological aspect By what means can cognition achieved?	Inductivism	Deductivism	**Hermeneutics**

book, the perspectives differ. Research on the technical aspects of software testing—i.e. the test tool—is computer science research with the aim of being valuable for the field of IS. In contrast to this, the project on organizational aspects of testing can be attributed to IS research that utilizes (or even relies on) knowledge from computer science. Most work can be attributed to software engineering (SE), which is seen as a discipline that combines IS and CS [8, p. 7].

Every research design underlies explicit or implicit assumptions about the world [9]. A framework is utilized to categorize the research presented in this book. The framework by Becker and Niehaves [10] is used in lieu of older attempts such as [11]. It is appropriate for the multi-disciplinary character of the presented work.

The framework divides the epistemological assumptions into five categories. These categories and their realizations are displayed in Table 3.1. Values printed bold are the assumptions that underpin the presented work.

With regard to the ontological aspect, a position based on Kantianism is taken. This aligns with the German interpretation of IS research (Wirtschaftsinformatik) [12, 13]. Furthermore, a constructivist approach has been chosen. Particularly for the IHK project we took a role as "participant and facilitator" [14]. Our aim was to accumulate knowledge through a "hermeneutical/dialectical process" in order to "transfer knowledge from one setting to another" [14]. In other words: knowledge that companies implicitly had was extracted in interviews, aggregated, and edited to become explicit recommendations.

Concerning the concept of truth, no uniform position was taken. Similar to the ontological aspect, the source of cognition capability is Kantianism. It is assumed that experiences are useless without interpretation, and intellectual thought requires experiences it can reflect on. Finally, with regard to the method research followed a design science approach. This implies that the underlying method of it is hermeneutics. Both implementing Muggl and the IHK project took several iterations in which refinements were made. Improvements were made based on the knowledge gained in the previous phase.

3.2 Research Method

The research paradigm used for the papers compiled in this book is *design science*. It is discussed in the next section. Afterwards, particularities that apply to the three threads of research are explained in sections of their own. All presented research either has a technical nature or concerns the application of technology for business needs. Especially, both rigorous and relevant [15] research is combined.

3.2.1 Design Science

Even though research on Muggl is based on the natural sciences [16] (in particular, computer science and mathematics[1]), the design science approach applies to all research presented in this book. According to Hevner et al. "research activities in design science are twofold: build and evaluate" [17]. This means, research is based on an iterative circle. First, an IT *artifact* [18] (e.g. software) is built. Secondly, it is checked with regard to the aims that are embedded in it and with regard to implications that can be learned from its creation [8, p. 5]. Usually, the knowledge derived from this process is used to improve the artifact, to learn for building further artifacts, and to contribute to the base of knowledge.

Design science as the main paradigm has been chosen for a number of reasons:

- Its "primary goal [...] is bringing about improvements in the phenomenon of interest" [19]. The phenomena of interest are the automated generation of test cases and the organizational implementation of testing; it is sought to improve both.
- Design science is capable of providing *satisficing* solutions [18].[2] With regard to testing, it hardly is possible to reach for optimality; that would be to prove a program to be free of defects and, hence, be testing no more. Solutions searched for, such as testing methods and strategies, should be satisfying and suffice with regard to the software quality that ought to be achieved.
- The outcome of research has been clear to only some extend a priori. Despite the formally studied ideas behind Muggl, finding ways to improve it requires trying out new approaches. This "learning via making" [21, p. 111] is a strength of design science research.
- It is possible to gain results without the need to rely on a theoretical base [22]. Both for Muggl and the IHK project the theory is studied and new approaches are

---

[1] In the characterization of research disciplines chosen by March and Smith [16], computer science (CS) and mathematics can be attributed to the natural sciences.

[2] The term, coined by Simon, first appeared in [20].

checked against the existing literature. Nevertheless, new paths of research which not yet have a theoretical foundation have to be tried out. This particularly applies to Muggl. While many of its basic ideas are described in the literature (e.g. on logic programming [23–26], constraint solving [27–29], and compiler construction [30, 31]), novel concepts have to be introduced. They are theorized after evaluation.

- Design science research "seeks to create IT artefacts intended to solve organizational problems" [32].[3] This holds for the IHK project research, but also Muggl promises to support businesses despite its prototypic status.
- A combination of software engineering and information systems research [33] is supported by design science.
- Design science not only draws from the "vast knowledge base of scientific theories and engineering methods" but also from "experience and expertise" and from "existing artifacts and processes [...] in the application domain" [34].

The output (also called *artifacts* [22]) of design science research can be constructs (including terms), models, methods, and implementations (or instantiations) [16]. An alternative terminology speaks of "ideas, practices, technical capabilities, and product[s]" [32]. *Constructs*, i.e. a "basic language of concepts" [16], are created in all three research threads. *Models* that "describe tasks, situations, or artifacts" [16] are particular to the IHK project in the form of recommendations. Some of the recommendations also have characteristics of *methods*. Research on Muggl led to the discovery of novel methods. *Implementations* exist, too: Muggl is the instantiation of concepts and models embodied by it; the IHK project led to a booklet, which is the "physical implementation" [16] of the project's outcome. Integrating Muggl and EASy led to another instantiation.

The included research has also been found to be compliant with guidelines for design science research (cf. [7, p. 63ff.]).

3.2.2 Particularities of Research on Technical Aspects

Two main particularities can be identified for the work on technical aspects. Firstly, methodology is less pronounced in the papers on Muggl. Secondly, the paper "output" in relation to the research effort is lower than for the other threads of research.

While IT research can be based on research methods from both natural science and humanities [16], pure computer science (CS) is based on natural science methods only. Methods seem to be driven by an inherent agreement on how to conduct research. Work on Muggl can be characterized as software engineering research [35] which shares its characteristics with design science. It focuses on constructing "new objects" [35] whereas *object* is another term for artifact. A simple Web search on Google [36] as well as searches on Google Scholar [37] and the ACM portal [38] show that while the IS community actively discusses, e.g. design science research,

---

[3] The reference was written in British English—thus artefact.

there are far less articles on computer science research methods. Most articles and Web pages found highlight the education of students in CS (for instance [39–41]). Articles that discuss methods or the philosophy of SE are often written from an IS perspective (cf. [42]).

Methods become important if a distinct research method is required to reach a defined aim, e.g. in empirical papers. Papers that describe *how* software (or a piece of it such as an algorithm) has been implemented, which instruments of CS are adequate to solve a given problem, or how to apply formal methods often do not have a section explaining the method used. However, papers of a given category follow a distinct organization; articles that are not structured in that way usually describe why they are built differently. Typically, an introductory section is followed by a section on related work. The remainder of the article is made up of sections that describe the solution applied to solve a problem. Usually, the earlier sections are rather descriptive while the later sections describe the author's contribution in detail. Often, a section which discusses the findings or an evaluation follows. Then, the paper is finalized with a concluding section.

The above considerations align with empirical studies on the methods used in CS research. A 1995 study by Tichy et al. [43] found that most papers focus on design and modeling. Its findings have been confirmed in 2009 [44]. The 2009 study analyzed 147 papers that were published in 2005 and that were randomly selected from the ACM portal. A categorization of "4% theory, 17% empirical, 4.7% hypothesis testing, 3.4% other, and 70% design and modeling" has been found [44]. While empirical and hypothesis testing papers require the explanation of their methodoly, this might be omitted in theoretic and experimental papers as well as in papers that describe design and modeling. Nevertheless, explicating a sound theoretical foundation of SE experiments is recommended [45].

The papers on Muggl and other technical aspects of software testing that are cited as the base of this book have a design focus, usually contain a (short) discussion, and an evaluation. The evaluation is done in terms of quantitative findings and experimentation. Typically, a proposed solution to a problem or a novel algorithm is checked with varying parameters and input data, and results are collected and analyzed. These papers do not contain a section on methods; usually, the chosen method can be derived from the context of the paper and its organization. Nevertheless, the papers include hints to the method and in the course of them it is argued why they have been written in the way they were.

In general, it appears that CS researchers put less attention to a section explaining why a certain method has been chosen; rather, they expect authors to explain their very steps and will (very) critically question why an algorithm has been implemented in the way it was, why a formal method has been applied, why experimental findings show particularities, and so on.

The second particularity concerns the research output. Chapter 4 is based on "only" three papers on technical aspects of software testing. There are three reasons for this.

The first reason is that work on a project for the creation of a tool for automated test case generation was continued. This eventually led to implementing the novel tool Muggl. Its predecessor GlassTT [46, 47] was discontinued.

It featured very promising concepts of which a number have been embedded into Muggl. Unfortunately, GlassTT suffered from problems with regard to the possibilities of generating test cases for a large variety of programs. Continuing the development of GlassTT and refining it was hindered by a lack of documentation—GlassTT was a certainly remarkable, but purely academic prototype not built to be maintained by other developers.

Muggl's core was implemented from scratch while trying to avoid the shortcomings GlassTT had. Even though the constraint solver of GlassTT [48] is integrated, a considerable amount of work was necessary. Implementation was done with much attention for details. As of May 2011, Muggl consists of 528 classes with 3,234 methods, 68 interfaces, and 44,436 LOC (excluding comments), in 2.67 MiB of source code. About 18 months were needed to reach a point at which Muggl was initially used. By then it contained profound functionality; the above compiled numbers underline that most of its components are no mere proof-of-concepts. For example, Muggl creates extensively documented, easy-to-read JUnit test cases that are even capable of setting up objects required for testing.

In the meantime, progress had been reported from projects that pursue similar ideas. Even though Muggl has much more functionality than GlassTT (cf. Sect. 4.3), most novel features were not yet evaluated exhaustively enough to publish findings at high-tier conferences. To cope with the extreme complexity of automatically generating test cases, Muggl is built with keeping its maintainability and extensibility in mind. However, more examples have to be found to motivate the approach, and the evaluation has to be extended. Experimentation is a laborious task due to finding suitable examples that combine clarity and sufficient complexity. As a consequence, progress in terms of published papers is slow, even though progress in terms of increasing functionality and extending the base of knowledge on automated TCG is considerable.

The second reason is directly connected to the first one. Progress with Muggl is fundamental research and published as such. Once it reaches a point of *break even*, there will be many possibilities for publishing articles on the progress. Currently, a stable prototype is implemented that constitutes the base of specific future research. With the experimentation needed for the above described approaches, some deficiencies are found. Identified possibilities for improvement are put to work.

Moreover, a very comprehensive documentation for Muggl is prepared. Each method and each class is documented according to the documentation standard from Oracle (formerly Sun) [49] using Javadoc [50] and following best practices [51]. There are inline comments for such algorithms that are not obvious to understand, either. Furthermore, a package documentations is provided. A well maintained documentation supports the long-term development of Muggl and provides parts of it as a library for similar projects. Besides, it enables other researchers to collaborate on automated TCG. Writing code with the mentioned level of documentation requires a notable additional effort compared to writing prototypic code without or with only a few comments. The additional endeavor will nevertheless pay out.

As a third reason, current interests of the research community have to be taken into account. For a couple of years, *model-based testing* has become very popular

[52–55]. It is not a niche technique anymore. There is model-based testing for Web services [56], for GUIs [57], and for embedded systems [58]; there is model-based testing advice for distinct programming languages (e.g. [59]) and an UML subset for model-based testing [60]. And there are considerations about the role of model-based testing [61], evaluations of model-based methods [62], and case studies about model-based test tools [63]. Along with the popularity of model-based testing, "classic" testing techniques have lost attention.

To revive attention, we aim at publishing papers on top-tier conferences. These papers have to be accompanied with a comprehensive experimental evaluation. Publishing theoretical considerations or articles on proposed features is hardly possible. In combination with the first two reasons, this further explains why progress of Muggl is not yet reflected by the number of publications. The vast amount of invested time serves a higher purpose.

3.2.3 Particularities of Research on Organizational Aspects

Design science is the basic paradigm for the research on organizational aspects. It is capable of building and evaluating artifacts that help managers to describe desired organizational states and develop actions to reach them [64, p. 204f.]. Due to the work with participating companies and the interviewed employees, research also has an empirical character. The number of participants was rather low (6 companies). Data collected in the project was analyzed using methods of qualitative research [65] despite some quantitative results were gained.

The project pursued with the IHK has a special character. While it is conducted with scientific rigor, it addresses practitioner's needs and is supported by the chamber of commerce, which has sovereign duties. Research methods need to adopt the requirements of practitioners. Executives from the companies had limited time for meetings and the companies were interested in results that could easily be implemented. Therefore, findings should not purely be theoretical but include actions that could be adopted by the companies. At the same time, an academic flavor and context should be kept to make sure project results mark research progress.

The project relied on the interviews of company representatives. They were the only source of data besides knowledge available from the literature. Hence, they had to be planned carefully and needed to be methodologically sound. We decided to conduct qualitative, semi-structured [4, 66] *expert interviews* [67, 68], which followed a rough guideline [69]. This approach has proven adequate to learn from experts and to gain as much insight as possible. Qualitative methods are not only advantageous for their capability to cope with a low number of participants. They help to "understand and explain in detail the personal experience of individuals" [70] and subsequently "experience research issues from a participant's perspective" [65, 70]. Insights can thus be put into context.

In contrast to most other forms of interviews (e.g. as part of journalism), an interviewed expert does not share intimate knowledge that still is supposed to be understandable by a non-expert. The interviewer is an expert himself or at least has proficiency in the context of the interview's topics. Therefore, expert interviews aim at the "reconstruction of (explicit) expert knowledge"[4] for research purposes [71]. Since interview partners were predominantly executives (managers) and senior software developers, an argumentative-discursive interview style was chosen.

Expert interviews are perfect to quickly gain high quality data [72]. The interviews were set up as *in-depth interviews*, which can take up to several hours [70]. The usual duration was between $1\frac{1}{2}$ and 3 h. In-depth interviews encourage the interviewee to talk and explicate answers, and they include to ask supplementary questions [70]. Almost anything discussed in the interview might be of value. In particular, thoughts narrated and procedures sketched by the interviewee often include details from the processes of his company. The "extended comment from respondents is the essence of the method" [70] which is by far "less structured than a questionnaire-based interview" [70]. In fact, the guideline (in this context also called checklist) [70] contained mainly *open* questions.

It has been found that in-depth expert interviews are especially suitable if the interviewees "are relatively few in number" [70] and the information obtained from each subject "is expected to vary considerably" [70]. In our case, companies were different in size, and both background and experience varied notably. This was not a disadvantage; in fact, it increased the amount of data gained even though it made the validation less convenient. Details on the questions dealt with in the interviews can be found in the papers (especially in [69]) and the booklet [73].

After the interviews were finished, findings were analyzed and arranged. The first aim of the project was to draw the status quo of testing in the Münsterland (to be specific in the region *Nord Westfalen* (northern Westphalia), which is the area of competence of the local chamber of commerce). Since research was driven by the practitioners' demands, we did not formulate hypotheses. It also would have hardly been possible to test them with a number of six participants only. A mere collection of data was unwanted; the project was not meant to prepare statistics. However, to draw conclusions about the region, findings and comments from participants had to be checked against the literature. This was done with much effort in order to add rigor to the research. Findings were also checked against the knowledge gained from further industry contacts. During the preparation of the booklet we conferred with employees of companies that did not take part in the project and discussed our impressions with them.

Even though it was tried to verify findings in various ways, the low number of participants abates the scientific value of drawing the status quo. A broader quantitative study would have been needed. Therefore, publications focus on the recommendations, which are significant despite being based on few participants. Nevertheless, evaluating the status quo is helpful as it offers local companies the possibility to judge their own status.

At an early point it became clear that recommendations for companies had to be put into a context that made them accessible. We noticed diversity in companies,

---

[4] Translated from the German original by the author.

differences among their stakeholders, and non-uniform willingness to change processes and to invest time and money. Therefore, a framework was created that is used to categorize recommendations. It is explained in Chap. 5. Each recommendation extracted from the interview data has been aligned with this framework.

To extract recommendations (i.e. best practices), the interviews were scanned for the description of successful strategies and any information that described good performance. We also searched for interrelations and differences between the companies and even between interviews with technical and organizational staff. Then, observations were put into relations with the company size, the kind of software a company develops, and further basic conditions and constraints. This led to the extraction of best practices and the (pre-)conditions under which they can be implemented. We also had to check whether similar recommendations were described in the literature. If so, it had to be retraced how differences to the description in the literature could be explained.

Recommendations found by the interview partners are not meant to describe a "definite" testing process. The project's aim was not to offer holistic advice on how to improve testing. Even the booklet only shortly introduces software testing. Recommendations are meant to complement the literature on software quality.

The qualitative approach is adequate since we had to understand phenomena "from the point of view of the participants" [65]. With the approach taken we were able to understand phenomena that "emerge from the interaction of people, organizations, and technology" [17]. The research directly "aims at improving IT performance" [16]. It might be criticized with regard to its rigor from a quantitative, social sciences-oriented standpoint, but it is highly relevant.

Further details of the research methodology and particularities with regard to the subtopic dealt with are explicated in the respective papers [69, 74–77].

3.2.4 Particularities of Research on E-Learning Aspects

To publish papers on e-learning, educational and didactical aspects have to be highlighted. They usually are considered more important by reviewers than technical details, a sophisticated method, or theoretical considerations. Moreover, at least a brief introduction into the subject has to be given if the paper is to be presented at the conference or published in a journal that has a general focus on e-learning. This is needed because both the e-learning context (for instance e-assessment) and in many cases details from a field of teaching have to be explained.

The term e-assessment describes the examination of student performance based on electronic systems, typically using a standard computer. E-assessment research deals with technical, organizational, educational, didactical, psychological, juridical, and financial issues of applying e-assessment technology. More details are given in Chap. 6, in handbooks such as [78, 79], and also in work of our colleagues (e.g. [80, 81]).

While the general approach behind our research on e-assessment is design science, the work was enriched with qualitative assessments. Surveys were set up in order to understand students' attitude towards the usage of e-assessment. Consequently, evaluating the system is accompanied with quantitative work. However, the methods of quantitative research [82–84] used were basic: both paper and Web based questionnaire forms were designed. They included questions that asked students to judge their experience with e-assessment prototypes or their attitude towards them as well as binary questions. Besides that, we usually provided a field for qualitative feedback. Students were asked to fill out the questionnaire; after that, results were evaluated with basic statistical methods to example determine a distribution. Eventually, results were transformed to figures such as histograms and interpreted graphically. No hypotheses testing was conducted.

3.3 Research Process

As explained at the beginning of this chapter, the research presented in this book is split into three threads. The course that research took in each of them is described in the corresponding chapters along with introducing the published work. Sections 4.4, 5.4 and 6.4 give details on each of the publications but also explain their relations and the order in which ideas were written down. This implicitly explains how the research questions drawn in Sect. 1.3 can be answered.

References

1. Becker, J.; Holten, R.; Knackstedt, R.; Niehaves, B.: Forschungsmethodische positionierung in der Wirtschaftsinformatik—epistemologische, ontologische und linguistische Leitfragen. In: Becker, J., Grob, H., Klein, S., Kuchen, H., Müller-Funk, H., Vossen, G. (eds.) Arbeitsbericht Nr. 93. Institut für Wirtschaftsinformatik, WWU, Münster (2003)
2. Braun, R.: Forschungsdesign in der Wirtschaftsinformatik. WISU—Das Wirtschaftsstudium **36**(1), S.61–S.66 (2007)
3. Williams, M., May, T.: Introduction to the Philosophy of Social Research. University College London Press, London (1996)
4. Bryman, A., Bell, E.: Business Research Methods. Oxford University Press, Oxford (2007)
5. Chalmers, A.F.: What is this Thing Called Science? 3rd edn. Hacket Publishing, Cambridge (1999)
6. Braun, R., Esswein, W.: Eine Methode zur Konzeption von Forschungsdesigns in der konzeptuellen Modellierungsforschung. In: Integration, Informationslogistik und Architektur Proceedings der DW2006 (2006)
7. Majchrzak, T.A.: Technical and organizational aspects of testing software. Ph.D. Thesis, University of Münster, Münster (2011)
8. Hevner, A., Chatterjee, S.: Design Research in Information Systems: Theory and Practice Integrated Series in Information Systems. Springer, Dordrecht (2010)
9. Burrell, G., Morgan, G.: Sociological Paradigms and Organizational Analysis: Elements of the Sociology of Corporate Life. Ashgate Publishing, London (1979)

10. Becker, J., Niehaves, B.: Epistemological perspectives on IS research—a framework for analyzing and systematizing epistemological assumptions. Inf. Syst. J. **17**(2), 197–214 (2007)
11. Hirschheim, R., Klein, H.K.: Four paradigms of information systems development. Commun. ACM **32**(10), 1199–1216 (1989)
12. Wilde, T., Hess, T.: Forschungsmethoden der Wirtschaftsinformatik. Wirtschaftsinformatik **49**(4), 280–287 (2007)
13. Frank, U.: Zur methodischen Fundierung der Forschung in der Wirtschaftsinformatik. In: Österle, H., Winter, R., Brenner, W. (eds.) Gestaltungsorientierte Wirtschaftsinformatik: Ein Plädoyer für Rigor und Relevanz, pp. 35–44. Infowerk, St. Gallen (2010)
14. Guba, E.G., Lincoln, Y.S.: Competing paradigms in qualitative research. In: Denzin, N.K., Lincoln, Y.S. (eds.) The Landscape of Qualitative Research, pp. 195–220. Sage Publications, Thousand Oaks (1998)
15. Applegate, L.: Rigor and relevance in MIS research: introduction. MIS Q. **23**(1), 1–2 (1999)
16. March, S.T., Smith, G.F.: Design and natural science research on information technology. Decis. Support Syst. **15**(4), 251–266 (1995)
17. Hevner, A.R., March, S.T., Park, J., Ram, S.: Design science in information systems research. MIS Q. **28**(1), 75–105 (2004)
18. Simon, H.A.: The Sciences of the Artificial, 3rd edn. MIT Press, Cambridge (1996)
19. Purao, S.: Design research in the technology of information systems: truth or dare. GSU Department of CIS Working Paper, Atlanta (2002). http://iris.nyit.edu/~kkhoo/Spring2008/Topics/DS/000DesignSc_TechISResearch-2002.pdf
20. Simon, H.A.: Rational choice and the structure of the environment. Psychol. Rev. **63**(2), 129–138 (1956)
21. Oates, B.J.: Researching Information Systems and Computing. Sage Publications, Thousand Oaks (2005)
22. Vaishnavi, V.K., Kuechler W., Jr.: Design Science Research Methods and Patterns: Innovating Information and Communication Technology. Auerbach Publications, Boston (2007)
23. Doets, K.: From Logic to Logic Programming. MIT Press, Cambridge (1994)
24. Bramer, M.: Logic Programming with Prolog. Springer, Secaucus (2005)
25. Antoy, S., Hanus, M.: Functional logic programming. Commun. ACM **53**(4), 74–85 (2010). http://doi.acm.org/10.1145/1721654.1721675
26. Hanus, M., Kuchen, H., Moreno-Navarro, J.: Curry: a truly functional logic language. In: Proceedings ILPS '95, pp. 95–107 (1995)
27. Tsang, E.: Foundations of Constraint Satisfaction. Academic Press, London (1993)
28. López-Fraguas, F.J., Rodríguez-Artalejo, M., Vírseda, R.V.: Constraint functional logic programming revisited. Electr. Notes Theor. Comput. Sci. **117**, 5–50 (2005). http://dx.doi.org/10.1016/j.entcs.2004.06.030
29. Comon, H., Dincbas, M., Jouannaud, J.P., Kirchner, C.: A methodological view of constraint solving. Constraints **4**(4), 337–361 (1999)
30. Aho, A.V., Lam, M.S., Sethi, R., Ullman, J.D.: Compilers: Principles, Techniques, and Tools with Gradiance, 2nd edn. Addison-Wesley, Essex (2007)
31. Srikant, Y.N., Shankar, P. (eds.): The Compiler Design Handbook: Optimizations and Machine Code Generation. CRC Press, Boca Raton (2002)
32. Niehaves, B., Stahl, B.: Criticality, epistemology, and behaviour versus design—information systems research across different sets of paradigms. In: 14th European Conference on Information Systems (ECIS 2006). Gothberg, Sweden (2006)
33. Morrison, J., George, J.: Exploring the software engineering component in MIS research. Commun. ACM **38**(7), 80–91 (1995)
34. Hevner, A.R.: The three cycle view of design science. Scand. J. Inf. Syst. **19**(2), 87–92 (2007)
35. Marcos, E.: Software engineering research versus software development. SIGSOFT Softw. Eng. Notes **30**(4), 1–7 (2005)
36. http://www.google.com/
37. http://scholar.google.com/
38. http://portal.acm.org/

39. Greening, T., Kay, J.: Undergraduate research experience in computer science education. SIGCSE Bull. **34**(3), 151–155 (2002)

40. Clear, T.: Valuing computer science education research? In: Proceedings of the 6th Baltic Sea Conference on Computing Education Research: Koli Calling 2006, Baltic Sea'06, pp. 8–18. ACM, New York (2006)

41. Hazzan, O., Dubinsky, Y., Eidelman, L., Sakhnini, V., Teif, M.: Qualitative research in computer science education. SIGCSE Bull. **38**(1), 408–412 (2006)

42. Gregg, D.G., Kulkarni, U.R., Vinzé, A.S.: Understanding the philosophical underpinnings of software engineering research in information systems. Inf. Syst. Front. **3**(2), 169–183 (2001)

43. Tichy, W.F., Lukowicz, P., Prechelt, L., Heinz, E.A.: Experimental evaluation in computer science: a quantitative study. J. Syst. Softw. **28**(1), 9–18 (1995)

44. Wainer, J., Novoa Barsottini, C.G., Lacerda, D., Magalhães de Marco, L.R.: Empirical evaluation in computer science research published by ACM. Inf. Softw. Technol. **51**(6), 1081–1085 (2009)

45. Wohlin, C., Runeson, P., Höst, M., Ohlsson, M.C., Regnell, B., Wesslén, A.: Experimentation in Software Engineering: an Introduction. Kluwer, Norwell (2000)

46. Mueller, R.A., Lembeck, C., Kuchen, H.: GlassTT—a symbolic java virtual machine using constraint solving techniques for glass-box test case generation. Technical Report, No. 102, Department of Information Systems, Arbeitsbericht Universitaet Muenster (2003)

47. Lembeck, C., Caballero, R., Mueller, R.A., Kuchen, H.: Constraint solving for generating glass-box test cases. In: Proceedings WFLP'04, pp. 19–32 (2004)

48. Mueller, R.A., Lembeck, C., Kuchen, H.: Generating glass-box test cases using a symbolic virtual machine. In: Proceedings IASTED SE 2004 (2004)

49. Oracle: How to Write Doc Comments for the Javadoc Tool (2004). http://www.oracle.com/technetwork/java/javase/documentation/index-137868.html

50. http://www.oracle.com/technetwork/java/javase/documentation/index-jsp-135444.html

51. Bloch, J.: Effective Java, 2nd edn. Prentice Hall, Upper Saddle River (2008)

52. Dias-Neto, A.C., Travassos, G.H.: Model-based testing approaches selection for software projects. Inf. Softw. Technol. **51**(11), 1487–1504 (2009)

53. Dias Neto, A.C., Subramanyan, R., Vieira, M., Travassos, G.H.: A survey on model-based testing approaches: a systematic review. In: Proceedings of the 1st ACM International Workshop on Empirical Assessment of Software Engineering Languages and Technologies, WEASELTech '07, pp. 31–36. ACM, New York (2007)

54. Pretschner, A., Prenninger, W., Wagner, S., Kühnel, C., Baumgartner, M., Sostawa, B., Zölch, R., Stauner, T.: One evaluation of model-based testing and its automation. In: Proceedings of the 27th International Conference on Software Engineering, ICSE '05, pp. 392–401. ACM, New York (2005)

55. Utting, M., Legeard, B.: Practical Model-Based Testing: a Tools Approach. Morgan Kaufmann, San Francisco (2006)

56. Jääskeläinen, A., Katara, M., Kervinen, A., Heiskanen, H., Maunumaa, M., Pääkkönen, T.: Model-based testing service on the web. In: Proceedings of the 20th IFIP TC 6/WG 6.1 International Conference on Testing of Software and Communicating Systems: 8th International Workshop, TestCom '08/FATES '08, pp. 38–53. Springer, Berlin (2008)

57. Nguyen, D.H., Strooper, P., Suess, J.G.: Model-based testing of multiple GUI variants using the GUI test generator. In: Proceedings of the 5th Workshop on Automation of Software Test, AST '10, pp. 24–30. ACM, New York (2010)

58. Conrad, M., Fey, I., Sadeghipour, S.: Systematic model-based testing of embedded automotive software. Electr. Notes Theor. Comput. Sci. **111**, 13–26 (2005)

59. Jacky, J., Veanes, M., Campbell, C., Schulte, W.: Model-Based Software Testing and Analysis with C#. Cambridge University Press, Cambridge (2007)

60. Bouquet, F., Grandpierre, C., Legeard, B., Peureux, F., Vacelet, N., Utting, M.: A subset of precise UML for model-based testing. In: Proceedings of the 3rd International Workshop on Advances in Model-based Testing, A-MOST'07, pp. 95–104. ACM, New York (2007)

61. Utting, M.: The role of model-based testing. In: Meyer, B., Woodcock, J. (eds.) Verified Software: Theories, Tools, Experiments, pp. 510–517. Springer, Berlin (2008)
62. Santos-Neto, P., Resende, R.F., Pádua, C.: An evaluation of a model-based testing method for information systems. In: Proceedings of the 2008 ACM Symposium on Applied Computing, SAC '08, pp. 770–776. ACM, New York (2008)
63. Sarma, M., Murthy, P.V.R., Jell, S., Ulrich, A.: Model-based testing in industry: a case study with two MBT tools. In: Proceedings of the 5th Workshop on Automation of Software Test, AST '10, pp. 87–90. ACM, New York (2010)
64. March, S.T., Vogus, T.J.: Design science in the management disciplines. In: Hevner, A., Chatterjee, S. (eds.) Design Research in Information Systems: Theory and Practice (Integrated Series in Information Systems). Springer, Heidelberg (2010)
65. Myers, M.D.: Qualitative research in information systems. MIS Q. **21**(2), 241–242 (1997)
66. Lamnek, S.: Qualitative Sozialforschung, 4th edn. Beltz, Weinheim (2005)
67. Bogner, A., Littig, B., Menz, W. (eds.): Das Experteninterview: Theorie, Methode, Anwendung, 2nd edn. VS Verlag für Sozialwissenschaften, Wiesbaden (2002)
68. Gläser, J., Laudel, G.: Experteninterviews und Qualitative Inhaltsanalyse, 3rd edn. VS Verlag Wiesbaden (2009)
69. Majchrzak, T.A., Kuchen, H.: Handlungsempfehlungen für erfolgreiches Testen von Software in Unternehmen. In: Becker, J., Grob, H., Hellingrath, B., Klein, S., Kuchen, H., Müller-Funk, U., Vossen, G. (eds.) Arbeitsbericht Nr. 127. Institut für Wirtschaftsinformatik, WWU Münster, Münster (2010)
70. Veal, A.J.: Business Research Methods: a Managerial Approach, 2nd edn. Pearson Addison Wesley, South Melbourne (2005)
71. Pfadenhauer, M.: Auf gleicher Augenhöhe reden—Das Experteninterview—ein Gespräch zwischen Experte und Quasi-Experte. In: Bogner, A., Littig, B., Menz, W. (eds.) Das Experteninterview: Theorie, Methode, Anwendung, 2nd edn. VS Verlag für Sozialwissenschaften, Wiesbaden (2002)
72. Bogner, A., Merz, W.: Expertenwissen und Forschungspraxis: die modernisierungstheoretische und die methodische Debatte um die Experten. In: Bogner, A., Littig, B., Menz, W. (eds.) Das Experteninterview: Theorie, Methode, Anwendung, 2nd edn. VS Verlag für Sozialwissenschaften, Wiesbaden (2002)
73. Majchrzak, T.A., Kuchen, H.: IHK-Projekt Softwaretests: Auswertung. In: Working Papers, No. 2. Förderkreis der Angewandten Informatik an der Westfälischen Wilhelms-Universität Münster e.V., Münster (2010)
74. Majchrzak, T.A.: Technische Aspekte des erfolgreichen Testens von Software in Unternehmen. In: Knoop, J., Prantl, A. (eds.) Schriftenreihe des Instituts für Computersprachen, Bericht 2009-X-1: 15. Kolloquium Programmiersprachen und Grundlagen der Programmierung, pp. 193–207. Technische Universität Wien, Maria Taferl, Vienna (2009)
75. Majchrzak, T.A.: Best practices for the organizational implementation of software testing. In: Proceedings of the 43th Annual Hawaii International Conference on System Sciences (HICSS-43), pp. 1–10. IEEE Computer Society, Washington, DC (2010)
76. Majchrzak, T.A.: Improving the technical aspects of software testing in enterprises. Int. J. Adv. Comput. Sci. Appl. **1**(4), 1–10 (2010)
77. Majchrzak, T.A.: Status quo of software testing—regional findings and global inductions. J. Inf. Sci. Technol. **7**(2), S.72–S.84 (2010)
78. Crisp, G.: The e-Assessment Handbook. Continuum, London (2007)
79. Iskander, M.: Innovative Techniques in Instruction Technology, E-learning, E-assessment and Education. Springer, Heidelberg (2008)
80. Gruttmann, S.: Formatives E-assessment in der Hochschullehre—Computerunterstützte Lernfortschrittskontrollen im informatikstudium. Ph.D. Thesis, University of Münster, Münster (2010)
81. Gruttmann, S., Böhm, D., Kuchen, H.: E-assessment of mathematical proofs: chances and challenges for students and tutors. In: Proceedings of the 2008 International Conference on Computer Science and Software Engineering, vol. 05, CSSE '08, pp. 612–615. IEEE Computer Society, Washington, DC (2008)

82. Straub, D., Gefen, D., Boudreau, M.C.: The ISWorld Quantitative, Positivist Research Methods Website (2004). http://dstraub.cis.gsu.edu:88/quant/
83. Creswell, J.W.: Research Design: Qualitative, Quantitative, and Mixed Methods Approaches, 3rd edn. Sage Publications, Thousand Oaks (2008)
84. Neuman, L.W.: Social Research Methods: Qualitative and Quantitative Approaches, 5th edn. Allyn & Bacon, Needham Heights (2002)

Chapter 4
Technical Aspects: Muggl

In this chapter the research on Muggl is introduced. It is the *technical* part of software testing included in this book.

4.1 Background

It will never be possible to produce software free of errors. The development process is too complex and no error-detecting approach will be able to cope with this [1]. Nonetheless, implementing software has to be economically feasible. *Economic feasibility* means to reach development aims with regard to both functionality and quality but without exceeding the estimated effort. Software testing is decisive to economically reach quality aims. As argued in Chap. 1, with the current state of software testing many software development projects do not meet their quality targets.

Putting more effort into testing can help to develop more economically because reaching quality aims can be very beneficial. In fact, producing high quality software can outweigh the increased effort. However, even with improving test processes, using highly efficient testing techniques and employing seasoned testers (cf. Chap. 2), there is an upper boundary for economically feasible testing. Further increasing the effort would not justify the increased costs. Thus, methodological improvements are necessary. An important idea is to automate testing. Computers can execute non-creative tasks in less time than humans would need to accomplish them. At the same time, modern systems are cheap in price and maintenance, and they provide vast computational power. While test tools are capable of automating *some* testing tasks or small *parts* of testing processes, tools for TCG promise to automatically provide and execute test cases. Theoretically, they can relieve humans of most testing activities.

Unsurprisingly, automatization is not a simple task. As discussed in Sect. 2.4.2, it is prone to many problems. Progress in automatization could dramatically rise the efficiency of software testing—probably almost without additional cost. Sophisticated automatization could even make testing more effective if techniques are found

T. A. Majchrzak, *Improving Software Testing*, SpringerBriefs in Information Systems, DOI: 10.1007/978-3-642-27464-0_4, © The Author(s) 2012

that deal with a level of complexity human testers cannot control. In conclusion, research on test automatization is a challenging yet reasonable approach.

Automatically generating test cases with no input but the program to test would strongly contribute to full test automatization. Recent approaches for TCG often rely on preconditions. Techniques based on model-checking for example require a program's specification in a processable format. Creating a feasible model requires additional effort and might be impossible in some cases. Approaches that do not rely on preconditions are either relatively simple (e.g. random testing, see Sect. 2.2.2.6, p. 33) or limited. Therefore, the Department of Information Systems of the WWU Münster, in particular the Chair for Practical Computer Science, investigates in novel methods for automated test case generation. Continuing the work that led to the tool *GlassTT*, *Muggl*—the **Mu**enster **g**enerator of **gl**ass-box test cases—was developed.

4.2 Related Work

Research on automated testing can be traced back to the 1960s (cf. [2]). The automated generation of test cases has been described as early as 1970 [3] with a number of papers following in the 1980s (for instance [4–6]). However, the amount of work spent in this field is immense; a study of it would be feasible for a survey paper but not for a brief overview of related work. Therefore, Muggl will be distinguished from other threads of research and similar ideas discussed in the literature. Furthermore, approaches that are very similar in some ideas while belonging to another context will be named.

Both symbolic execution and test data/test case generation—and even their combination [7]—are not new. Symbolic execution has entered general textbooks on testing such as [8, 9]; test case generation is part of very recent articles such as [10, 11]. Most of these papers have a different focus, though. Symbolic execution is used for a variety of aims and test case generation is based on a set of entirely different techniques. To keep the overview of related work concise, only newer approaches are discussed. Loosely related, mostly older work is mentioned in the papers on Muggl's predecessor [12–14]. A general overview of automated test case generation is given in [15] and [16]. It also has to be noted that many papers describe special approaches that provide test case generation under fixed conditions or for distinct fields. Examples are approaches that are model-driven [17] or based on UML [18, 19]. Interestingly, it is often tried to combine other testing techniques—for instance slicing [20], cf. Sect. 2.2.1.2—with test case generation.

Three approaches are suitable for comparison with Muggl:

- *IBIS* [21] uses symbolic execution of Java bytecode in combination with constraint solving. It internally employs a Prolog representation of class files. The constraint solver is an external component. Unfortunately, no papers on progress have recently been published and results are initial. For example, not the full set of bytecode instructions is covered.

- Fischer and Kuchen present a similar approach for functional logic programming, in particular for Curry [22, 23]. Despite being quite similar in theoretic foundations, differences apply if nothing else for the differences between the programming paradigms. To handle object orientation, Muggl requires different strategies than Fischer and Kuchen's approach does. For example, arrays are not dealt with. Moreover, Fischer and Kuchen do not include a constraint solver.
- *Pex* [24–26] is a tool developed by Microsoft research. It can be seen as the counterpart of Muggl for .NET based programs. Pex instruments the Common Language Infrastructure (CLI) of the Microsoft .NET framework. It uses dynamic symbolic execution and employs a constraint solver. Even though Pex is based on path-bounded *model checking*, it has many similarities to Muggl. In contrast to Muggl, Pex does not feature an own VM but instruments the *.NET profiling API*. Additionally, its search strategy differs. It uses Z3 [27] which is a constraint solver of its own. However, it is a *satisfiability modulo theory* (SMT) solver and therefore different in design to Muggl's constraint solver. For example, Z3 natively supports data structures such as arrays. Research on Pex is ongoing [28]. It has found its way into new articles [29] and has even led to follow-up projects such as *Rex* [30].

Symstra [31] and *ATGen* [32] have similar ideas compared to Muggl. However, Symstra's techniques resemble symbolic model checking; ATGen has been written for a subset of *Ada* and does not feature coverage tracking.

In general, also work on *constraint logic programming* [33] can be related. However, it only is used for test case generation by some authors (cf. [34, 35]).

The first two papers on Muggl are based on control flow and data flow coverage [36, 37]. A wealth of work has been published on this subject and techniques needed are well understood. First of all, only related work that combines bytecode analysis is of interest—using flow information is reported for many other purposes that hardly have a relation to our ideas. Generation of CFGs from Java bytecode is utilized for various purposes, for instance bytecode rewriting [38] and verification [39]. A comprehensive introduction into control graph generation from Java bytecode is given in [40]. There is also a plug-in for *Eclipse* [41], the arguably most popular integrated development environment (IDE), called *Control Flow Graph Factory* [42]. It visualizes CFGs for Java source code and bytecode. Analysis of data-flow generated from bytecode can be found in the context of bytecode verification [43, 44]. Another approach is to generate unit tests from formal proofs [45]. Even though this work is related w.r.t. using coverage criteria, its focus on proofs renders it incomparable to Muggl.

Furthermore, there are approaches that try to achieve high structural coverage [46] but not necessarily work on bytecode. Pinte et al. [47] use evolutionary algorithms to heuristically generate test cases. They try to maximize coverage and especially keep track of def-use chains. Similarly, test cases can be generated from the CFG based on genetic algorithms. Sofokleous and Andreou try to find a "near to optimum set of test cases with respect to the edge/condition coverage criterion" [48]. The idea to use genetic approaches to maximize coverage is also discussed in [49]. *DyGen* derives test cases from analyzing execution traces [50]. Finally, Yang et al. present a study of "17 coverage-based test tools primarily focusing on, but not restricted to, coverage measurement" [51]. Some tools also deal with the "automatic generation of test cases" [51].

A second aspect of Muggl that can be compared to related work is utilizing so called *generators*. We could not identify any directly related work but various generators have been used for test data generation in other approaches. The *Spring Web Development Framework* [52] uses the inversion of control (IoC) pattern [53, 54]. Spring projects include a pre-configured structure for object generation that can (besides other purposes) be used for testing. Demankov et al. use abstract models to generate test data with complex structures [55]. In contrast, Muggl is not based on abstract models but uses custom approaches for each data structure. Many approaches on automated test data generation [56] consider the description of generators for data that is used to test systems [57]. However, they do not provide empirical results about the suitability of alternative generators.

Generating objects is also used in the context of integration and system testing, in which *mock objects* are used to simulate the behavior of components that have not yet been added to the system or must not be used for testing [58]. Whereas this can be automated [59] and advanced approaches exist [60], it only is loosely related to Muggl since it needs the generated objects in order to generate test cases and not to properly execute them. Besides the discussed approaches, much work can be found that is about (object) generators or generation. Examining it reveals that the context is different, though. This example applies to *parser generators*. Similar to generators, so called *validators* can be used to check data structures for test case generation [61].

4.3 Muggl

In the following sections, Muggl and its main techniques are briefly introduced. Moreover, an overview of experimental results is given. Whereas the following sections are a summary, all aspects of Muggl are described with much detail in a recently published paper [62]. It also shows additional screenshots, which are out of scope here.

4.3.1 Java Virtual Machine Basics

Muggl implements the Java virtual machine (JVM) specifications [63]. It provides a non-symbolic virtual machine and extensions for symbolic execution. Thus, a very brief introduction of the JVM is given, which bases on [63].

The JVM is an abstract computing machine that has been built to execute Java code. Java is a platform independent object oriented programming language [64]. The JVM is the interface between intermediary code compiled from Java source code[1]

---

[1] Since the JVM has been introduced, many other programming languages from various programming paradigms have been equipped with compiling support to Java bytecode.

Table 4.1 Types supported by the JVM [63, Chaps. 2.4, 2.5, 3.2, and 3.3]

Type	Format	Length[a]	Bytecode prefix	Initial value
boolean	Boolean value	1	z	false
byte	signed integer	8	b	(byte) 0
char	Unicode sign	16	c	\u0000
double	IEEE754 float	64	d	0.0
flout	IEEE754 float	32	f	0.0F
int	signed integer	32	i	0
long	signed integer	64	l	0L
reference	reference pointer	32	a	null
return address	address pointer	32	a	*(no default)*
short	signed integer	16	s	(short) 0

[a] The actual memory utilization of many types is higher

(i.e. bytecode) and hardware and operation system. Hence, JVM implementations are platform dependent. Bytecode is stored in a per-class representation in class files, which can be bundled in jar archives.

Bytecode is verified before run by the JVM [63, Chap. 4.9]. This is required since class files might origin from untrusted sources. Bytecode is statically typed; explicit conversion of types are necessary but for primitive integer types despite automatic conversion and auto-boxing being supported in Java source code. A list of supported types is given in Table 4.1. All types can be explicitly used with the exception of *return address*, which is an internal address pointer. Memory management is automated in the JVM; allocated memory not anymore used is deallocated using *garbage collection*.

During execution, the JVM uses several runtime *data areas* [63, Chap. 3.5]. The *pc register* stores the address of the instruction currently executed. Objects are stored on a *heap*. A *method area* and the *runtime constant pool* are used to store data loaded from class files and required during execution. Finally, the *JVM stacks* store so called *frames* which are currently suspended. The latter are used for method execution. Besides additional functions, they provide access to *local variables* of a method and an *operand stack* [63, Chap. 3.6].

For methods that implementation is provided in a class file (i.e. non-native ones that are not interfaces), an array of byte values describes the instructions. Each instruction is denoted by a one byte value, thus, there are 256 instructions possible. There are 205 instructions actually assigned [63, Chap. 6]. Some of them use additional bytes, e.g. to specify a jump address. Since the JVM is a stack-based machine, most instruction do not have additional bytes but expect operands on the stack. Many instructions exist in type sensitive variants. They are summarized in Table 4.2. A more detailed explanation of the instructions' functionality is given in [62] and [63, Chap. 6].

Besides the type sensitive instructions, further instructions can be categorized as follows:

Table 4.2 Type sensitive bytecode instructions

Category	Opcode	Byte	Char	Double	Float	Int	Long	Short	Reference
Push constants	xconst			dconst_0	fconst_0	iconst_0	lconst_0		aconst_null
				dconst_1	fconst_1	iconst_1	lconst_1		
						iconst_2			
						iconst_3			
						iconst_4			
						iconst_5			
						iconst_m1			
	xipush	bipush						sipush	
Load / store local variable[a]	xload_n			dload_n	fload_n	iload_n	lload_n		aload_n
	xload			dload	fload	iload	lload		aload
	xstore_n			dstore_n	fstore_n	istore_n	lstore_n		astore_n
	xstore			dstore	fstore	istore	lstore		astore
Load to / store from array	xaload	baload	caload	daload	faload	iaload	laload	saload	aaload
	xastore	bastore	castore	dastore	fastore	iastore	lastore	sastore	aastore
Arithmetic operations	xadd			dadd	fadd	iadd	ladd		
	xdiv			ddiv	fdiv	idiv	ldiv		
	xmul			dmul	fmul	imul	lmul		
	xrem			drem	frem	irem	lrem		
	xneg			dneg	fneg	ineg	lneg		
	xsub			dsub	fsub	isub	lsub		
Bit shifting	xshl					ishl	lshl		
	xshr					ishr	lshr		

(continued)

Table 4.2 (Continued)

Category	Opcode	Byte	Char	Double	Float	Int	Long	Short	Reference
	xushr					iushr	lushr		
Incrementation	xinc					iinc			
Logic operations	xand					iand	land		
	xor					ior	lor		
	xxor					ixor	lxor		
Long and float comparison	xcmp						lcmp		
	xcmpl			dcmpl	fcmpl				
	xcmpg			dcmpg	fcmpg				
Conversion	d2x				d2f	d2i	d2l		
	f2x			f2d		f2i	f2l		
	i2x	i2b	i2c	i2d	i2f		i2l	i2s	
	l2x			l2d	l2f	l2i			
Conditional jumps	if_xcmpOP					if_icmpeq			if_acmpeq
						if_icmpne			if_acmpne
						if_icmplt			
						if_icmpge			
						if_icmpgt			
						if_icmple			
	ifOP					ifeq			ifnull
						ifne			ifnonnull
						iflt			
						ifge			
						ifgt			
						ifle			
Return from method	xreturn			dreturn	freturn	return	lreturn		areturn

[a]There is one instruction for each value of $n \in \{0, 1, 2, 3\}$

- Fetching literals from the constant pool: `ldc`, `ldc_w`, and `ldc2_w`.
- Operations on the operand stack: `pop`, `pop2`, `dup`, `dup_x1`, `dup_x2`, `dup2`, `dup2_x1`, `dup2_x2`, and `swap`.
- Switches: `tableswitch` and `lookupswitch`.
- Return from method with void return type: `return`.
- Field access: `getstatic`, `pustatic`, `getfield`, and `putfield`.
- Method invocation: `invokevirtual`, `invokespecial`, `invokestatic`, `invokeinterface`, and `invokedynamic`.
- Object and array initialization: `anewarray`, `new`, `newarray`, and `multianewarray`.
- Unconditional jump: `goto` and `goto_w`.
- Checking reference types: `checkcast` and `instanceof`.
- Synchronization: `monitorenter` and `monitorexit`.
- Widened access to other instructions: `wide`.
- Explicitly throwing an exception: `athrow`.
- Getting an array's length: `arraylength`.
- Implementation of `finally`: `jsr`, `jsr_w`, and `ret`.
- Doing nothing: `nop` and `xxxunusedxxx`.
- Reserved for debugging: `breakpoint`, `impdep1`, and `impdep2`.

The JVM offers a number of sophisticated concepts for optimization. In particular, execution undergoes runtime optimization. This can significantly enhance performance (cf. [65]). Dynamic optimization of the JVM is an active field of research [66, 67].

4.3.2 Basic Functions and Execution Principles

Muggl implements the JVM specification [63] and directly executes Java bytecode. It thereby takes compiler optimizations into consideration and can easily be extended to other programming languages than Java. While Muggl implements the full set of bytecode instructions, some features of Java 1.5 and 1.6 are currently incomplete. Most notably, Muggl does not provide threading.

While Muggl can be directly invoked through its API (as done for its integration with EASy, cf. Sect. 6.3.3), it also offers a comprehensive GUI. The GUI is used to select `class` files and set up execution, to configured Muggl, to inspect `class` files, and to visualize the execution process. Muggl allows execution of arbitrary methods—initiating execution is not limited to `public static void main(String ... args)`. Execution is possible in normal, i.e. constant mode, or symbolically.

For symbolic execution, input parameters are treated as logic variables as known from logic programming languages [68, 69]. In the course of execution, variables are bound to terms consisting of constants, operation symbols (such as arithmetic operators), and variables. Terms are changed by executing instructions. When instructions

Table 4.3 Simple symbolic execution example including a conditional jump

Offset	Bytecode	Java	Explanation
	method invocation		
00	**iload_0**	a	Push **int** a onto the stack.
01	**iload_1**	b	Push **int** b onto the stack.
02	**if_icmpge** 0 7	if $(a < b)$	Jump to offset 09 if $(a < b)$.
05	**iload_0**	a	Push **int** a onto the stack.
06	**iload_1**	b	Push **int** b onto the stack.
07	**isub**	$a - b$	Subtract the two topmost **int** variables after popping them from the stack and push the result.
08	**ireturn**	return $a - b$	Pop the topmost **int** from the stack and return it.
09	**iload_0**	a	Push **int** a onto the stack.
10	**iload_1**	b	Push **int** b onto the stack.
11	**iadd**	$a + b$	Add the two topmost **int** variables after popping them from the stack and push the result.
12	**ireturn**	return $a + b$	Pop the topmost **int** from the stack and return it.

are executed that require a choice to be taken, constraints (e.g. in form of inequations) are built. An example is given in Listing 4.3. The column *offset* denotes the bytecode instruction's offset in the array of instructions. The second column denotes the bytecode instruction along with additional bytes. The third column represents the corresponding Java statement; the fourth column provides an explanation. A comprehensive example is given in [62], which this example was adapted from Table 4.3.

Each time a choice is taken, e.g. at the conditional jump at offset 02 of the example, a *choice point* is generated. The choice point saves the constraint that describes the choice being taken. Along with it, a *trail* is set up. With each instruction subsequentially executed, data on state changes is added to the trail. Execution finishes when a `return` instruction has been executed and no frames are left on the JVM stack. Muggl then uses *backtracking* to revert the virtual machine (VM) state to that encountered when the last choice point was generated. This is done by processing the trail in reversed order (*last-in-first-out*). It is checked whether the choice points provides another possible path of execution. In case of conditional jumps, this is the non-jumping branch. Using the trail only adds little computational overhead but is very efficient w.r.t. memory utilization. If no more choices are left for a choice point, backtracking continues until the parent choice point is reached. Should a choice point have no parent, execution is finished since all possible states have been visited.

With the described way of execution, a search tree is created. Muggl processes the tree using an iterative-deepening depth-first strategy. Each valid path found corresponds to a distinct test case. This test case (to be precise, the *solution* found) is made up of the constraints describing the input parameters and a constraint describing the expected result from computation. To calculate constant values for test cases, Muggl uses its built-in constraint solver. The solver is also used during execution. Each time a choice point is generated and each time it is checked whether another branch is provided by a choice point, the solver is used to check the constraint describing the choice. By taking into account the set of constraints built throughout computation, it becomes clear whether the condition describing the choice to branch can be satisfied. In many cases, not all branches have to be visited as execution will never yield values that satisfy the required condition. This massively decreases the number of states that have to be visited; ideally, sub-trees of the search tree can be cut off.

Constraint solving can be clarified with a simple example. Consider the source code statement $if(a > b)$. Both branches—jump and sequential execution following the corresponding bytecode instruction—have to be visited. However, assume b had been defined as $2a$ and $a < -4$ was known. Since a has a negative value, it will always be greater than b in this case. Thus, one of the two branches does not have to be visited. Constraint solving becomes far more complex for real problems. To counter the *state space explosion* and create test cases within an acceptable amount of time, Muggl employs many sophisticated techniques. Details are out of scope of this book; some details on notable functions are given in Sect. 4.3.5.

After finishing execution, Muggl eliminates redundant test cases and creates a JUnit [70] test case file. Elimination is based on coverage data and dramatically reduces the number of test cases, thus making their assessment by humans much easier. The elimination algorithm and its applicability are described in [36]; code examples are given in [62]. Muggl's approach for test case elimination is suitable for being used in other approaches for automated TCG.

To support execution, Muggl offers extensive logging functions. Moreover, it is highly configurable. While standard settings are feasible for generating test cases for most programs, a variety of settings can be changed if execution is not successful.

4.3.3 Architecture

Muggl is divided into its GUI and the execution core (Fig. 4.1). The GUI provides the capabilities to set up execution. The execution core is made up by the symbolic JVM (SJVM) and additional components, namely the constraint solver, the solution processors, and components for control flow and data flow coverage tracking. The JVM adheres to the specification and is augmented with components for symbolic execution. In order to read class files, it utilizes a bytecode parser. Furthermore, the *native wrapper* enables access to code not written in Java. For symbolic execution, the choice point generator and a variety of additional components are provided.

Muggl's architecture is modular; many components are interchangeable. Moreover, it provides a high number of interfaces, which allow extension. For example, processing a choice point is standardized. ChoicePoint however is an interface implemented by a variety of different choice points. Using object orientation tech-

Fig. 4.1 The architecture of Muggl

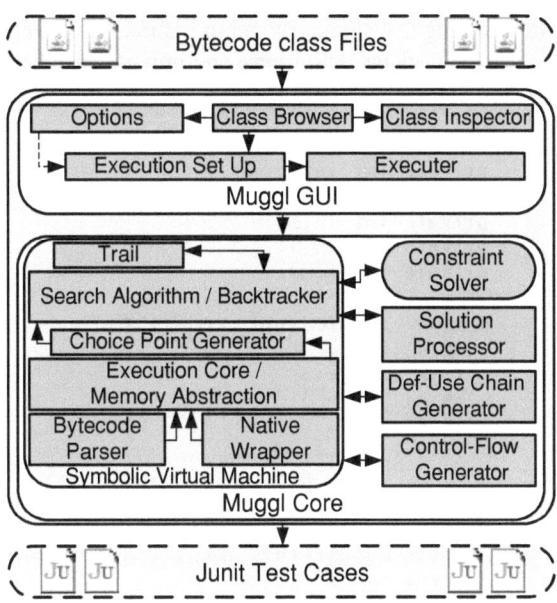

niques in Muggl's programming keeps its extension flexible. At the same time, parts of Muggl can easily be extracted and provided as libraries to other programs.

4.3.4 Example Test Case

Consider the example implementation of the *greatest-common-divisor* algorithm in Listing 4.1. After elimination, Muggl writes a JUnit test case file that comprises three distinct tests. The first one invokes the algorithm with a value for *m* that is less than *n*. Thus, values are swapped and gcd(int, int) is recursively invoked until the greatest common divisor 1 is returned. All possible paths are thereby covered. The following two tests trigger the exceptions for input integers that are less than zero.

Listing 4.1 Example implementation of the greatest-common-divisor algorithm

```
1  public static int gcd(int m, int n){
2      if (m < 0) throw new IllegalArgumentException("No natural
           number.");
3      if (n < 0) throw new IllegalArgumentException("No natural
           number.");
4
5      if (m < n) {int t = m; m = n; n = t;}
6      int r = m - n;
7      if (r == 0) return n;
8      return gcd(n, r);
9  }
```

The resulting test case is shown in Listing 4.2. Comments (but in the `try-catch` block), the package definitions, and imports have been removed for brevity.

Listing 4.2 Test case generated by Muggl for gcd (int, int)

```
1   public class TestCase {
2       private int int1;
3       private int int3;
4       private int int5;
5       private int int0;
6       private int intm1;
7
8       @Before public void setUp() {
9           this.int1 = 1;
10          this.int3 = 3;
11          this.int5 = 5;
12          this.int0 = 0;
13          this.intm1 = -1;
14      }
15
16      @Test public void testIt() {
17          assertEquals(this.int1, Gcd.gcd(this.int3, this.int5));
18          try {
19              Gcd.gcd(this.int0, this.intm1);
20              fail("Expected a java.lang.IllegalArgumentException to be
                        thrown.");
21          } catch (java.lang.IllegalArgumentException e) {
22              // Do nothing - this is what we expect to happen!
23          }
24          try {
25              Gcd.gcd(this.intm1, this.int0);
26              fail("Expected a java.lang.IllegalArgumentException to be
                        thrown.");
27          } catch (java.lang.IllegalArgumentException e) {
28              // Do nothing - this is what we expect to happen!
29          }
30      }
31
32      public static void main(String args[]) {
33          org.junit.runner.JUnitCore.main("TestCase");
34      }
35
36  }
```

4.3.5 Notable Functions

Muggl does not only comprise components that have been implemented for its basic functionality. Several distinct and in parts novel techniques have as well been embedded into it. The most notable ones are briefly sketched:

Iterative-Deepening Depth-First Search

Using an iterative-deepening approach, Muggl realizes the low memory footprint of
depth-first search without suffering from its problems. In particular, test cases are
found very quickly. Depth-first search can run into problems if execution is continued
in branches that result from unpropitious loops (cf. Listing 4.3). Due to cycles and
very high depth, execution does not reach any leaf nodes or takes extremely long in
doing so. With iterative-deepening, backtracking is invoked when a pre-set depth has
been reached. If execution is finished and no abortion criterion is met, the maximum
search depth is incremented by a predefined value and execution is restarted. Even
for an increment of only 1, only a small number of branches are visited again. For
simplification, consider a search tree in that each node has exactly two children. The
number of nodes for a given depth n is 2^{n-1}. For search depth n, the number of nodes
to discover is $2^n - 1$. For an increment of 1, the number of states that have to be
processed again is only $2^{n-1} - 1$. In addition to the search algorithm, Muggl checks
for loops that are executed for a very high number of cycles; with standard setting,
backtracking is invoked after 200 cycles without leaving the loop.

Listing 4.3 Unpropitious loop for high values of `limit`

```
1   for (int i = 0; i < limit; i++) {
2     // Do something.
3   }
```

Step-by-Step GUI

Muggl provided a step-by-step GUI which can be used for trace debugging Java
bytecode. This is helpful for debugging programs, for understanding how the JVM
works, and for debugging Muggl. The *step-by-step execution window* is shown in
Fig. 4.2. It visualizes the state of the JVM along with additional information on
symbolic execution. Using the buttons at the bottom of it, executing one or multiple steps is enabled. Furthermore, it is possible to jump to the state encountered
after executing a specified number of instructions. If it is known from non-stepped
execution that a problem is encountered after a high number of executed instructions, jumping to this very event is possible in order to monitor the state changes to
the VM.

Configurability

Muggl provides over 60 settings that can be configured. They can either be changed
by altering the configuration XML file or using Muggl's GUI. Settings address visualization in the GUI, optimization of the JVM performance, and symbolic execution.
Extensive options ensure that many examples can be run by Muggl; changing options
can greatly reduce execution time or improve results.

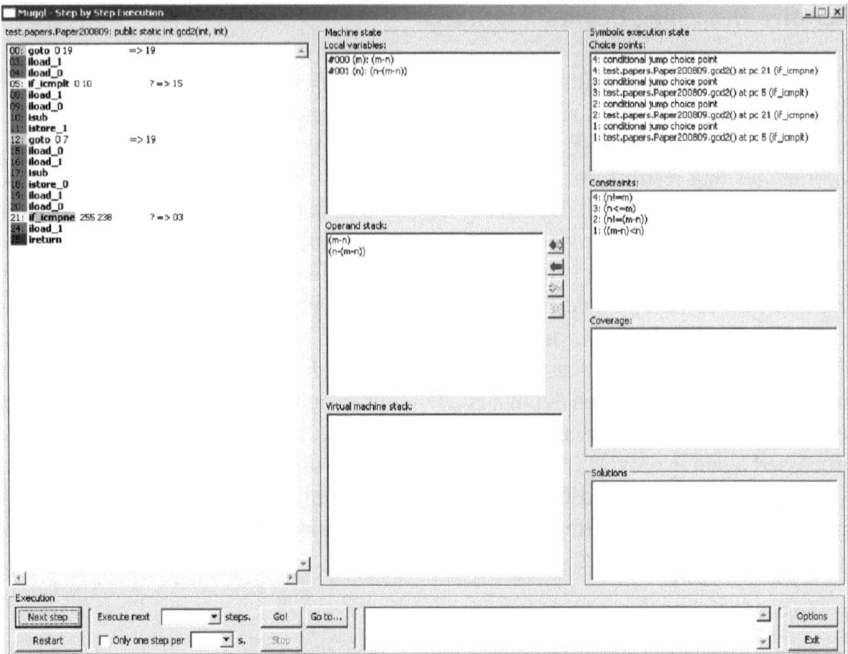

Fig. 4.2 Muggl's step-by-step execution window

`Class` File Inspection

To provide reasonable support for debugging and since Muggl has the capabilities to
read and write `class` files, it has the functionality to visualize them. Visualization
is done in a tree-like form that shows the dependence of structures of `class` files.
The tree can be expanded; thereby, only those structured are shown that are of current
interest. Furthermore, string values from the *constant pool* of `class` files can be
modified, which directly affects execution. It also is possible to save the changed
`class` to a new file. An example of the window is depicted in Fig. 4.3. It shows
parts of the constant pool, the access flags, and parts of the structure of a method.

Java `Class` File Representation by Java Classes

`Class` file inspection relies on Muggl's internal representation of `class` files. It
is implemented as a number of depended Java classes and interfaces. These data
structures not only simplify Muggl's internal handling of Java classes but can also
be used by other tools and for other purposes. They ensure high performance when
reading and writing Java `class` files. An API reference is given in [62].

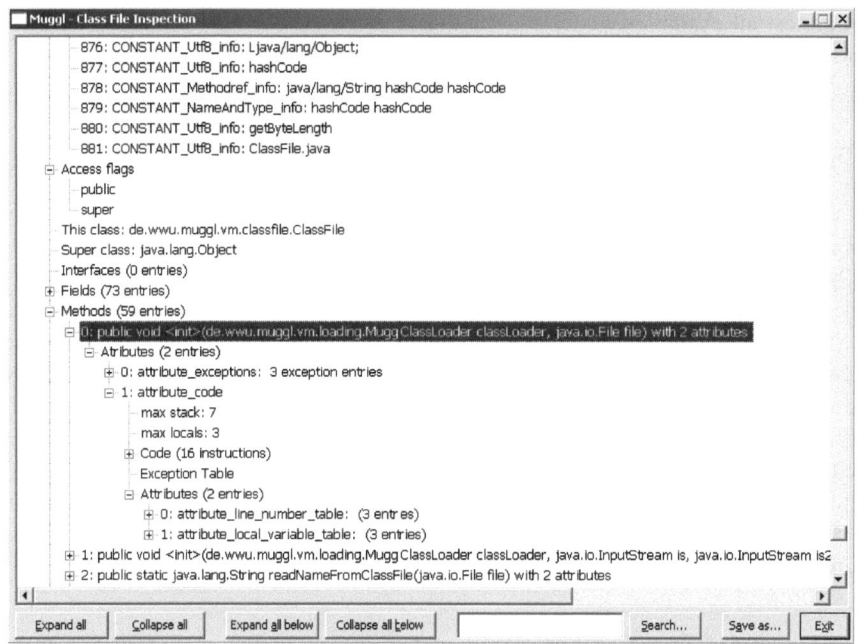

Fig. 4.3 Muggl's `class` file inspection window

Control Flow and Data Flow Coverage

Covering control flow and data flow is an important criterion for assessing test cases (see Chap. 2). Muggl is capable of tracking control flow and data flow by building control flow graphs (CFG) and by generating def-use (DU) chains. Specifically, the generation of interprocedural def-use chains is a sophisticated task. Muggl generates flow information statically and dynamically tracks coverage. This greatly decreases the memory footprint since coverage information for each test case can be saved in a simple array of **boolean** values. Furthermore, execution can be aborted once full coverage is detected.

Test Case Elimination

Muggl eliminates test cases based on coverage information. Symbolic execution leads to a high number of found test cases. However, most of them are redundant despite having different values for the input parameters of the tested program. They can be eliminated based on an assumption: a test case that neither contributes to control flow nor to data flow coverage is *redundant*. With given coverage information, the minimal set of test cases is searched that still covers all CFG edges and DU chains found to be coverable. Muggl uses a *greedy algorithm* for this set-coverage problem.

In almost all examples we tested, it reduced the set to the optimal number of test cases. In few cases, one or two additional test cases were kept.

Dynamic Optimization

Due to dynamic optimization, the official JVM is able to execute code with a very high performance. In fact, due to using information available at runtime, code ideally executes faster than native code. To increase execution speed, Muggl supports the replacement of instructions with optimized ones. The basic idea is simple: some instructions are computationally very expensive. However, they perform the same action whenever they are executed. Thus, the results or at least an intermediary result from execution can be saved in an alternative instruction. It replaces the original instruction. When executed the next time, the result can be used without the requirement of expensive execution. This for example speeds up access to the runtime constant pool dramatically. Muggl employs instruction replacement for `ldc_w`, `ldc2_w`, and `invokestatic`. Results are very promising; the experimental feature will be extended to more instruction in the future.

Native Wrapper

Some of the method from the Java libraries rely on platform dependent, so called *native* code. For example, writing to the console requires communication with the operation system, which is possible trough methods implemented in C. As a Java application, Muggl cannot invoke such code. However, it provides a wrapper to invoke native methods through the system's Java Runtime Environment (JRE). The overhead is negligible for symbolic execution. At the same time, the number of programs executable by Muggl is increased greatly. Native wrapping is either done by providing the required functionality as a special class within Muggl or by redirecting method calls to the JVM that runs Muggl. The latter requires conversion of data structures from Muggl's representation to the ones used by the system's JRE. This is a very complex and computationally costly process. Therefore, Muggl uses special wrapper classes instead of forwarding for performance critical methods. For example, calls to the native method `System.arraycopy(Object, int, Object, int, int)` are internally handled by Muggl with hardly any penalty in performance.

Array Generation

Muggl's solver cannot represent arrays of variable length. Since many programs use arrays, array generation is a strategy to circumvent this limitation. When an element from an array is to be loaded, Muggl created an *array generation choice point*. It provides as many elements as are specified by the predefined *generation strategy*. One element is provided each time backtracking is used to return to the state encountered at this choice point. The generated arrays vary in length. Their elements are symbolic (i.e. logic variables) if the array type is primitive or one of the wrapper classes for primitive types (e.g. `java.lang.Integer` for **int**). Dependent on the tested program, there are two successful strategies. The first one is to provide several arrays with a low number of elements. The second one is to provide some arrays with a low number of elements and some with a high number of elements. Besides, additionally providing an empty array (i.e. an array of zero length) and the `null` reference often leads to further test cases. Muggl currently provides four distinct generation strategies; details on generation are out of scope of this short summary but included in [62].

4.3.6 Performance

No elaborate experimentation data can be given in a short book. However, Muggl's performance has to be examined; detailed results are compiled in the papers [36, 62].

First of all, Muggl is capable of successfully generating test cases for a large number of examples. This includes both a three-digit number of artificial examples and a two-digit number of algorithms used in other programs. Artificial examples were required to assess Muggl's functionality—most of these examples are rather simple. Tested algorithms comprise typically used programs for sorting, search, and basic calculation. Moreover, Muggl was used in combination with e-assessment. Results are described in Chap. 6. This application demonstrates Muggl's feasibility for actual problems—it had to quickly process programs uploaded by students with a predefined set of options. This was by far more challenging than testing programs with ample available time and the possibility to try out varying settings.

Experimentation shows that test case elimination is successful. In particular, it is very fast. In many cases, Muggl finds test cases within a very short time. Examples that do not lead to an abortion after a few second of execution, usually spend much time in unpropitious data structures or lead to problems with the solver that ends in an infinite loop. In most cases, feasible test cases have still been found and once the time limit is met a suitable JUnit test case file is created. Only in a small number of examples that we tested, a number of test cases was found that is too small or execution failed at all. In the first case, problems could be tracked down to erroneous computation in the solver; these problems are currently being fixed. With the exception of these problems, the solver has proven to be flexible and powerful. In the latter case, problems are hard to fix.

Due to the size of Muggl (over 44,000 LOC excluding comments) and the extreme complexity of some of its components, some conceptual problems yet reside in it. After all, Muggl is a prototype. *Removing* these defects usually is simple since the general conception of Muggl is sound and well proven; however, *finding* them is very hard. In the few examples in which execution fails with an `Error` being thrown by Muggl's SJVM, the reasons are not obvious. They cannot be derived from information that accompany the error. Using the step-by-step execution GUI helps, but finding defects can still be very laborious. We removed defects that lead to SJVM malfunction after the execution of ten thousands of instructions as seen from the point of execution at which they originated. Removing only one such defect can attribute for a high two-digit figure of man hours of debugging. Notwithstanding, both problems with the solver and Muggl malfunction only occurs in a very small number of examples.

For large examples, execution currently is not possible. Muggl utilizes memory very defensively and its techniques dramatically reduce the number of states to explore. However, for testing programs of commercial scale, additional techniques have to be found. Execution does not come to an end in a reasonable amount of time or Muggl runs out of memory.

Results from execution are highly dependent on the chosen settings. Optimized settings often improve performance or results. However, no means to automatically configure Muggl have been found, yet.

4.3.7 Intermediate Conclusion

Despite being the thread of research presented in this book that has been pursued for the longest time, work on Muggl is not finished. Its code base is very large and Muggl is capable of generating test cases for many examples. It provides functionality that goes far beyond automated TCG. Due to its extensibility, additional usage scenarios are planned. However, some problems with execution reside and will have to be addressed in future work. Ongoing research is discussed in Chap. 8.

4.4 Overview of Published Work

To conclude this chapter, an overview of published work is presented. For each paper, title and abstract are given followed by a discussion how it applies to the context of this book. Eventually, the full citation is given.

Automatische Testfallerzeugung auf Basis der Überdeckungsanalyse

Abstract Wir stellen ein Werkzeug für die automatische Generierung von Testfällen vor. Es führt Java Bytecode symbolisch aus, um Ausführungspfade durch ein Programm zu finden. Dazu nutzt es Constraint Solving, die Erzeugung von Entscheidungspunkten und Backtracking. Da die Zahl der gefundenen Testfälle sehr hoch werden kann und die meisten von ihnen redundant sind, regen wir an, Testfälle anhand ihres Beitrags zur globalen Kontroll- und Datenflussüberdeckung zu eliminieren. Neben den dazu benötigten Techniken zeigen wir experimentelle Ergebnisse, um die Machbarkeit des Ansatzes zu demonstrieren.

This paper is a translation and adaption of the next paper, *Automated Test Case Generation based on Coverage Analysis*, for a workshop held in Bad Honnef. It was published priorly due to a much shorter publication process. More details on its content are given in the following Section.

Full citation: Tim A. Majchrzak and Herbert Kuchen. Automatische Testfallerzeugung auf Basis der Überdeckungsanalyse. In Michael Hanus and Bernd Brassel, editors, Technischer Bericht des Instituts für Informatik Nr. 0915: 26. Workshop der GI-Fachgruppe "Programmiersprachen und Rechenkonzepte", pp. 14–25, Bad Honnef, Germany, May 2009. Christian-Albrechts-Universität Kiel.

Automated Test Case Generation Based on Coverage Analysis

Abstract We present a tool for the automated generation of unit tests. It symbolically executes Java bytecode in order to find execution paths through a program. To efficiently accomplish this task, it uses constraint solving, choice-point generation and backtracking. As the number of test cases found might be very high and most of them are redundant, we propose a novel way to eliminate test cases based on their contribution to the global coverage of the control-flow and data-flow. Besides discussing the techniques used to achieve this, we present experimental results to prove the feasibility of our approach.

This paper introduces Muggl and presents a novel approach to keep the set of automatically generated test cases small. Since it was the first conference paper on Muggl, a comprehensive introduction into Muggl had to be included. Therefore, not only the basics of Muggl are described but also some advanced techniques that are not found in other systems or that base on ideas not priorly used in the context of Muggl. The combination of generating coverage data and using it for elimination is novel. Moreover, the sophisticated technique to generate def-use chains from Java bytecode had not been published as such before. Therefore, this paper is the base for future publications and at the same time presents an important contribution. Techniques for generating and tracking coverage information as well as for test case elimination can seamlessly be used in other tools for test automatization. Besides, the paper marks the transition from GlassTT to its successor Muggl.

Full citation: Tim A. Majchrzak and Herbert Kuchen. Automated test case generation based on coverage analysis. In TASE '09: Proceedings of the 2009 3rd IEEE International Symposium on Theoretical Aspects of Software Engineering. IEEE Computer Society, 2009.

Muggl: The Muenster Generator of Glass-box Test Cases

Abstract Testing is a task that requires much effort, yet it is essential for developing software. Automated test case generation (TCG) promises to relieve humans of manual work. We introduce Muggl (the Muenster generator of glass-box test cases), which is developed at our institute. Muggl generates test cases for Java bytecode. It symbolically executes code and uses constraint solving techniques. While papers on Muggl have already been published, no comprehensive introduction of the tool exist. This working paper fills this gap.

This paper summarizes the development status of Muggl. Since the last paper was published in 2009, this paper includes information about all additions to Muggl. It also describes the general functionality more comprehensively than the yet published papers. Furthermore, it compiles experimental results and statistical data that helps to understand Muggl's capabilities and performance. Therefore, the paper supports an assessment of the contribution Muggl makes.

Full citation: Tim A. Majchrzak and Herbert Kuchen. Muggl: The Muenster Generator of Glass-box Test Cases. In Becker, J. et al., editors, Working Papers No. 10, European Research Center for Information Systems (ERCIS), Münster, 2010.

References

1. Glass, R.L.: Two mistakes and error-free Software: a confession. IEEE Softw. **25**(4), 96 (2008)
2. Hamburger, P.: On an automated method of symbolically analyzing times of computer programs. Commun. ACM **9**(7), 481 (1966)
3. Hanford, K.V.: Automatic generation of test cases. IBM Syst. J. **9**(4), 242–257 (1970)
4. Bird, D.L., Munoz, C.U.: Automatic generation of random self-checking test cases. IBM Syst. J. **22**(3), 229–245 (1983)
5. Tsai, W.T., Volovik, D., Keefe, T.F.: Automated test case generation for programs specified by relational algebra queries. IEEE Trans. Softw. Eng. **16**(3), 316–324 (1990)
6. Kilperäinen, P., Mannila, H.: Generation of test cases for simple Prolog programs. Acta Cybern. **9**(3), 235–246 (1990)
7. Gotlieb, A., Botella, B., Rueher, M.: Automatic test data generation using constraint solving techniques. SIGSOFT Softw. Eng. Notes **23**(2), 53–62 (1998). http://doi.acm.org/10.1145/271775.271790
8. Liggesmeyer, P.: Software-Qualität: Testen, Analysieren und Verifizieren von Software, 2nd edn. Spektrum-Akademischer, Berlin (2009)
9. Wallmüller, E.: Software-Qualitätsmanagement in der Praxis, 2nd edn. Hanser, München (2001)
10. Hoffman, D., Wang, H.Y., Chang, M., Ly-Gagnon, D., Sobotkiewicz, L., Strooper, P.: Two case studies in grammar-based test generation. J. Syst. Softw. **83**(12), 2369–2378 (2010)
11. Chatterjee, R., Johari, K.: A prolific approach for automated generation of test cases from informal requirements. SIGSOFT Softw. Eng. Notes **35**(5), 1–11 (2010)
12. Mueller, R.A., Lembeck, C., Kuchen, H.: Generating glass-box test cases using a symbolic virtual machine. In: Proceedings IASTED SE 2004 (2004)

13. Mueller, R.A., Lembeck, C., Kuchen, H.: GlassTT—a symbolic Java virtual machine using constraint solving techniques for glass-box test case generation. Technical Report, No. 102. Department of Information Systems, Arbeitsbericht Universitaet Muenster (2003)

14. Lembeck, C., Caballero, R., Mueller, R.A., Kuchen, H.: Constraint solving for generating glass-box test cases. In: Proceedings WFLP '04, pp. 19–32 (2004)

15. Prasanna, M., Sivanandam, S., Venkatesan, R., Sundarrajan, R.: A survey on automatic test case generation. Acad. Open Internet J. **15**, 1–6 (2005)

16. Edvardsson, J.: A survey on automatic test data generation. In: Proceedings of the Second Conference on Computer Science and Engineering in Linköping, pp. 21–28. ECSEL (1999)

17. Liu, Y., Li, Y., Wang, P.: Design and implementation of automatic generation of test cases based on model driven architecture. In: Proceedings of the 2010 Second International Conference on Information Technology and Computer Science, ITCS '10, pp. 344–347. IEEE Computer Society, Washington, DC (2009)

18. Ogata, S., Matsuura, S.: A method of automatic integration test case generation from UML-based scenario. WSEAS Trans. Info. Sci. App. **7**(4), 598–607 (2010)

19. Chen, M., Qiu, X., Xu, W., Wang, L., Zhao, J., Li, X.: UML activity diagram-based automatic test case generation For Java programs. Comput. J. **52**(5), 545–556 (2009)

20. Samuel, P., Mall, R.: Slicing-based test case generation from UML activity diagrams. SIG-SOFT Softw. Eng. Notes **34**(6), 1–14 (2009)

21. Doyle, J., Meudec, C.: IBIS: an Interactive Bytecode Inspection System, using symbolic execution and constraint logic programming. In: PPPJ '03: Proceedings, pp. 55–58. New York (2003)

22. Fischer, S., Kuchen, H.: Systematic generation of glass-box test cases for functional logic programs. In: PPDP '07: Proceedings of the 9th ACM SIGPLAN International Conference on Principles and Practice of Declarative Programming, pp. 63–74. ACM, New York (2007)

23. Fischer, S., Kuchen, H.: Data-flow testing of declarative programs. In: ICFP'08: Proceedings of the 13th ACM SIGPLAN International Conference on Functional Programming, pp. 201–212. ACM, New York (2008)

24. Tillmann, N., de Halleux, J.: Pex-white box test generation for .NET. In: 2nd International Conference on Tests and Proofs, pp. 134–153 (2008)

25. Godefroid, P., de Halleux, P., Nori, A.V., Rajamani, S.K., Schulte, W., Tillmann, N., Levin, M.Y.: Automating software testing using program analysis. IEEE Softw. **25**(5), 30–37 (2008)

26. Tillmann, N., Schulte, W.: Unit tests reloaded: parameterized unit testing with symbolic execution. IEEE Softw. **23**(4), 38–47 (2006)

27. de Moura, L., Bjoerner, N.: Z3: an efficient SMT solver, LNCS, vol. 4963/2008, pp. 337–340. Springer, Berlin (2008)

28. http://research.microsoft.com/en-us/projects/pex/

29. Tillmann, N., de Halleux, J., Xie, T.: Parameterized unit testing: theory and practice. In: Proceedings of the 32nd ACM/IEEE International Conference on Software Engineering, vol. 2, ICSE'10, pp. 483–484. ACM, New York (2010)

30. Veanes, M., Halleux, P.D., Tillmann, N.: Rex: symbolic regular expression explorer. In: Proceedings of the 2010 Third International Conference on Software Testing, Verification and Validation, ICST '10, pp. 498–507. IEEE Computer Society, Washington, DC (2010)

31. Xie, T., Marinov, D., Schulte, W., Notkin, D.: Symstra: a framework for generating object-oriented unit tests using symbolic execution. In: 11th International Conference on Tools and Algorithms for the Construction and Analysis of Systems, LNCS, pp. 365–381. Springer, Berlin (2005)

32. Meudec, C.: ATGen: automatic test data generation using constraint logic programming and symbolic execution. Softw. Test. Verif. Reliab. **11**(2), 81–96 (2001)

33. Gavanelli, M., Rossi, F.: Constraint logic programming. In: Dovier, A., Pontelli, E. (eds.) A 25-Year Perspective on Logic Programming, pp. 64–86. Springer, Berlin (2010)

34. Colin, S., Legeard, B., Peureux, F.: Preamble computation in automated test case generation using constraint logic programming: research articles. Softw. Test. Verif. Reliab. **14**(3), 213–235 (2004)

35. Zeng, Z., Ciesielski, M.J., Rouzeyre, B.: Functional test generation using constraint logic programming. In: Proceedings of the IFIP TC10/WG10.5 Eleventh International Conference on Very Large Scale Integration of Systems-on/Chip: SOC Design Methodologies, VLSISOC '01, pp. 375–387. Kluwer, Deventer (2002)

36. Majchrzak, T.A., Kuchen, H.: Automated test case generation based on coverage analysis. In: TASE '09: Proceedings of the 2009 3rd IEEE International Symposium on Theoretical Aspects of Software Engineering, pp. 259–266. IEEE Computer Society, Washington, DC (2009)

37. Majchrzak, T.A., Kuchen, H.: Automatische Testfallerzeugung auf Basis der Überdeckungsanalyse. In: Hanus, M., Brassel, B. (eds.) Technischer Bericht des Instituts für Informatik Nr. 0915: 26. Workshop der GI-Fachgruppe "Programmiersprachen und Rechenkonzepte", pp. 14–25. Christian-Albrechts-Universität Kiel, Bad Honnef (2009)

38. Balland, E., Moreau, P.E., Reilles, A.: Bytecode rewriting in Tom. Electron. Notes Theor. Comput. Sci. **190**(1), 19–33 (2007)

39. Bernardeschi, C., Francesco, N.D., Martini, L.: Efficient bytecode verification using immediate postdominators in control flow graphs. In: OTM Workshops, Lecture Notes in Computer Science, vol. 2889, pp. 425–436. Springer, Berlin (2003)

40. Zhao, J.: Analyzing control flow in Java bytecode. In: Proceedings of the 16th Conference of Japan Society for Software Science and Technology, pp. 313–316 (1999)

41. http://www.eclipse.org/

42. http://www.drgarbage.com/control-flow-graph-factory-3-3.html

43. Klein, G.: Verified Java bytecode verification. Inf. Technol. **47**(2), 107–110 (2005)

44. Qian, Z.: Constraint-based specification and dataflow analysis for Java TM byte code verification. Technical Report, Kestrel Institute (1997)

45. Engel, C., Haehnle, R.: Generating unit tests from formal proofs. In: Proceedings of the Testing and Proofs. Springer, Berlin (2007)

46. Baluda, M., Braione, P., Denaro, G., Pezzè, M.: Structural coverage of feasible code. In: Proceedings of the 5th Workshop on Automation of Software Test, AST '10, pp. 59–66. ACM, New York (2010)

47. Pinte, F., Oster, N., Saglietti, F.: Techniques and tools for the automatic generation of optimal test data at code, model and interface level. In: ICSE Companion '08: Companion of the 30th International Conference on Software Engineering, pp. 927–928. ACM, New York (2008)

48. Sofokleous, A.A., Andreou, A.S.: Automatic, evolutionary test data generation for dynamic software testing. J. Syst. Softw. **81**(11), 1883–1898 (2008)

49. Dharsana, C.S.S., Jennifer, D.N., Askarunisha, A., Ramaraj, N.: Java based test case generation and optimization using evolutionary testing. In: Proceedings of the International Conference on Computational Intelligence and Multimedia Applications (ICCIMA 2007), vol. 01, pp. 44–49. IEEE Computer Society, Washington, DC (2007)

50. Thummalapenta, S., de Halleux, J., Tillmann, N., Wadsworth, S.: DyGen: automatic generation of high-coverage tests via mining gigabytes of dynamic traces. In: Proceedings of the 4th International Conference on Tests and proofs, TAP'10, pp. 77–93. Springer, Berlin (2010)

51. Yang, Q., Li, J.J., Weiss, D.: A survey of coverage based testing tools. In: Proceedings of the 2006 International Workshop on Automation of Software Test, AST'06, pp. 99–103. ACM, New York (2006)

52. Johnson, R., Hoeller, J., Arendsen, A., Risberg, T., Kopylenko, D.: Professional Java Development with the Spring Framework. Wrox, Birmingham (2005)

53. Ladd, S., Davison, D., Devijver, S., Yates, C.: Expert Spring MVC and Web Flow. Apress, Berkely (2006)

54. Minter, D.: Beginning Spring 2: From Novice to Professional. Apress, Berkely (2007)

55. Demakov, A.V., Zelenov, S.V., Zelenova, S.A.: Using abstract models for the generation of test data with a complex structure. Program. Comput. Softw. 34(6), 341–350 (2008). http://dx.doi.org/10.1134/S0361768808060054

56. Korel, B.: Automated software test data generation. IEEE Trans. Softw. Eng. **16**(8), 870–879 (1990). http://dx.doi.org/10.1109/32.57624

57. Zhao, R., Li, Q.: Automatic test generation for dynamic data structures. In: Proceedings SERA '07, pp. 545–549. IEEE Computer Society, Washington, DC (2007). http://dx.doi.org/10.1109/SERA.2007.59

58. Thomas, D., Hunt, A.: Mock objects. IEEE Softw. **19**(3), 22–24 (2002)

59. Tillmann, N., Schulte, W.: Mock-object generation with behavior. In: Proceedings ASE '06, pp. 365–368. IEEE Computer Society, Washington, DC (2006). http://dx.doi.org/10.1109/ASE.2006.51

60. Galler, S.J., Maller, A., Wotawa, F.: Automatically extracting mock object behavior from design by contract specification for test data generation. In: Proceedings AST '10, pp. 43–50. ACM, New York (2010). http://doi.acm.org/10.1145/1808266.1808273

61. Liu, H., Tan, H.B.K.: Automated verification and test case generation for input validation. In: Proceedings of the 2006 International Workshop on Automation of Software Test, AST '06, pp. 29–35. ACM, New York (2006)

62. Majchrzak, T.A., Kuchen, H.: Muggl: the Muenster generator of glass-box test cases. In: Becker, J., Backhaus, K., Grob, H., Hellingrath, B., Hoeren, T., Klein, S., Kuchen, H., Müller-Funk, U., Thonemann, U.W., Vossen, G. (eds.) Working Papers, No. 10. European Research Center for Information Systems (ERCIS) (2011)

63. Lindholm, T., Yellin, F.: The Java Virtual Machine Specification, 2nd edn. Prentice Hall, Englewood Cliffs (1999)

64. Gosling, J., Joy, B., Steele, G., Bracha, G.: Java(TM) Language Specification, 3rd edn. Addison-Wesley, Boston (2005)

65. Oracle: Java 2 Platform, Standard Edition (J2SE Platform), version 1.4.2 Performance White Paper (2010). http://java.sun.com/j2se/1.4.2/1.4.2_whitepaper.html

66. Suganuma, T., Yasue, T., Kawahito, M., Komatsu, H., Nakatani, T.: Design and evaluation of dynamic optimizations for a Java just-in-time compiler. ACM Trans. Program. Lang. Syst. **27**, 732–785 (2005)

67. Hoste, K., Georges, A., Eeckhout, L.: Automated just-in-time compiler tuning. In: Proceedings of the 8th Annual IEEE/ACM International Symposium on Code Generation and Optimization, CGO '10, pp. 62–72. ACM, New York (2010)

68. Doets, K.: From Logic to Logic Programming. MIT Press, Cambridge (1994)

69. Bramer, M.: Logic Programming with Prolog. Springer, Secaucus (2005)

70. http://www.junit.org/

Chapter 5
Organizational Aspects: The IHK Project

The IHK project evolved to a main part of the research included in this book. It is introduced in the following sections.

5.1 Background

As discussed in earlier chapters, testing is a very challenging task. Literature gives much advice on testing techniques and provides recommendations for testing management. Unfortunately, it does not provide practitioners with *solutions* to their business problems.

The region of the IHK Nord Westfalen [1] (the chamber of commerce in the region of North Westphalia) and in particular the Münsterland are home to a number of companies that rely on testing software and on quality management of software. Firstly, many small to medium size software developing companies and software vendors produce individual software solutions and standard software. Secondly, several large financial service providers with far over 1,000 employees are based in Münster— the economic center of the Münsterland. Due to the criticality of software for their business, they develop software on their own, customize standard software, or test licensed software products in order to check their quality. All companies are members of the IHK. The IHK supports the IAI [2] which is an academically managed research institute financially funded by the *Förderkreis* (board of supporters) of the IAI. Members of the IAI or commissioned scientist work on research projects that mean to solve IT problems of the local businesses with academic means.

There is a frequent exchange between supporters, IAI directors, and the IHK. It thereby was learned that companies were dissatisfied with their software testing efforts or sought to increase the quality of their software products without rising their expenditures. Despite these ambitions, they did not know how to reach the aims or lacked the time to investigate in ways to improve their testing. As a consequence, the project "software testing" was initiated (in the following: *IHK project*) and assigned to the Chair for Practical Computer Science of the WWU Münster.

T. A. Majchrzak, *Improving Software Testing*, SpringerBriefs in Information Systems, DOI: 10.1007/978-3-642-27464-0_5, © The Author(s) 2012

The project had two main aims. Firstly, the status quo of testing of companies in the region should be drawn. Secondly, best practices for testing should be collected and provided to the companies. The second aim is based on the following idea. While companies strive for improvements w.r.t. their testing, they are not economically endangered. In fact, they successfully test software. In conclusion, they must have developed strategies that helped them in achieving software quality. Due to the diversity of companies, it was expected that successful strategies (*strength*) would at least partly be distinct. Software testing is influenced by the corporate culture, processes, used standards, and especially by the employees. Consequently, best practices developed by single companies would complement each other. Each participating company could expect to learn *some* successful strategies that were not yet implemented by it.

Best practices learned from companies were to be aggregated as recommendations and published as a booklet. Because the IAI is based on the work of academics, it also strives for scientific progress. IAI projects are conducted with academic *rigor* in order to gain theoretical knowledge. The other way around, testing academic theories in practice is vital [3]. Theoretical considerations could thus be verified in collaboration with practitioners.

5.2 Related Work

There are vast amounts of papers and textbooks published on software testing. In comparison to it, the number of papers on *software testing best practices, recommendations*, and *process optimization* is low. Papers that can be identified usually have a rather special focus, i.e. they deal with a subtopic of testing or only apply in a narrow context [4–7]. Alternatively, they are presented as sector specific case studies [8, 9], have been published at least a decade ago [10, 11], or only as a doctoral thesis without directly related papers [12]. Other authors rather discuss challenges [13, 14] or why best practices are *not* used [15]. It is indisputable that these papers—in parts greatly—contribute to the body of software testing knowledge. But they do not compile best practices for testing in companies that develop or customize software.

The standard literature that was used to compile Chap. 2 of this work comprises notes on testing best practices. However, such books typically present the general knowledge with some author-specific or subtopic-focused additions. In particular, these books do not mean to give advice on how to improve testing processes or the organizational background of testing—this task is left to the reader. Liggesmeyer [16] for example closes each of his chapter with a checklist of $\frac{1}{2}$ to 1 page. The checklists summarize operational advice. Moreover, he concludes the book with a ten page chapter on practical guidelines [16, Chap. 15]. This—by far—exceeds practical hints given in common textbooks. Cleff for example summarizes seven guidelines on 4 pages [17]. Similarly, Zeller proposes how to prevent "unknown problems" and gives recommendations such as "test first", "test often" and "test enough" [18, p. 77ff.]. However, such recommendations are subordinate in textbooks. Comparing newer titles to older ones such as the 1993 title from Kaner et al. [19], no increased focus on practical advice can be identified.

Besides general textbooks, specialized books compile best practices without naming them as such. This example applies to books on special topics in testing [20] or on software quality management [21]. Some of these books even have "effective" in their name [22]. Business oriented books such as [23–25] give recommendations for the organization of testing processes.

Newer textbooks try to provide advice that either can be applied to business problems directly or that helps to improve testing processes. Two examples are the books by De Grood [26] and Henry [27]. Both combine academic rigor with hands-on experience. De Grood presents a holistic approach for result-driven testing that tries to optimize all phases of the testing process [26]. The book of Henry is much more specialized and comprehensively addresses testing in large software projects [27]. Both books can be seen as part of a new generation of testing books. Instead of giving an overview of testing, they present basics only very concisely. Rather, they give in-depth advice for testing strategies or typical problems domains.

Finally, some authors present directly usable advice. A technical report of IBM compiles "software testing best practices" [28]. Unfortunately, with hardly 11 pages in length it does not comprise many recommendations. Perry and Rice present "10 golden rules for software testing" [29]. Despite being limited to 10 recommendations, their suggestions can be applied to business problems. Literature such as the *Test Engineer's Handbook* [30] addresses professionals. While it focuses on giving certification related knowledge, it can be seen as a practical guideline. Dustin presents a compilation of "50 Ways to Improve [...] Software Testing" [31]. The book covers fields such as test-planning, staffing a test team, testing strategy, and test automatization. It has a holistic approach and tries to give hints for many important testing subtopics. In [32], 23 essays are compiled on software testing best practices. Most of them have been written by practitioners.

Besides the literature that can be related to the IHK project as a whole, there is related work for each of the recommendations. It is mentioned in the respective chapter of the published work; it is not reasonable to repeat this discussion here.

5.3 Findings of the IHK Project

The following sections will tersely present the findings of the project. Details are given in the booklet [33], which is publicly available [34]. It will not explicitly be cited as it is the reference for all following subsections. Additional details can be found in the other papers on the IHK project. They are introduced in Sect. 5.4.

5.3.1 Participants

For publication purposes, participating companies must not be named. Neither can interview protocols be published without anonymization. Nevertheless, an overview of some key figures can be given.

Six companies were chosen for detailed expert interviews. One company falls into the range of 1–50 employees (*small*), two employ between 51 and 250 employees (*medium*), and three—in parts vastly—have more than 1,000 employees (*very large*). For two of them software development is a means to an end. They are financial service providers who develop software to support their core business. The other companies' core business is software development. Two companies offer standard software; the remaining four focus on individual development by contract. The typical project size correlates with the size of the company. However, the smaller companies reported that they take part in joint projects which can be larger.

5.3.2 Status Quo of Testing

The status quo just hints how testing is done in the Münsterland region. Despite being informally verified with several company representatives from the region, and even despite receiving reports of similar findings in other regions worldwide, findings are *not* significant and do not adhere to quantitative research methods. Nevertheless, they are noteworthy. For summarization, findings will be presented quantitatively in that general observations and overall trends are mentioned.

On all conferences we talked about the IHK project, we were told of similar findings by both practitioners and scientists. Neither of them had quantitative results but all of them concordantly reported similar observations. Even with the low sample size, the findings of the IHK project seem to be typical, if not representative. Quantitative confirmation is a future task (see Chap. 8).

In general, results were very heterogeneous. Findings align with company sizes, though. Smaller companies test informally whereas larger companies have a structured testing process and a sophisticated testing organization. They also have less trouble in justifying testing. Customers of smaller companies do not accept higher development costs due to testing. At the same time, fixing defects after shipping a software product is common. For financial service providers this is not acceptable: products ought to have a very high quality upon completion.

Smaller companies usually do not distinguish between developers and testers. Testing is an ad hoc *activity*. Typically, it follows an approach similar to Extreme Programming [35]. Larger companies do not only have this distinction but have fixed roles and their processes include formal approvals of quality. They also employ a *test center*, which coordinates tests, provides guidelines, and supports staffing. Moreover, they follow a staging based testing process (cf. Sect. 2.3.1) with distinct phases and fixed roles.

High testing effort was observed for companies that use staging. In contrast, ad hoc testing usually goes along with less testing effort. While the overall testing effort is static in larger companies, smaller companies vary tests in connection to a project's progress and background. They also try to substitute testing activities by carefully surveying requirements.

With regard to the kinds of tests, practitioners do not distinguish between glass-box tests and black-box tests. Furthermore, they hardly use test automatization. In particular, advanced automatization (cf. Sect. 2.4.2) techniques are not used. Considering component, integration, system, and acceptance tests, all companies roughly follow the recommendations given in the literature. Acceptance tests are especially important for software developed by contract as it usually includes the approval by customers.

Only one of the companies reported tests that target the data abstraction or databases. Obligatory stress testing was reported by none of the companies. However, rather informal assessments of programs' performance are common. Several companies reported that it is more important for them to satisfy their customers than to develop technically sound software—in particular with regard to its performance.

While regression testing is widely used, it usually is not supported by test tools. In general, usage of test tools is low and companies are dissatisfied with them. Only large companies employ systems for test case management or sophisticated (and expensive) test tools. Usage of small tools such as unit testing programs is common. Besides, some companies described positive experiences with individually implemented test tools.

In conclusion, testing is very heterogeneous while the general structure, effort, and complexity correlate with a company's size. Tool usage is low and even in large companies not universal. Test automatization is neglected.

5.3.3 Framework

In a project that tries to compile best practices, diversity is both a blessing and a curse [36]. It guarantees that many successful strategies, likely to be unknown to other companies, are described. They can be expected to be valuable to them. At the same time, best practices rely on organizational preconditions. Not all best practices apply to all companies. The effort to adopt them is subject to the organizational background.

To help companies judge whether a recommendation in the booklet applies to them and to estimate the effort of adopting it, we designed a graphical categorization framework. An example is given in Fig. 5.1 (p. 100).

The framework is made up of a matrix and three additional bars. The matrix dimensions are *level of demand* and *phase* of testing. The level of demand describes how much effort is needed to adopt a recommendation; at the same time it hints to the impact it will have. Levels are *basic*, *advanced*, and *target state*. Phases are the four main phases of testing: *component*, *integration*, *system*, and *acceptance* test. A tick

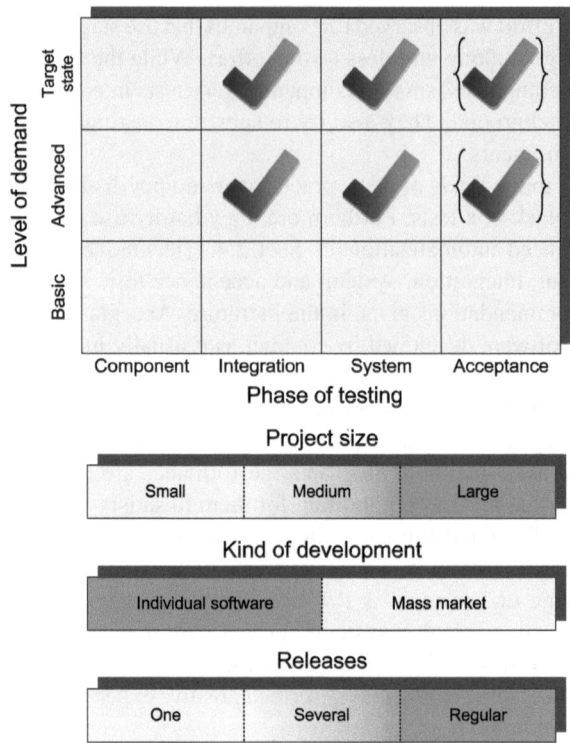

Fig. 5.1 Exemplary use of the categorization framework

in the matrix indicates that a recommendation applies to a phase at the corresponding level of demand. Ticks can be put in brackets to indicate optionality. Recommendations might apply to multiple phases and implementation can be possible with more than one level of demand.

Bars are separated into areas. If their background is dark gray, they apply to a recommendation. More than one area can apply; fading indicates that the corresponding value applies for the recommendation while the values with a dark gray background are the main values.

In the first bar, *project size* is depicted. The IHK project showed that testing in software development project varies with their size. Therefore, *small*, *medium*, and *large* projects are distinguished.

Some best practices only apply for distinct kinds of software development. The second bar shows the *kind of development*. The framework distinguishes between *individual software* (developed by contract) and *mass market* software (standard software).

Finally, the number of *releases* has impact on testing, in particular on regression testing. Thus, it is distinguished between *one* release, *several*, and *regular* releases.

Software developed by contract often is released only once upon delivery to the customer. Mass market software usually is developed continuously with regular releases.
The example in Fig. 5.1 can be read as follows:

• Mainly the phases of integration and system testing benefit from the application of the recommendation. Positive effects can also be expected for acceptance testing.
• Adopting the recommendation requires considerable effort but will lead to advanced improvements. With even higher effort outstanding results could be achieved.
• The recommendation applies to large projects. Medium sized projects that are similar in character to large projects will also be improved.
• Software is addressed that is individually developed by contract but that at least regularly is released.

All recommendations in the booklet and in the corresponding research papers have been categorized using the framework.

5.3.4 Recommendations

The booklet comprises 29 recommendations in two categories. Besides, a compilation of additional findings is included. Recommendation categories and information about additional findings are introduced in the following sections. No concrete recommendation is discussed at this point since they are in the booklet.

5.3.4.1 Organizational

Many organizational recommendations are not surprising. They base on common aims: well-defined organizational structures, defined processes, and unambiguous responsibilities. Nevertheless, most companies do not adhere to them. Small companies often do not deem a structured approach essential since testing is seen as a "necessary evil". However, a *culture of testing* can improve software quality in all companies that develop software [37].

Most recommendations compiled in the fifth chapter of the booklet address organizational issues that deal with the recognition and the structuring of testing. Many of them apply to most project sizes, kinds of developed software, and number of releases. Some of them are unsuitable for small projects or lower number of releases. Considerable differences apply to the effort required to adopt them. Moreover, many recommendations can be adopted in multiple steps from a basic adoption to reaching a target state.

Examples for organizational recommendations include to define roles for testers and developers, to define processes, to adhere to a staged testing process, and to set up a *test controlling*.

There are 15 organizational recommendations in total. They are included in Chap. 5 of the booklet.

5.3.4.2 Technical

Testing in the broader sense includes manifold organizational aspects. Testing in the narrow sense is a technical activity. Technical recommendations therefore do no rely that much on a project's size or the kind of software development. Technical aspects are also more heterogeneous and range from the technical test organization to actual testing methods. Most recommendations only apply to one or two phases.

Examples for technical recommendations are the usage of modern integrated development environments (IDE), employing a test case management system, aligning testing and productive systems, integration test tools, and aligning tools with processes.

There are 14 technical recommendations in total. They are included in Chap. 6 of the booklet.

5.3.5 Additional Findings

Besides the recommendations, the booklet includes two appendix chapters. The first one compiles directives that are important for software testing. In particular, official directives (i.e. laws or regulations) dictate certain testing practices or—more general—quality aims that are mandatory for software development in companies. Some of them only apply to specific branches, e.g. to financial service providers.

The second appendix compiles *free* test tools. We have learned of some tools in the project, but most interview partners lamented a lack of tool support. Therefore, we compiled tools that are available free of charge and that are often customizable as they are released as *open source* software. Categories in the booklet are test case management, management of requirements and bugs, GUI testing, database testing, stub and mock object generation, performance testing, measurement of metrics, coverage checking, checking of code quality, and special tools. Additionally, links to further tools are provided. Each tool is described in one or two sentences along with a download link. The number of featured tools is very high.

5.4 Overview of Published Work

To conclude this chapter, an overview of published work is presented. For each paper, title and abstract are given followed by a discussion how it applies to the context of this book. Eventually, the full citation is given.

Best Practices for the Organizational Implementation of Software Testing

Abstract Software testing as a main part of the development process is essential for the successful production of highest quality software. We have cooperated with regional companies in order to capture their problems with software development and to learn their distinct best practices in software testing. Based on our observations we created a framework to categorize recommendations for testing. In this paper we present the research methodology used and the framework built. We further illustrate four major recommendations considering the organizational implementation and strategic alignment of testing. They are derived from the analysis of the companies' status quo and best practices. Each recommendation is classified using the framework to show the conditions its application depends on.

This paper is the first that has been published on the IHK project. While the booklet was almost finished but publication and comments from the participants were pending, it was decided to publish a part of the results as an academic paper. Due to its IS focus, we picked organizational recommendations and selected the momentous "Competitive Strategy, Economics and IS" minitrack of the Hawaii International Conference on System Sciences (HICSS). The paper comprises four recommendations along with an introduction into the project and a on methodology. The latter is not comprehensively mentioned in the booklet because of its low relevance for practitioners. Recommendations were picked based on their novelty and in order to align well with each other.

Full citation: Tim A. Majchrzak. Best practices for the organizational implementation of software testing. In Proceedings of the 43rd Annual Hawaii International Conference on System Sciences (HICSS-43). IEEE Computer Society, 2010.

Technische Aspekte des erfolgreichen Testens von Software in Unternehmen

Abstract Um Softwareprodukte von hoher Qualität zu erstellen ist das Testen unerlässlich. Da es sich bei Softwaretests um eine teure Aufgabe handelt, die nur schwierig zu beherrschen ist, muss ihre organisatorische Einbettung wohlüberlegt sein. Wir haben mit regionalen Unternehmen zusammengearbeitet, um ihre individuellen Stärken und Schwächen hinsichtlich der Entwicklung und insbesondere des Testens von Software kennenzulernen. In der Folge war es uns möglich, erfolgreiche Vorgehensweisen ("best practices") abzuleiten und Empfehlungen zu formulieren. In diesem Artikel wird das Projekt und die gewählte Forschungsmethodik vorgestellt.

Danach werden fünf Empfehlungen vorgestellt, deren Fokus auf technischen bzw. technologischen Aspekten des Testens liegt. Es wird insbesondere auch berücksichtigt, welchen Einfluss Programmierpraktiken sowie-paradigmen bzw. die Wahl der Programmiersprache haben. Für jede Empfehlung wird erörtert, unter welchem Gegebenheiten sich ihre Umsetzung anbietet.

This paper has been written in German. It is the second scientific publication on the IHK project. It is similar in style and structure to the first paper but comprises technical recommendations. In particular, recommendations relate to the usage of programming languages. Recommendations have been chosen to be suitable for the German speaking colloquium they were presented at.

Full citation: Tim A. Majchrzak. Technische Aspekte des erfolgreichen Testens von Software in Unternehmen. In Jens Knoop and Adrian Prantl, editors, Schriftenreihe des Instituts für Computersprachen, Bericht 2009-X-1: 15. Kolloquium Programmiersprachen und Grundlagen der Programmierung, pp. 193–207, Maria Taferl, Austria, 2009. Technische Universität Wien.

Handlungsempfehlungen für erfolgreiches Testen von Software in Unternehmen

Abstract Softwaretests sind als ein Hauptbestandteil des Entwicklungsprozesses ausschlaggebend für das Erstellen hochqualitativer Software. Wir haben mit regionalen Unternehmen zusammengearbeitet, um ihre Stärken und Schwächen bezüglich des Testens von Software kennenzulernen. Darauf aufbauend haben wir Handlungsempfehlungen erarbeitet, die über bisher in der Literatur zu findende Ratschläge hinausgehen. In diesem Bericht stellen wir das zugrundeliegende Projekt vor und skizzieren die gewählte Forschungsmethodik. Wir führen in einen Ordnungsrahmen für die Kategorisierung der Empfehlungen ein. Schließlich stellen wir exemplarisch vier besonders aussichtsreiche Handlungsempfehlungen vor und geben Implementierungshinweise. Dieser Bericht ergänzt die bisher zum Projekt erschienenen Artikel.

This paper has been written in German. Following the first two publications, we prepared another paper in the same manner. Its contribution are four further recommendations. They address the underlying processes of software testing.

Full citation: Tim A. Majchrzak and Herbert Kuchen. Handlungsempfehlungen für erfolgreiches Testen von Software in Unternehmen. In J. Becker, H.L. Grob, B. Hellingrath, S. Klein, H. Kuchen, U. Müller-Funk, and G. Vossen, editors, Arbeitsbericht Nr. 127. Institut für Wirtschaftsinformatik, WWU Münster, 2010.

Status Quo of Software Testing—Regional Findings and Global Inductions

Abstract Software testing is an important part of the development process. It is essential for producing software of high quality. However, testing is seen as a cumbersome and costly task, and even with testing many software development projects fail. In a joint project with local companies we analyzed the status quo of software testing. Semi-structured expert-interviews were conducted. We suggest that understanding how software is tested in companies will help to improve testing and to cut down costs. In this work we describe the project's background and sketch our research method. We then present the detailed results of the qualitative analysis along with notable comments from the participants. Results are generalized and discussed in order to induce general findings.

With the recommendations being of general scientific interest, we checked whether results from the status quo assessment would be of interest to the scientific community. They are very limited in generality as the status quo has been drawn from case studies rather than from a quantitative analysis. However, the status can be presented for the Münsterland region, regional findings can be discussed, and connections to the global status of testing can be drawn.

Full citation: Tim A. Majchrzak. Status quo of software testing—regional findings and global inductions. In Proceedings of the 9th ISOneWorld Conference. The Information Institute, 2010.

Best Practices for Technical Aspects of Software Testing in Enterprises

Abstract Software testing is essential for the creation of high quality software products. Since it is an expensive task and hard to manage, its organizational implementation has to be well founded. We worked with regional companies in order to learn about their distinct weaknesses and strengths in software development. Eventually, we induced best practices for software testing. In this paper we sketch the research methodology used. We present four important best practices focusing on technical aspects of testing in organizations. For each of the four recommendations we give implementation advice based on a categorization framework.

Following the first three papers on recommendations and finalizing these publications, we wrote an article about technical recommendations. In contrast to the paper on recommendations with a relation to programming languages, recommendations chosen for this paper concern the technical *background* of successful testing. Thus, it has a technical focus but is written with keeping test management in mind. With the paper's publication, about half of the recommendations of the booklet were published in scientific papers. The "remaining" recommendations are either too specific or no novelty in a scientific sense. An example is the recommendation to test with decision tables [33, p. 94ff.]. It was found to be a best practice in the project, but the underlying technique is already described in the literature (see Sect. 2.2.2.2).

Full citation: Tim A. Majchrzak. Best practices for technical aspects of software testing in enterprises. In Proceedings of the International Conference on Information Society (i-Society 2010). IEEE Computer Society, 2010.

IHK-Projekt Softwaretests—Auswertung

This publication is a booklet rather than an article, there is no abstract in the classical sense.

With the need for much coordination, it took a while until the booklet for the IHK project could be published. It comprises an introduction into the topic, an overview of the status quo, an explanation of the categorization framework, and the recommendations. Moreover, it has extensive appendices that compile relevant norms and standards and lists a myriad of *free* test tools.

Full citation: Tim A. Majchrzak and Herbert Kuchen. IHK-Projekt Softwaretests: Auswertung. In Working Papers, number 2. Förderkreis der Angewandten Informatik an der Westfälischen Wilhelms-Universität Münster e.V., 2010.

Status Quo of Software Testing—Regional Findings and Global Inductions

Abstract Software testing is an important part of the development process. It is essential for producing software of high quality. However, testing is seen as a cumbersome and costly task and even with testing many software development projects fail. In a joint project with local companies we analyzed the status quo of software testing. Semi-structured expert-interviews were conducted. We suggest that understanding how software is tested in companies will help to improve testing and to cut down costs. In this work we describe the project's background and sketch our research method. We then present the detailed results of the qualitative analysis along with notable comments from the participants. Results are generalized and discussed in order to induce general findings.

This article is the journal version of the paper presented at ISOneWorld 2010. It has been slightly extended and modified in accordance with comments we got at the conference.

Full citation: Tim A. Majchrzak. Status quo of software testing—regional findings and global inductions. Journal of Information Science and Technology (JIST), 7(2), 2010.

Improving the Technical Aspects of Software Testing in Enterprises

Abstract Many software developments projects fail due to quality problems. Software testing enables the creation of high quality software products. Since it is a cumbersome and expensive task, and often hard to manage, both its technical background and its organizational implementation have to be well founded. We worked with regional companies that develop software in order to learn about their distinct weaknesses and strengths with regard to testing. Analyzing and comparing the strengths, we derived best practices. In this paper we explain the project's back-ground and sketch the design science research methodology used. We then introduce a graphical categorization framework that helps companies in judging the applicability of recommendations. Eventually, we present details on five recommendations for technical aspects of testing. For each recommendation we give implementation advice based on the categorization framework.

This article is the journal version of the paper presented at i-Society 2010. It has been slightly extended and its title has been changed in accordance with the journal's guidelines.

Full citation: Tim A. Majchrzak. Improving the technical aspects of software testing in enterprises. International Journal of Advanced Computer Science and Applications (IJACSA), 1(4), 2010.

References

1. http://www.ihk-nordwestfalen.de/
2. http://www.wi.uni-muenster.de/pi/iai/
3. Glass, R.L.: Goodbye! IEEE Softw. **26**(6), 96 (2009)
4. Drabick, R.: Best Practices for the Formal Software Testing Process: A Menu of Testing Tasks. Dorset House Publishing, New York (2004)
5. Berner, S., Weber, R., Keller, R.K.: Observations and lessons learned from automated testing. In: Proceedings of the 27th International Conference on Software Engineering, ICSE '05, pp. 571–579. ACM, New York (2005)

6. Lou, H., Zeng, H.: Some recommendations for performance testing using TTCN-3. In: Proceedings of the 2009 International Conference on Electronic Computer Technology, pp. 249–253. IEEE Computer Society, Washington, DC (2009)
7. Wieczorek, S., Stefanescu, A.: Improving testing of enterprise systems by model-based testing on graphical user interfaces. In: Proceedings of the 2010 17th IEEE International Conference and Workshops on the Engineering of Computer-Based Systems, ECBS '10, pp. 352–357. IEEE Computer Society, Washington, DC (2010)
8. Maatta, J., Harkonen, J., Jokinen, T., Mottonen, M., Belt, P., Muhos, M., Haapasalo, H.: Managing testing activities in telecommunications: a case study. J. Eng. Technol. Manag. **26**(1–2), 73–96 (2009)
9. Guan, J., Offutt, J., Ammann, P.: An industrial case study of structural testing applied to safety-critical embedded software. In: Proceedings of the 2006 ACM/IEEE International Symposium on Empirical Software Engineering, ISESE '06, pp. 272–277. ACM, New York (2006)
10. Barrett, N., Martin, S., Dislis, C.: Test process optimization: closing the gap in the defect spectrum. In: Proceedings of the 1999 IEEE International Test Conference, ITC '99, pp. 124–129. IEEE Computer Society, Washington, DC (1999)
11. Moore, T.J.: A test process optimization and cost modeling tool. In: Proceedings of the IEEE International Test Conference on TEST: The Next 25 Years, pp. 103–110. IEEE Computer Society, Washington, DC (1994)
12. Stringfellow, C.V.: An integrated method for improving testing effectiveness and efficiency. Ph.D. Thesis, Colorado State University, Fort Collins (2000)
13. Lazic, L.: The software testing challenges and methods. In: Proceedings of the 9th WSEAS International Conference on Communications, vol. 30, pp. 1–17. World Scientific and Engineering Academy and Society (WSEAS), Stevens Point (2005)
14. Perry, W.E., Rice, R.W.: Surviving the Top Ten Challenges of Software Testing: A People-Oriented Approach. Dorset House Publishing, New York (1998)
15. Jackelen, G., Jackelen, M.: When standards and best practices are ignored. In: Proceedings of the 4th IEEE International Symposium and Forum on Software Engineering Standards, pp. 111–118. IEEE Computer Society, Washington, DC (1999)
16. Liggesmeyer, P.: Software-Qualität: Testen, Analysieren und Verifizieren von Software, 2nd edn. Spektrum-Akademischer, Berlin (2009)
17. Cleff, T.: Basiswissen Testen von Software. W3L GmbH (2010)
18. Zeller, A.: Why Programs Fail: A Guide to Systematic Debugging. Morgan Kaufmann, San Francisco (2006)
19. Kaner, C., Nguyen, H.Q., Falk, J.L.: Testing Computer Software. Wiley, New York (1993)
20. McGregor, J.D., Sykes, D.A.: A Practical Guide to Testing Object-Oriented Software. Addison-Wesley, Boston (2001)
21. Wallmüller, E.: Software-Qualitätsmanagement in der Praxis, 2nd edn. Hanser, München (2001)
22. Perry, W.: Effective Methods for Software Testing, 3rd edn. Wiley, New York (2006)
23. Beck, K.: Test-Driven Development by Example. Addison-Wesley, Boston (2002)
24. Black, R.: Managing the Testing Process, 3rd edn. Wiley, Indianapolis (2009)
25. Watkins, J.: Testing IT: An Off-the-Shelf Software Testing Process. Cambridge University Press, New York (2001)
26. Grood, D.: TestGoal: Result-Driven Testing. Springer, Heidelberg (2008)
27. Henry, P.: The Testing Network: An Integral Approach to Test Activities in Large Software Projects. Springer, Heidelberg (2008)
28. Chillarege, R.: Software testing best practices. Report RC 21457, Log 96856, IBM Research (1999)
29. Perry, W.E., Rice, R.W.: Die zehn goldenen Regeln des Software-Testens. mitp (2002)
30. Bath, G., McKay, J.: The Software Test Engineer's Handbook: A Study Guide for the ISTQB Test Analyst and Technical Analyst Advanced Level Certificates. Rocky Nook, Santa Barbara (2008)

31. Dustin, E.: Effective Software Testing: 50 Ways to Improve Your Software Testing. Addison-Wesley, Boston (2002)
32. Riley, T., Goucher, A.: Beautiful Testing: Leading Professionals Reveal How they Improve Software. O'Reilly Media, Sebastopol (2009)
33. Majchrzak, T.A., Kuchen, H.: IHK-Projekt Softwaretests: Auswertung. In: Working Papers, no. 2. Förderkreis der Angewandten Informatik an der Westfälischen Wilhelms-Universität Münster e.V. (2010)
34. http://www.wi.uni-muenster.de/pi/iai/publikationen/iai2.pdf
35. Beck, K.: Extreme Programming Explained: Embrace Change. Addison-Wesley, Boston (1999)
36. Majchrzak, T.A.: Best practices for technical aspects of software testing in enterprises. In: Proceedings of the International Conference on Information Society (i-Society 2010), pp. 205–212. IEEE Computer Society, Washington, DC (2010)
37. Majchrzak, T.A.: Best practices for the organizational implementation of software testing. In: Proceedings of the 43th Annual Hawaii International Conference on System Sciences (HICSS-43), pp. 1–10. IEEE Computer Society, Washington, DC (2010)

Chapter 6
Testing and E-Assessment

This chapter introduces E-learning and e-assessment and their connection to software testing.

6.1 Background

E-assessment [1, 2] in higher education is a rather new emergence. Typically, examinations are paper based or alternatively oral.[1] The term is also used synonymously for *online assessment* which describes the assessment of job candidates with the help of software [4, 5]. This kind of e-assessment is used for longer than a decade [6].

Assessments are essential for teaching and learning in higher education. They help to measure an individual's learning success—both for himself and for grading purposes. Additionally, assessment is an indicator for lecture improvements [7]. Manual assessment is very laborious for personnel in higher education [8]. For this reason, e-assessment systems receive an increasing interest [9]. They promise to save "time, space, material and personnel" and to carry out examinations "more precise" with "greater neutrality and objectivity" [10]. Currently available systems are not suitable to assess complex cognitive abilities or creative tasks [11]. Rather, they focus on multiple choice questions or insertion of text into boxes. Such systems are particularly unsuitable for computer science, which focuses on developing analytic, creative, and constructive skills (cf. with the guidelines for computer science (CS) education [12]).

Three basic types of assessments can be distinguished: "summative assessments like formal exams, formative assessments like weekly exercises, and voluntary or obligatory (self-)assessments for diagnostic reasons" [8]. Assessments can also be used to reach teaching aims. Students who solve exercises that are based on lecture content consolidate their newly acquired theoretical knowledge. Besides, they

---

[1] A general introduction to "classroom assessment" is example given by Black and Wiliam [3].

T. A. Majchrzak, *Improving Software Testing*, SpringerBriefs in Information Systems,
DOI: 10.1007/978-3-642-27464-0_6, © The Author(s) 2012

become aware of their learning success while lecturers gain an overview of the course participants' performance. Ideally, this information can be used to improve lectures.

To provide e-assessment support for CS courses and to investigate into novel e-assessment methods, EASy (*EASy*) has been developed. EASy is a Web based e-assessment tool that particularly offers modules for assessment in mathematic sciences and CS. Currently, EASy provides exercise modules for multiple choice questions, simple programming exercises, and mathematical proofs [13–15]. Developments described in this book are the modules for software verification proofs and for Java programming in combination with testing.

At the moment, EASy is used for voluntary practical examinations offered as preparation for the exams at the end of terms. Therefore, aspects of e-assessment for exams that effect grading do not need to be kept in mind. This includes organizational embedding, security, and legal issues [16], which significantly increase complexity.

6.2 Related Work

E-assessment software is widely used to support teaching and examination in academic courses. Almost universally, current systems are limited to simple forms of assessment like multiple choice or free text input [15]. Analytic, creative, and constructive tasks are not supported. Thus, the assessment of software verification proofs is not possible. In general, most e-assessment systems are inappropriate for adoption in CS [8].

A few systems support assessment of programming exercises in object oriented [17] and functional [18] programming languages. Moreover, several tools support graph based exercises like drawing UML classes (for instance [19]). Three systems are particularly notable: Praktomat, DUESIE and ELP. They offer functionality to assess Java programming exercises.

- Praktomat [20] supports programming courses. It offers static and dynamic testing of programs developed by students in order to check them before they hand them in as exercise solutions.
- DUESIE [21] offers static and dynamic tests, too. It also checks coding style and functionality of students' program code. However, programs of students cannot be checked before being handed in. Both DUESIE and Praktomat are based on style checking and unit testing tools. Solutions are manually corrected by tutors.
- ELP [22] provides very simple exercises for programming novices. Handed in solution are compared with stored example solutions. A feedback according to the structural similarity can be given immediately. However, it is limited to small, well-defined exercises. ELP can mainly be used for self-assessment.

There are some systems used in academic education that are capable of demonstrating formal methods for software verification; however, they do not provide assessment functionality. An example is the Fredge Program Prover (FPP), which is a Web based tool. It is used to semi-automatically verify the consistency of a specification and a program written in Ada [23]. FPP is a teaching tool and focuses on visualizing proving strategies. Since FPP is not interactive and provides no assessment functionality, it cannot be used for examination. Similarly, the New Paltz Program Verifier (NPPV) [24] for programs written in Pascal cannot be used for e-assessment. Java Program Verifier (JPV) II [25] optionally offers manual verification. Students can take part in the proving process by applying rules in a step-by-step approach. JPV does not support assessment, though.

A discussion of related work for Muggl is not repeated here; it can be found in Sect. 4.2. We identified one work that deals with a combination of e-assessment and TCG. Ihantola presents an approach based on the Java PathFinder model checker [26]. It tries to automatically generate test data and to visualize it. While the author also discusses assessment strategies, his work does not include testing strategies. In a recent paper that apparently follows up with the earlier work, inclusion of mutation analysis and code coverage is discussed [27].

Despite a high number of general e-assessment publications, no other approaches but the above mentioned could be identified that directly relate to the work presented in this chapter. For a broader overview of tools please refer to [15].

6.3 The E-Assessment System EASy

At the beginning, an overview of the e-assessment system EASy is given. Then, work on the two new modules is summarized. First, the module for software verification proofs is described. An introduction of the module for programming and testing follows. For both modules, results from an initial evaluation are summarized. More details are given in the papers on EASy. They are introduced in Sect. 6.4.

6.3.1 Basics

EASy has been implemented as a modular Web application. Students and tutors can use it both from home and at on-faculty terminals. Furthermore, a modular design keeps it convenient to maintain and suitable for addition of new modules. EASy aims at providing a *single* system to support electronic assessment in the CS education. Modularization is required to enable successive extension of the available exercise types. Modules are loosely coupled with the surrounding platform. Hence, modification of the platform does not affect modules.

Support for exercises is meant to be holistic. In the ideal case, exercises are prepared, disseminated, solved, collected, corrected, and graded using EASy. Moreover, the system has to manage students' scores and provide help in end-of-term grading. While the current implementation provides self-assessment and assessment of practical course, future versions could be expanded to be used for exams.

Fig. 6.1 GUI screenshot of the verification proofs module

To separate concerns, EASy uses so called portlets [28]. Portlets are distinct con-figurable components that are combined to form a GUI. They are typically managed by a portal server, which is provided by an application server. For Java programs, two portlet specifications exist (JSR 168 [29] and JSR 286 [30]). EASy also employs Ajax technology [31]. This makes EASy convenient to use despite being accessible by Web browsers. While portlets (i.e. exercise modules) provide task specific exer-cises, general concerns such as administration and security are coped with by the EASy core platform.

The design and implementation of EASy is not focused on in this work. In par-ticular, the book's contribution concerns two novel modules but not the EASy core. Therefore, no verbose introduction is given. For more details please refer to [13, 15]. Furthermore, existing work such as the modules for mathematical proofs [14, 32] is not described. A screenshot of EASy's GUI is shown in the next section (Fig. 6.1, p. 114).

6.3.2 The Module for Software Verification Proofs

Firstly, software verification is introduced. Then the EASy module for Hoare Logic correctness assertions is explained. Finally, brief evaluation results are presented.

Table 6.1 Hoare Logic rules (cf. [34])

Rule name	Rule
Rule for skip	$\{P\}\,\text{skip}\,\{Q\}$
Rule for assignments	$\{Q[x/e]\}\,x := e\,\{Q\}$
Rule for sequencing	$\dfrac{\{P\}\,c_1\,\{R\},\{R\}\,c_2\,\{Q\}}{\{P\}\,c_1;c_2\,\{Q\}}$
Rule for conditionals	$\dfrac{\{P\wedge b\}\,c_1\,\{Q\},\{P\wedge\neg b\}\,c_2\,\{Q\}}{\{P\}\,\text{if}\,b\,\text{then}\,c_1\,\text{else}\,c_2\,\{Q\}}$
Rule for while loops	$\dfrac{\{P\wedge b\}\,c\,\{P\}}{\{P\}\,\text{while}\,b\,\text{do}\,c\{P\wedge\neg b\}}$
Consequence rule	$\dfrac{\models(P\Rightarrow P')\;\{P'\}\,c\,\{Q'\}\;\models(Q\Rightarrow Q')}{\{P\}\,c\,\{Q\}}$

6.3.2.1 Software Verification with Hoare Logic

Software verification is an important part of the CS education. It typically is taught in lectures on theoretical CS and in advanced CS lectures such as *Formal Specification*.[2] Software verification proofs can be based on *Hoare Logic*, which is a formal system consisting of proof rules. Each rule allows to assert partial correctness of a program [33]. A partial correctness assertion has the form $\{P\}\,c\,\{Q\}$ whereas c is a code fragment, $\{P\}$ is a precondition, and $\{Q\}$ is a postcondition. For a correctness proof, Hoare rules as well as arithmetic or boolean transformations have to be applied successively. The Hoare Logic rules have been compiled in Table 6.1.

To give an example, the so called *Hoare Triple* for multiplication by repeated addition is

$$\underbrace{\{x = n \wedge s = 0 \wedge x \geq 0\}}_{\{P\}}\quad \underbrace{\text{while}\,(x > 0)\,\text{do}\,s \leftarrow s + y; x \leftarrow x - 1}_{c}\quad \underbrace{\{s = (n * y)\}}_{\{Q\}}$$

Software verification proofs can become very complex. Without prior knowledge of proof strategies, they are hard to accomplish. Checking and grading them is a very time consuming task. Students might find ways to do the proof that differ from the exemplary solution. If they do not succeed with the proof, it has to be decided if their progress is partly correct and graded correspondingly.

6.3.2.2 Implementation of the Module for Hoare Logic Correctness Assertions

To accomplish a proof, EASy provides students with a comprehensive set of proof strategies as well as with arithmetic and boolean transformation rules. They are combined in a GUI, which shows applicable rules along with the progress in solving the proof (if applicable with sub proofs). An example is given in Fig. 6.1.

---

[2] Formal Specification is a lecture offered in the IS studies at the WWU Münster.

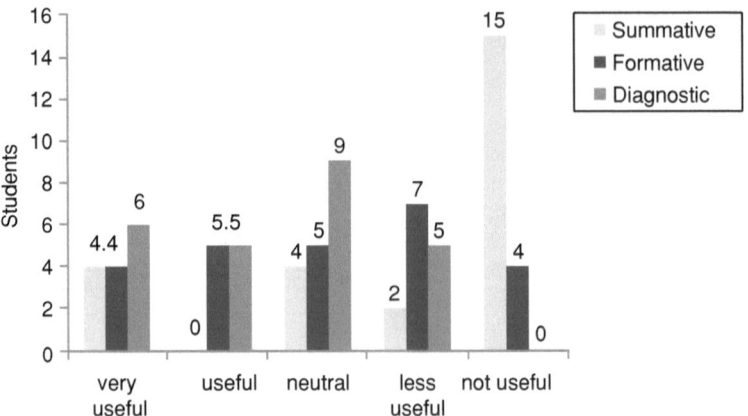

Fig. 6.2 Evaluation of the EASy module for software verification: attitude of students towards using EASy [8]

While students have to chose consequent rules, EASy checks whether they are applicable or not. Students cannot proceed with steps that are mathematically incorrect. This particularly helps students that have little exercise with proofs. Students do not need to finish a proof at once. It can be saved and reopened at any time. Sub proofs that have been finished successfully are highlighted. Due to the structuring of proofs they are not only easier to conduct but tutors are supported in checking them.

6.3.2.3 Evaluation of the Module

To assess the feasibility of the approach and its acceptance by students, an evaluation has been done. It was conducted with students from the Formal Specification lecture when the new module was used for the first time. Students had to do a proof using Hoare Logic and could use EASy to accomplish this task. Out of 39 students that attended the lecture, 25 participated in the survey.

The survey's main findings are that while the usability of EASy has to be improved, it helped most students in accomplishing the proof. 86% of them reported that using EASy took them longer than they expected for doing the proof manually. However, 60% thought that the number of mistakes they did was reduced by using EASy. In general, students had a positive attitude towards using EASy but were very skeptical w.r.t. using it for exams. As depicted in Fig. 6.2, 44% had a positive attitude towards using EASy (or similar systems) for diagnostic self-assessment and 36% stated they would like to use it for formative assessment of exercises. While only 20% had a negative attitude towards self-assessments, 68% opposed to using EASy (or similar systems) in summative assessments (such as written exams). The high number of students with a neutral opinion indicates their uncertainty. Apparently, they were not sure whether they would benefit from using e-assessment.

Using EASy for the correction proof was optional; students could also hand in manual solutions. One notable finding is that students who used EASy did considerable better in the Hoare Logic exercise that was part of the end-of-term exam. This effect cannot exclusively be attributed to EASy; nevertheless, it underlines the merits of using EASy.

6.3.3 The Module for Programming and Testing

Firstly, implementation of the module is described. Then an application scenario and evaluation results are briefly discussed.

6.3.3.1 Implementation of the Module that Combines EASy and Muggl

EASy already provided support for Java programming exercises. A programming exercise in EASy may include multiple Java classes. In general, students are provided with class interfaces or a description of the class layout. Two assessment stages are offered: students can upload programs and receive automatically checked results as often as they desire to, and they can finally upload the program as an exercise solution. Thereby, students are able to continuously refine their solutions until they have a satisfying result. This approach is recommended for didactic reasons [35]. EASy offers an automated check of style and functionality. Results can be used for automated correction or grading, but tutors should check them to avoid inconsistencies.

To encourage students to develop in a test-driven manner (see Sect. 2.3.2, p. 48) and to motivate the usage of testing techniques such as back-to-back testing (see Sect. 2.2.2.6, p. 40), a combination of EASy and Muggl was realized. We did not only intend it to be beneficial w.r.t. education but also to learn more about Muggl's performance under realistic conditions. In fact, the integration demonstrates Muggl's capabilities and can be seen as a "real world" application.

Integrating EASy and Muggl can be described in two steps. Firstly, interfaces for the coupling have to be provided. Secondly, they have to be integrated.

Due to EASy's modular structure, providing an interface was simple. In an enhanced module, functionality to invoke Muggl was implemented. Specifically, an adequate representation of Muggl's results had to be found. Since test case generation requires considerable resources both w.r.t. processing power and memory, EASy invokes a new thread to wrap Muggl. It is ensured that this thread does not negatively influence EASy, i.e. EASy keeps enough resources to process requests.[3]

Muggl does not depend on a GUI. The symbolic JVM (SJVM) can be invoked as a service. It provides interfaces to control execution, to request results, and to

---

[3] Running EASy and Muggl on distinct machines would be no challenge with the current architecture. It was not required for the initial scenario, though.

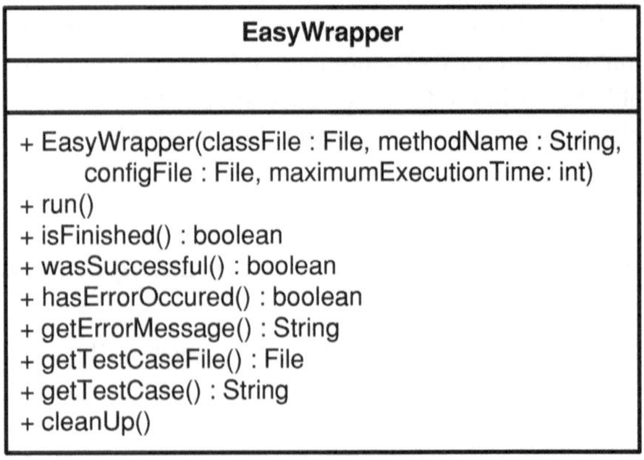

Fig. 6.3 UML class diagram
for the EASy wrapper of
Muggl

EasyWrapper
+ EasyWrapper(classFile : File, methodName : String, configFile : File, maximumExecutionTime: int) + run() + isFinished() : boolean + wasSuccessful() : boolean + hasErrorOccured() : boolean + getErrorMessage() : String + getTestCaseFile() : File + getTestCase() : String + cleanUp()

monitor the JVM state. However, providing the full functionality is not necessary. In fact, it adds unwanted complexity. Consequently, a wrapper for EASy is provided. It does not offer access to the full Muggl application programming interface (API) but a limited set of methods. Its public interface is depicted in Fig. 6.3. The wrapper is initialized with data that specifies the class to generate test cases for. Furthermore, it provides methods to start execution, to monitor the execution process, and to fetch results (i.e. a test case)—or an error message in case of problems.

The wrapper also controls the maximum runtime. Since students are to be provided with results (almost) immediately, we deem a runtime of more than five seconds to be unacceptable. For simple programs, Muggl usually finds test cases and terminates within this time. Even if it does not terminate, the set of test cases derived within five seconds is sufficient in most cases. Besides, longer runtimes often hint to serious flaws in students' solutions.

Students working with EASy can upload their programs to it. EASy then asynchronously invokes Muggl as a background task. While Muggl runs, students are provided with a message. Once Muggl reports the end of execution, students are either provided with the textual representation of a test case or a message describing the encountered problem. EASy eventually shuts down the SJVM. This process is depicted in Fig. 6.4. For simplification, it does not show the asynchronous polling of isFinished() in a loop and the successive request of the result.

6.3.3.2 Evaluation of the Module

The new EASy module was evaluated in a first term course of programming with about 280 students of CS, IS, and related studies. Students were provided with the specification of a simple algorithm that takes an Integer array containing pixels of an image. The algorithm blurs the image and returns the resulting array. This task is sufficiently easy, yet it provides some challenges with regard to programming style and finding a well performing solution. We provided students also with a test case

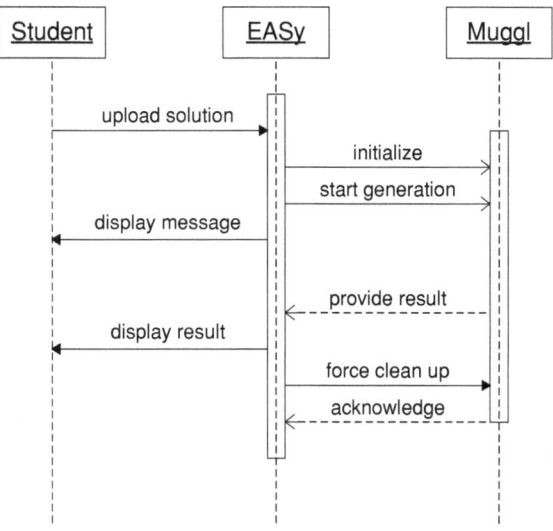

Fig. 6.4 UML sequence diagram for the (simplified) usage of EASy and Muggl

generated by Muggl for our exemplary solution. Our exemplary solution is shown in Listing 6.1. Comments are omitted but for the most important ones; formatting has been modified for print (e.g. optional brackets were removed). Listing 6.2 shows the exemplary test case. Its verbose comments have been omitted.

Students were asked to write a program that satisfied the test case. They could then upload their program to EASy and were immediately provided with a test case generated for it. Comparing their test case to the one provided should encourage them to judge their program's quality. Thus, they did not only learn about test driven development (TDD) and back-to-back testing, but also to reason from test cases. Students had to decide whether differences in test cases were mere variations due to a slightly different structuring or if they resulted from problems with their program. In the latter case, they had to find out how the test case reflected the flaws in their program.

Along with the exercise, students were asked to participate in a survey to find out about the approach's effectiveness and usability. It was answered by 187 students ($\frac{2}{3}$ of the course participants). In general, the attitude towards using EASy and the exercise was positive. Many students were able to improve their programs after receiving an automatically generated test case. 75% of all students deemed the approach to be at least to some degree helpful (Fig. 6.5). 49% of the students reported that working test driven and being able to generate test cases for their programs motivated them. While detailed results are out of scope, the evaluation was very encouraging. It proves the general feasibility of the approach. Concludingly, it has to be noticed that many students expressed they were glad to participate in an evaluation that supported research. Despite much scepticism towards using e-assessment in exams, the general attitude towards computer supported learning was very positive.

Listing 6.1 Exemplary solution for the blur algorithm

```
1  public static int[] simpleBlur(int[] image) {
2    if (image == null)
3      throw new IllegalArgumentException("Null specified.");
4    int length = image.length;
5    if (length == 0)
6      throw new IllegalArgumentException("Cannot blur empty
           image.");
7
8    // Check whether the image is quadratic.
9    int n = length;
10   while (n * n != length) {
11     n /= 2;
12     if (n == 1)
13       throw new IllegalArgumentException("Not quadratic.");
14   }
15   if (n < 3)
16     throw new IllegalArgumentException("Sides are too short.");
17
18   int[] image2 = new int[length];
19   for (int a = 0; a < length; a++) {
20     int neighbours = 0;
21     long pixel = 0L;
22
23     if (a % n != 0) { // Left pixel.
24       neighbours++;
25       pixel += image[a - 1];
26     }
27     if (a >= n) { // Upper pixel.
28       neighbours++;
29       pixel += image[a - n];
30     }
31     if (a % n != n - 1) { // Right pixel.
32       neighbours++;
33       pixel += image[a + 1];
34     }
35     if (a < length - n) { // Lower pixel.
36       neighbours++;
37       pixel += image[a + n];
38     }
39     // Calculate the new value and round it to get precise
           results
40     pixel += (8 - neighbours) * image[a];
41     pixel = ((pixel * 10 / 8L) + 5) / 10;
42     image2[a] = (int) pixel;
43   }
44
45   return image2;
46 }
```

Listing 6.2 Test case for the blur algorithm

```
1   public class TestCase {
2     private int [] returnedArray0 =
         {19,55,156,63,84,90,121,138,82,82,136,110,163,73,82,129};
3     private int [] array0 =
         {8,12,236,12,94,132,44,197,65,43,223,61,196,60,44,155};
4     private int [] array1 = null;
5     private int [] array2 = new int [0];
6     private int [] array3 = {219};
7     private int [] array4 = {131,121};
8
9     @Before public void setUp() {}
10
11    @Test public void testIt() {
12      assertArrayEquals(this.returnedArray0,
           Blur.simpleBlur(this.array0));
13      try {
14        Blur.simpleBlur(this.array1);
15        fail("Expected a java.lang.IllegalArgumentException to be
              thrown.");
16      } catch (java.lang.IllegalArgumentException e) {
17        // Do nothing – this is what we expect to happen!
18      }
19      try {
20        Blur.simpleBlur(this.array2);
21        fail("Expected a java.lang.IllegalArgumentException to be
              thrown.");
22      } catch (java.lang.IllegalArgumentException e) {
23        // Do nothing – this is what we expect to happen!
24      }
25      try {
26        Blur.simpleBlur(this.array3);
27        fail("Expected a java.lang.IllegalArgumentException to be
              thrown.");
28      } catch (java.lang.IllegalArgumentException e) {
29        // Do nothing – this is what we expect to happen!
30      }
31      try {
32        Blur.simpleBlur(this.array4);
33        fail("Expected a java.lang.IllegalArgumentException to be
              thrown.");
34      } catch (java.lang.IllegalArgumentException e) {
35        // Do nothing – this is what we expect to happen!
36      }
37    }
38
39  }
```

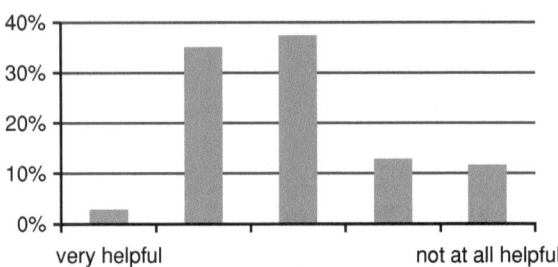

Fig. 6.5 Evaluation of the EASy module for programming and testing: how helpful did students deem generated test cases [36]

6.4 Overview of Published Work

To conclude this chapter, an overview of published work is presented. For each paper, title and abstract are given followed by a discussion how it applies to the context of this book. Eventually, the full citation is given.

Formative E-Assessment of Software Verification Skills in Higher Education

Abstract Conventional e-assessment systems often are not suited for examining analytic, creative and constructive skills; the few existing ones have very limited functionality. On this account the e-assessment system EASy, which focuses on the examination of formative assessments, has been developed. Besides exercise modules for multiple-choice questions, programming exercises and mathematical proofs the system recently has been extended by a module for the computer-supported examination of software verification proofs based on the Hoare Logic. In this work we discuss the module for automated assessment of these proofs. To demonstrate the feasibility of our approach, the applicability, usability and acceptance of the Hoare-Logic module have been evaluated in a lecture on formal specification.

This paper was prepared when the book's author taught the practical course of the Formal Specification lecture. One part of the lecture are correctness proofs using Hoare logic. Since the EASy system had been extended to support mathematical proofs [14], the next step was to include formal verification. The required functionality was added. Then, EASy was used in the practical course for actual assessment. Afterwards, a questionnaire was prepared that was used to evaluate the new module. Supporting formal verification is a first step towards a variety of modules to support assessment of CS courses.

Full citation: Claus A. Usener, Susanne Gruttmann, Tim A. Majchrzak, and Herbert Kuchen. Formative e-assessment of software verification skills in higher education. In Proceedings of the IADIS International Conference e-Learning 2010 (eL2010). IADIS Press, 2010.

Computer-Supported Assessment of Software Verification Proofs—Towards High-Quality E-Assessments in Computer Science Education

Abstract Most conventional e-assessment systems are not suited for examining analytic, creative and constructive skills and the few existing ones have too limited functionality to appropriately support Computer Science assessments. On this account the e-assessment system EASy has been developed which example provides relevant exercise modules for Computer Science tasks. Recently the system has been extended by a module for the computer-supported examination of software verification proofs based on the Hoare Logic. In this work we discuss this module and evaluate its applicability, usability and acceptance in terms of a lecture on Formal Specification.

Extending the first paper on e-assessment of formal verification proofs, this paper adds more details.

Full citation: Claus A. Usener, Susanne Gruttmann, Tim A. Majchrzak, and Herbert Kuchen. Computer-supported assessment of software verification proofs—towards high quality e-assessments in computer science education. In Proceedings of the 2010 International Conference on Educational and Information Technology (ICEIT). IEEE Computer Society, 2010.

Combining State of the Art Software Engineering and E-Assessment

Abstract Assessments are an integral part of teaching and learning. To overcome the high manual effort for teaching personnel, e-assessment systems are used. We propose an extension of EASy, a system for e-assessment in computer science and mathematics sciences education. It offers assessment of exercises that require higher-order cognitive skills. Our extension allows assessing programming exercises in conjunction with state of the art software development, in particular test-driven-development and back-to-back testing. It integrates a tool for automated test case generation. Test cases are provided for students that upload their solution of programming exercises. They can use them to improve their solution and gain knowledge on software testing at the same time. Besides introducing our extension of EASy and distinguishing it from related work, we present an exemplary scenario. To prove the effectiveness of our approach, we discuss findings from a survey. It was conducted with almost 200 students from a programming lecture. The study provided us both with quantitative results and qualitative feedback. Most students reflected positively on using EASy. Our general approach is feasible. However, several details require further investigation.

This e-assessment paper is the first to describe the combination of Muggl and EASy. Similar to the first two papers, it combines the description of the Software Engineering approach to build a system and its evaluation. In contrast to them, it does not solely describe EASy but also introduces Muggl. Consequently, related work of Muggl is discussed, too.

Full citation: Claus A. Usener, Tim A. Majchrzak, and Herbert Kuchen. Combining State of the Art Software Engineering and E-Assessment. In Proceedings of the IADIS International Conference e-Learning 2011 (eL2011). IADIS Press, 2011.

Evaluating the Synergies of Integrating E-Assessment and Software Testing

Abstract Teaching and learning rely on assessments. E-assessment systems are used to reduce the high manual effort for teaching personnel. We propose an extension of the tool EASy and present its evaluation. EASy is used for assessments in the computer science and mathematics science education and particularly addresses exercises that require higher-order cognitive skills. Extending the module for programming exercises, we present the integration of test driven development and back-to-back testing. Specifically, a test case generation tool interacts with EASy. We not only introduce the extension of EASy and discuss related work but present results from an initial evaluation with almost 200 undergraduate students from a programming course. We gained both quantitative findings and qualitative insights. While the general perception of our approach is positive, required steps towards a holistic e-assessment solution could be identified.

Extending the first paper on the combination of Muggl and EASy, this paper adds more details.

Full citation: Tim A. Majchrzak and Claus A. Usener. Evaluating the Synergies of Integrating E-Assessment and Software Testing. In Proceedings of the 20th International Conference on Information Systems Development (ISD2011). Springer, 2011.

References

1. Laumer, S., von Stetten, A., Eckhardt, A.: E-assessment. Bus. Inf. Syst. Eng. **1**(3), 263–265 (2009)
2. Ruedel, C.: Was ist E-assessment. In: Ruedel, C., Mandel, S. (eds.) E-Assessment: Einsatzszenarien und Erfahrungen an Hochschulen. Waxmann, Münster (2010)
3. Black, P., Wiliam, D.: Assessment and classroom learning. Assess. Educ. Princ. Pol. Pract. **5**(1), 7–74 (1998)
4. Konradt, U., Sarges, W. (eds.): E-Recruitment und E-Assessment: Rekrutierung, Auswahl und Beratung von Personal im Inter- und Intranet. Hogrefe, Göttingen (2003)

5. Steiner, H. (ed.): Online-Assessment: Grundlagen und Anwendung von Online-Tests in der Unternehmenspraxis. Springer, Heidelberg (2009)
6. Schmidt, J.U., Gutschow, K. (eds.): Vom Papier zum Bildschirm: computergestützte Prüfungsformen. Bertelsmann, Bielefeld (1999)
7. Pellegrino, W.J., Chudowsky, N., Glas, R.: Knowing What Students Know: The Science and Design of Educational Assessment. National Academy Press, Washington, DC (2001)
8. Usener, C.A., Gruttmann, S., Majchrzak, T.A., Kuchen, H.: Computer-supported assessment of software verification proofs—towards high-quality E-assessments in computer science education. In: Proceedings of the 2010 International Conference on Educational and Information Technology (ICEIT), pp. 115–121. IEEE Computer Society, New York (2010)
9. n. A.: SQA Guidelines on Online Assessment for Further Education. Scottish Qualifications Authority (SQA), Glasgow (2003)
10. Kröll, M.: E-assessment: a suitable alternative for measuring competences? In: Proceedings of the 13th International Conference on Human–Computer Interaction. Part IV: Interacting in Various Application Domains, pp. 543–550. Springer, Berlin (2009)
11. Heywood, J.: Assessment in Higher Education: Student Learning, Teaching, Programmes and Institutions. Jessica Kingsley, London (2000)
12. http://www.gi-ev.de/fileadmin/redaktion/empfehlungen/GI-Empfehlung_BaMa2005.pdf
13. Gruttmann, S., Usener, C., Kuchen, H.: Das E-Assessment-System EASy: Computerunterstützer Übungsbetrieb im Informatikstudium. Praxisbericht für e-teaching.org, Tübingen (2010)
14. Gruttmann, S., Böhm, D., Kuchen, H.: E-assessment of mathematical proofs: chances and challenges for students and tutors. In: Proceedings of the 2008 International Conference on Computer Science and Software Engineering, vol. 05, CSSE'08, pp. 612–615. IEEE Computer Society, Washington, DC (2008)
15. Gruttmann, S.: Formatives E-assessment in der Hochschullehre—Computerunterstützte Lernfortschrittskontrollen im informatikstudium. Ph.D. Thesis, University of Münster, Münster (2010)
16. Wannemacher, K.: Computergestützte Prüfungsverfahren: Aspekte der Betriebswirtschaftslehre und Informatik. In: Breitner, M.H., Bruns, B., Lehner, F. (eds.) Neue Trends im E-Learning. Aspekte der Betriebswirtschaftslehre und Informatik, pp. 427–440. Physica, Heidelberg (2007)
17. Striewe, M., Balz, M., Goedicke, M.: A flexible and modular software architecture for computer aided assessments and automated marking. In: Cordeiro, J.A.M., Shishkov, B., Verbraeck, A., Helfert, M. (eds.) Proceedings of the First International Conference on Computer Supported Education (CSEDU), pp. 54–61. INSTICC Press, Montreal (2009)
18. Rösner, D., Amelung, M., Piotrowski, M.: LlsChecker—ein CAA-System für die Lehre im Bereich Programmiersprachen. In: DeLFI2005: 3. Deutsche e-Learning Fachtagung Informatik der Gesellschaft für Informatik e.V., Lecture Notes in Informatics (LNI)—Proceedings, pp. 307–318. GI-Verlag, Bonn (2005)
19. Jayal, A., Shepperd, M.: An improved method for label matching in e-assessment of diagrams. Innov. Teach. Learn. Inf. Comput. Sci. 8(1), 3–16 (2009)
20. Krinke, J., Störzer, M., Zeller, A.: Web-basierte programmierpraktika mit praktomat. Softwaretechnik-Trends 22(3), S.51–S.53 (2002)
21. Hoffmann, A., Quast, A., Wismüller, R.: Online-Übungssystem für die programmierausbildung zur Einführung in die informatik. In: Seehusen, S., Lucke, U., Fischer, S. (eds.) DeLFI 2008: Die 6. e-Learning Fachtagung Informatik der Gesellschaft für Informatik e.V., LNI, vol. 132, pp. 173–184 (2008)
22. Truong, N., Roe, P., Bancroft, P.: Static analysis of students' Java programs. In: Proceedings of the Sixth Conference on Australasian Computing Education, vol. 30, ACE'04, pp. 317–325. Australian Computer Society, Darlinghurst (2004)
23. Winkler, J.F.H.: The Fredge program prover FPP. In: 42. Internationales Wissenschaftliches Kolloquium, pp. 116–121. Technische Universität Ilmenau (1997)

24. Freining, C., Kauer, S., Winkler, J.F.H.: Ein Vergleich der programmbeweiser FPP, NPPV und SPARK. In: Winkler, J.F.H., Denecker, P., Keller, H.B., Tonndorf, M. (eds.) Ada Deutschland Tagung 2002: Software für sicherheitskritische Systeme, pp. 127–145. Shaker Verlag, Aachen (2002)

25. Schaefer, U., Hohmann, C., Ockenfels, S., Viehmeyer, M.: Weiterentwicklung eines programmverifizierers in Java. Technical Report, Philipps-Universität Marburg (2004)

26. Ihantola, P.: Creating and visualizing test data from programming exercises. Inf. Educ. **6**, 81–102 (2007)

27. Aaltonen, K., Ihantola, P., Seppälä, O.: Mutation analysis versus code coverage in automated assessment of students' testing skills. In: Proceedings of the ACM International Conference Companion on Object Oriented Programming Systems Languages and Applications Companion, SPLASH'10, pp. 153–160. ACM, New York (2010)

28. Linwood, J., Minter, D.: Building Portals with the Java Portlet API (Expert's Voice). Apress, Berkely (2004)

29. http://jcp.org/aboutJava/communityprocess/final/jsr168/

30. http://www.jcp.org/en/jsr/detail?id=286

31. http://www.adaptivepath.com/ideas/essays/archives/000385.php

32. Gruttmann, S., Kuchen, H.: A framework for formative E-assessments of mathematical proofs. In: Proceedings of the 2008 Symposium on e-Assessment in Practice (2008)

33. Hoare, C.A.R.: An axiomatic basis for computer programming. Commun. ACM **12**(10), 576–580 (1969)

34. Winskel, G.: The Formal Semantics of Programming Languages: An Introduction. MIT Press, Cambridge (1993)

35. Weicker, N., Weicker, K.: Didaktische Anmerkungen zur Unterstützung der Programmierlehre durch E-Learning. In: Haake, J.M., Lucke, U., Tavangarian, D. (eds.) DeLFI 2005: 3. Deutsche e-Learning Fachtagung Informatik, pp. 435–446. Gesellschaft für Informatik e.V., Bonn (2005)

36. Usener, C.A., Majchrzak, T.A., Kuchen, H.: Combining state of the art software engineering and E-assessment. In: Proceedings of the IADIS International Conference e-Learning 2011 (eL2011). IADIS Press, Amsterdam (2011)

Chapter 7
Conclusion

To conclude the book, a synopsis of the work is given. It is then checked whether the research questions stated in Sect. 1.3 were answered and how the book and the mentioned papers contributed to the body of knowledge. Eventually, findings are briefly discussed and research's limitations are sketched.

7.1 Synopsis

In the book at hand, technical aspects and organizational aspects of software testing as well as an approach for combining testing with e-assessment have been presented.

In Chap. 1, software testing was motivated as an integral constituent of software development. It is a necessity for the development of high quality software and required to countervail problems due to the complexity of software and the entailed failures of projects. Eventually, ten research questions were stated.

Papers present facets of research; a Springer Brief should not repeat papers but summarize them and highlight the course of research. Reading a book on current research threads is greatly aided by providing a concise introduction into the context of the research papers. Chapter 2 gave an all-embracing overview of the software testing discipline. Testing basics were explained, the ideas of almost all important testing techniques were sketched, and the organizational background of testing was described. Furthermore, using test tools and test automatization was discussed. The chapter can be read completely to get a brief overview of all facts of testing or treated as a reference. For the latter, the index (p. 149ff.) should turn out to be helpful.

Another noteworthiness of this book is summing-up the research papers. On this account, the underlying research design should be explained. This was done in Chap. 3. The design science research method was introduced and particularities of the three threads of research were explained. For Muggl, the methodology usually is not explicated. The IHK project required additional research methods, e.g. with respect to the expert interviews. The e-assessment research was combined with quantitative surveys.

T. A. Majchrzak, *Improving Software Testing*, SpringerBriefs in Information Systems, 127
DOI: 10.1007/978-3-642-27464-0_7, © The Author(s) 2012

Chapters 4, 5, and 6 sketched the three threads of research. All three chapters have been structured in the same way. Firstly, the background of the research thread was drawn. Then, closely related work was described. A brief introduction into the research results followed. Eventually, an overview of the published work was given including abstracts of papers and short commentary.

Chapter 4 dealt with technical aspects of software testing. In particular, implementing the tool Muggl was described. Therefore, the JVM was briefly introduced. Muggl provides a JVM along with an extension for symbolic execution. It implements the full bytecode instruction set both for *normal* and symbolic execution.

Muggl symbolically executes Java bytecode in order to derive test cases from its structure. It employs a constrain solver to reduce the number of states it has to discover. Furthermore, Muggl includes a number of sophisticated techniques that both improve execution and provide additional functionality that aids testers and developers. Examples are a step-by-step GUI as well as control flow and data flow tracking. Muggl's architecture is modular. Top-level components are a GUI and an execution core. Many components of the execution core are interchangeable and adaptable; besides, the symbolic JVM's functionality is provided as an API and can be used by other programs.

Muggl successfully generates test cases for a large number of examples. However, some problems remain and test case execution currently fails for large programs. The general approach has been proven feasible, but Muggl is still a prototype. Due to the profound code base and the detailed documentation, Muggl offers good preconditions for further development. Three papers have so far been published.

Organizational aspects of testing were the central theme of Chap. 5. It introduced work on the IHK project which was conducted in cooperation with enterprises from the Münsterland region. Expert interviews facilitated insight into the companies' testing processes. It could be concluded that testing activities change with company size and the criticality software quality has for it. Surprisingly, the usage of test tools and test automatization is very low.

Since the project led to the preparation of 29 recommendations, a categorization framework was designed and introduced. Recommendations were put into two categories: organizational and technical. They range from basic hints to advanced best practices. Seven papers and a booklet have been published on the project's findings. Papers were presented both on IS and technically oriented conferences; moreover, two conference papers were invited for extension and issued in scientific journals.

Research on e-assessment was introduced in Chap. 6. E-assessment is an area of e-learning and deals with assessing students' performance with technical means. EASy is an e-assessment system that is developed at the Chair for Practical Computer Science at the WWU Münster. Two modules for it have been developed and evaluated with students of the accompanying practical courses of lectures.

The first module concerns software verification proofs. It enables students to do Hoare Logic proofs in EASy. Despite some criticism w.r.t. the usability, students considered it helpful and concluded that by using it they did less mistakes than they would have done in a manual, paper based proof. The second module combines testing with e-assessment. An interface between EASy and Muggl has been implemented that allows to create test cases for students using EASy's programming exercise module. Using it encourages test driven development and motivates students to learn from test cases. Students found this approach to be adjuvant. In particularly, it encouraged them to ponder on the test case they got and thereupon to improve their programs. Moreover, the approach underlines the possibilities of Muggl. Three papers on e-assessment have been published. Two additional articles are currently in preparation.

This chapter (Chap. 7) draws a conclusion from the book. After giving this synopsis, the lessons learned will be sketched and the limitations discussed. The next chapter then highlights future work.

7.2 Lessons Learned

At the beginning of this book, a number of research questions were risen. It has to be checked whether the questions could be answered, what the findings are, and what lessons have been learned. This also summarizes the contributions made.

Research on Muggl

The first three questions concerned technical aspects of testing. Research on Muggl meant to find out *by which technical means the automated creation of test cases is possible* (first question). Some of the basic techniques used by Muggl were adopted from its predecessor. They had been proven to be feasible in general; however, the number of examples that the old tool GlassTT could successfully execute test cases for was low. With the continued work on Muggl, the general approach of symbolically executing Java bytecode in combination with constraint solving has proven to be feasible. Furthermore, statically generating CFGs and interprocedural def-use chains, dynamically covering them, and using coverage data to eliminate test cases is a very valuable contribution. The new approaches currently investigated are promising despite results being preliminary. This particularly applies to the work on generators. A number of additional techniques have been developed. They help to answer the second and third question (see below). Answering them also helps to better understand the challenges of the first question. Besides its general functionality, Muggl has been programmed with much love for detail. Consequently, it has much functionality that improves test case generation. For example, Muggl uses a wrapper for native method invocations, which greatly expands the number of methods that can be tested. Even with just one greater addition to the body of knowledge yet published, working on Muggl has led to a number of useful smaller contributions. More detail is given in Chap. 4 and the papers on Muggl.

The second question was derived from the experience with GlassTT and the early research on Muggl. In order to successfully find test cases, it has to be found *how the state space explosion encountered in tools for the automated test case generation can be controlled*. Using a constraint solver is a strategy adopted from GlassTT. For Muggl, the search algorithm was optimized. Using iterative-deepening depth-first search with a low starting depth helps to find a high number of relevant test cases in a short execution time. In addition, Muggl uses a variety of abortion criteria to stop execution once a *feasible* number of test cases has been found. For example, execution can be stopped if no new test cases have been found after executing a specified number of instructions. To cope with loops with unpropitious bounds, Muggl has a "soft" abortion criterion. If a loop is run for a specified number of times, execution is not aborted but Muggl backtracks to the last choice point it had created. Strictly speaking, using generators also helps to keep control of the state space. By testing programs with appropriate data, no invalid states are executed. Furthermore, many smaller techniques further keep the number of states to discover low or speed up execution of existing states. An example is the dynamic replacement of instructions by optimized ones.

Automatically generating test cases is very helpful, but they have to be assessable by humans. Furthermore, the effort to configure TCG tools should be kept low. The third question therefore is *whether it is possible to support software developers and testers in working with automatically generated test cases*. Supporting testers is possible, but the level of support depends on the actions offered by tools (also cf. Sect. 2.4). Muggl offers two means towards the aim of relieving humans from as much manual effort as possible.

Firstly, Muggl eliminates as many redundant test cases as possible. Keeping the number of test cases low helps testers to check them. The less test cases they need to check, the easier their work becomes. For most examples tested, Muggl finds the minimal or a nearly minimal set of test cases that covers all coverable control flow (CF) edges and def-use chains. Muggl also tries to find parameters for test cases that are as simple as possible. This further disburdens testers.

Secondly, Muggl tries to relieve testers of configuring settings before running it. While the GUI offers detailed options, most of them have default values found to be suitable in *most* cases. Moreover, testers can specify a maximum running time after which execution is aborted. Aborting by running time is not a *scientific criterion* but convenient. For practical use, the possibility to abort while keeping the test cases yet found is crucial.

Research on the IHK Project

The following questions concern the IHK project. The fourth questions asked *how companies tested software and how successful they were in doing so*. Globally answering this question in the scope of a short book is impossible. However, an answer for a limited region (the Münsterland) is given and described in the published booklet and two papers. It was also tried to generalize some of the findings in alignment with the existing literature. Evidence for a misalignment of active knowledge in companies and the body of knowledge documented in the literature was found.

The two aims of the IHK project were to draw the status quo of testing in the Münsterland region and to describe testing best practices. Thus, it had to be asked *whether it is possible to explicate the implicit knowledge of companies on optimizing software testing processes and in setting up a suitable technical background for testing* (fifth question). This is a precondition for drawing recommendations from interviews with company representatives. It was unclear to which extend this would be possible. After finishing the expert interviews, it became visible that a vast amount of data had been gained. Fortunately, it contained much intimate knowledge on processes and successful methods. Therefore, it was possible to extract best practices from it. The approach did not only succeed for the field of software testing but it should be able to adopt it for other topics in software development. It strongly relies on the cooperation with industry partner, though.

Best practices gained from the interviews ought to be presented as recommendations that could be applied by the participating companies. Thus, the sixth research question was *how explicated knowledge could be prepared in a form that makes it accessible for practitioners*. For this reason, a categorization framework was designed. The framework helps to judge whether a recommendation is useful for a company by showing preconditions under that it is effectual. Moreover, it helps to estimate the required effort to implement a recommendation. All recommendations were categorized with the framework. Additionally, detailed advice on how to adopt a recommendation is given where applicable. Being invited to the practitioners' conference *Belgium Testing Days 2011* for a talk on testing best practices[1] demonstrates the value our work has for companies.

The IHK project was initiated as a joint project between academia and practice. However, the first aim was to create a booklet for practitioners. It was unclear whether *theoretical knowledge could be derived from the explicated knowledge* (seventh question). Aligning the recommendations with the published theoretical literature enabled the process of theorizing it. This was supported by the fact that the framework proved helpful in this process. Besides theorizing the knowledge on best practices, the methodological approach had to be described in detail. Fortunately, the chosen methodology was sound and compatible with the expectations of the research community. Consequently, publication and presentation of a number of papers on the project succeeded.

Research on Testing and E-Assessment

The last three questions concern combining software testing and e-assessment. The eighth question was *how lectures in computer science could be supported by e-assessment*. After the author's colleagues had shown that e-assessment was feasible for mathematical proofs in prior work, we jointly extended their system for the assessment of formal verification. Formal verification is a small facet of computer science (CS) only. Nevertheless, the successful implementation in EASy shows

---

[1] The talk *Best Practices for Software Testing: Proposing a Culture of Testing* was given on 2011-02-15 in Brussels.

that e-assessment of complex CS topics *is* possible. Due to the lack of competing solutions and related work in general, EASy can be seen as an important *milestone*. Which other topics can be assessed is a question for future research.

Even though we had the idea to combine the research effort on EASy and Muggl, it was unclear *whether it would be possible to combine technical work on software testing with other subjects of IS research* (ninth question). It directly can be asked *how such combinations could look like and what the experiences with them are* (tenth question). Programming is an important part of the CS curriculum. Providing e-assessment support for it would be very valuable. Assessing programming lends itself to incorporate testing. We therefore implemented an interface between EASy and Muggl. It was successfully used for the assessment in a programming lecture. This also contributes to answering the first research question: Muggl obviously is a feasible tool.

7.3 Discussion and Limitations

In the light of the findings, impact and limitations of the research have to be analyzed. A discussion of the findings and in particular their boundaries and limitations is the base of future research.

It can be claimed without exaggeration that research on Muggl could have dramatic impact. As discussed earlier, there only is one other project (*Pex*) that follows a similar holistic approach. Would Muggl become able to process large commercial programs without the need for much configuration, it would completely change the way software is tested in enterprises. The presented work, however, only marks steps towards that aim—and towards finding out if it is reachable at all.

The method for coverage based test case elimination might be adopted by other researchers. It is too early to speculate about the impact of Muggl's other features. In general, it can be expected that single features that will be used in other research projects will have more impact than the tool as such. Muggl, nevertheless, suffers from a number of limitations. First of all, the number of examples that can be executed is still relatively low. Many small algorithms typically used for demonstration and teaching can be executed. However, for some examples execution fails for yet undiscovered reasons. Large programs seem to execute successfully but not all test cases are found in a reasonable amount of time. Alternatively, execution is aborted after running short of memory.

The complexity of Muggl is immense and there are problems to debug it. Examples have shown that errors in execution might occur after a 6- or 7-digit number of instructions have been processed. The erroneous operation might have occurred thousands of instructions earlier but revealed itself after a myriad of state changes. Consequently, some general defects that hinder the execution of more examples are expected to reside in Muggl. Moreover, its methods to keep the state space small are not (yet) capable of controlling the explosion of states for medium to large programs. While the progress with Muggl is notable, these limitations are the greatest challenges for future development. It also has to be noted that developing Muggl in a very small team requires prioritizing tasks. Instead of quickly publishing many superficial papers on hardly mature components, we decided to carefully design the system. Thus, remaining defects are expected to be hard-to-track conceptional misconceptions rather than simple programming mistakes. Moreover, Muggl is *very* thoroughly documented and adheres to a standard-conform programming style (cf. [1, 2]). Choosing this style limited the time available to actually program functionality. But it greatly enhances maintainability and simplifies future development.

With regard to actual functionality, minor limitations can be named. The def-use generator of Muggl becomes slow (i.e. runtime rises) if generating intraprocedural chains for larger programs. While the generator framework is finished, no set of *general purpose generators* for common data structures exist. Moreover, no ways have yet been found to easily implement generators. Finally, the native wrapper does not support execution of arbitrary third party libraries.

Ultimately, it has to be mentioned that Muggl does not support threading. While parallelizing execution is in preparation, executing multiple threads of a program is currently not intended to be added. Implementing threading for non symbolic execution would merely require a diligent implementation of the specification [3], but this would not aid symbolic execution. Not all of Muggl's concepts apply to multi-threaded execution. At least new concepts have to be found to use symbolic execution with the nondeterminism in threading. There is a number of research papers—mostly on verification [4–6] but also on testing [7]—but the effort of getting even initial and immature results can be expected to be extremely high.

Even with scientific restraint, the IHK project can be seen as a significant success. Not only did it satisfy the participating companies, but a number of scientific papers could be published. Additionally, the research method has proven to be suitable. At the same time, a number of limitations apply:

- The project was limited to the Münsterland. As a consequence, the status quo only applies to a narrow region.
- Drawing the status quo and gaining significant results would have required a quantitative study. Therefore, quantitative statements are very limited. Qualitative statements cannot be verified for significance.
- Despite finding 29 recommendations, the booklet is limited in scope. It does neither present a general introduction into testing in companies nor does it present a general testing process. Recommendations address distinct topics of testing and only partly support each other. Admittedly, no book exists that would holistically deal with all issues of testing in companies.
- From an academic viewpoint not all findings are new. Hence, theorizing was limited to novel findings or contexts of the finding not yet described.
- The framework could be refined. Moreover, it is not theoretically justified.
- A number of recommendations is not useful for small companies because they have preconditions with regard to organizational structures or the effort that needs to be put into realizing the recommendation.
- More attention could be given to *agile* testing.

Besides answering the research questions, the IHK project led to additional findings. Obviously, the reality of testing in companies is not yet captured by the literature. Textbooks fail to give concise and operational advice on testing in companies. At the same time, findings suggest that practitioners only slowly adopt knowledge documented in the literature. Some of the visited companies did *not* use methods that are comprehensively described in many books, easy to implement, and without question in their positive effects.

Research on e-assessment is mainly limited in scope. Software verification proofs are a tiny fragment of the CS curriculum only. Programming in Java is *an example* for assessing programming tasks. Therefore, research shows the producibility of e-assessment for CS courses and gives hints how it could look like. It does not offer *solutions* or even *products*. To our knowledge, it did not (yet) help companies to build such products. Up to now, research keeps the character of showing proof-of-concepts and presenting examples. Nevertheless, our approaches will continue to be used in actual courses.

Furthermore, evaluating the e-assessment solutions is limited to classes selected from the WWU Münster. Using EASy at least partly was voluntarily. It is unclear whether e-assessment would be accepted as a mandatory part of practical work. Moreover, it is questionable whether it could be used in exams. Evaluation results are limited to being applicable to similar CS courses. For example, intercultural differences or variations in education systems could derogate our findings' applicability to other courses.

Most of these limitations are inevitable in basic research. After all, e-assessment in higher education is an initial approach but for very simple assessment tasks. Therefore, limitations are severe but do not impair the value of our research.

References

1. Bloch, J.: Effective Java, 2nd edn. Prentice Hall, Upper Saddle River (2008)
2. Oracle: How to write Doc comments for the Javadoc tool (2004). http://www.oracle.com/technetwork/java/javase/documentation/index-137868.html
3. Lindholm, T., Yellin, F.: The Java Virtual Machine Specification, 2nd edn. Prentice Hall, Englewood Cliffs (1999)
4. Bäumler, S., Balser, M., Nafz, F., Reif, W., Schellhorn, G.: Interactive verification of concurrent systems using symbolic execution. AI Commun. **23**(2–3), 285–307 (2010)
5. Vernier, I.: Symbolic executions of symmetrical parallel programs. In: Proceedings of the 4th Euromicro Workshop on Parallel and Distributed Processing (PDP '96), PDP '96, p. 327. IEEE Computer Society, Washington, DC (1996)
6. Siegel, S.F., Mironova, A., Avrunin, G.S., Clarke, L.A.: Combining symbolic execution with model checking to verify parallel numerical programs. ACM Trans. Softw. Eng. Methodol. **17**(2), 10:1–10:34 (2008)
7. Staats, M., Păsăreanu, C.: Parallel symbolic execution for structural test generation. In: Proceedings of the 19th International Symposium on Software Testing and Analysis, ISSTA '10, pp. 183–194. ACM, New York (2010)

Chapter 8
Future Work

Research on the introduced topics is not finished with finishing this book. Two of the threads are continued. Moreover, the findings can be the start for new research threads. Possible future research is not limited to our work at the Chair for Practical Computer Science, though. Some questions remain open and some have been risen during the course of work.

8.1 Open Questions

None of the research questions Muggl tries to answer is conclusively answered. While much progress was achieved, research has shown that more work is needed. To enable Muggl to run more examples, its methods have to be refined. To include larger examples, it has to control the state space even more effectively. And to be suited for practical usage, Muggl should not merely rely on default values. Rather, it should examine programs before it executes them in order to find suitable settings. Ideally, this should be possible without human intervention.

In consequence, it will not only be needed to keep up the current research on Muggl, but also new ways to deal with the existing problems have to be found. Finding suitable settings for execution will require a new approach. More work is also needed with respect to Muggl's constraint solver. It could be observed that it neatly works for many examples but that runtime is very high for others. For a small number of examples it even is unsuitable; it runs into an endless loop or it takes so much time to solve constraint systems that execution is degraded below practicability. Optimizing the constraint solver thus is an open issue of research.

Moreover, it will have to be checked whether all techniques incorporated in Muggl already are optimal. For example, redundant test cases are currently eliminated based on their contribution to CF edge and def-use chain coverage. Only those test cases are deleted that contribute to neither coverage. In addition, coverage is tracked intraprocedural. In current examples, no test cases were deleted by mistake. Theoretically, a

T. A. Majchrzak, *Improving Software Testing*, SpringerBriefs in Information Systems, 135
DOI: 10.1007/978-3-642-27464-0_8, © The Author(s) 2012

test case could be deleted even though it would help to detect an additional defect. It remains an open question whether such examples exist, how they can be identified, and how they should be dealt with. Furthermore, generators promise to be very helpful but they might not be the definite solution to all problems of data structure generation. This particularly applies to handling arrays. A future task could be to directly compare *Pex*, the glass-box test tool of Microsoft research, with Muggl in order to benefit from both approaches. Especially, it could be tried to use its constraint solver Z3 in Muggl. Z3 natively supports arrays.

However, Z3 does not have an interface to Java, which would require using the Java native interface (JNI). A wrapper component that transforms Muggl's internal data structures for constraints as well as a native interface would be needed. This would not only be a laborious task but also massively slow down execution. Finding novel ways to improve Muggl nevertheless remains an open question and unaccustomed or even seemingly digressive ways could prove themselves worthy. After all, research on Muggl is low level work and fundamental research.

While the IHK project is finished, a number of open questions remain. First of all, the status quo of testing has not yet been described on a global level. Literature usually describes project failures or single success stories. Analyzing how companies test would—in particular with a focus on national differences—require a sophisticated method and enormous effort in terms of personnel. A quantitative study could go much further than the IHK project. For example, it is unclear whether the claim that "software quality improvement should be seen as an investment" [1] can be supported quantitatively. Similarly, the typical return on investment (ROI) for software development [1] could be determined where appropriate in relation to techniques or development processes. Furthermore, the effectivity of testing techniques and also of (assumed) testing best practices could be checked. This could also be used to give strong empirical proof for recommendations' effectiveness.

Regarding qualitative questions, only some answers could be given by the IHK project. It remains an open question how companies can be supported with effective testing processes. Besides, questions related to many testing subtasks require further attention. It can be expected that testing and its economic feasibility will stay an important topic of research.

E-assessment of cognitively demanding and creative tasks in higher education has an initial state of research. Many research questions remain and new ones arise in the course of progress. However, we will focus on computer science related tasks. Addressing the requirements for e-assessment in further subjects requires interdisciplinary work with professionals from these subjects.

It has to be checked which topics of computer science education are suitable for e-assessment. Systems that are feasible for actual assessment have to be built and evaluated. It is unclear whether e-assessment can be adopted for all topics. Furthermore, it is questionable whether it will be helpful in terms of improving education for all topics that it can be used for. In addition, how e-assessment can be used for course examinations is unclear. Subordinate research questions arise with each topic e-assessment is extended to. Challenges in the fields of designing e-assessment systems are accompanied by sociological, juridical, and managerial questions.

Research on the combination of e-assessment and testing is not finished, either. Results are initial and have to be verified in further studies. Moreover, it can be checked whether including testing in assessment can be extended or changed in a way that either relieves tutors from work or has a higher educational value (or, ideally, both).

8.2 Ongoing Research

General progress of the research on software testing seems to be rather slow. Comparing textbooks that were published around the year 2000 with textbooks published in the last year, the differences are humble. For example, consider Liggesmeyer's books on software quality. The editions from 2002 and 2009 are not only almost identical in length, but their table of contents is nearly equal [2, 3]. The second edition has been augmented with a chapter on model checking. Model checking *is* an innovation of the last ten years that has received much attention (cf. Sect. 2.1.3, p. 16). This shows that most published techniques are well understood but that there have been hardly any breakthroughs. In particular, the merits (and problems) of test automatization have already been described ten years ago [4]. The same applies to the management of testing and software quality [5]. Both topics are up-to-date. Neither automatization nor test management work as smooth as they ought to. Therefore, they remain topics which are discussed in the current literature. The problems mentioned have hardly changed.

The above conclusion does not mean that there is no or too little research on software testing. As already mentioned, there has been considerable progress in some testing related disciplines. The ACM portal [6] lists over 100000 documents for the search query "software test" that have been indexed in 2000 or later. Google Scholar [7] even finds almost twice as much. It is needless to say that many of these documents are only loosely related to software testing. However, as there also is an active community that organizes conferences on software testing, it can be concluded that testing still is a very active field of research. It regrettably does not come up with many noticeable innovations at the moment.

In the light of the research that the was conducted in the last four years, above considerations encourage to go on with the research. In particular, the following topics will be investigated by the book's author and the research group at the Chair for Practical Computer Science:

- We will test the generator framework for Muggl with a number of examples. Generators for common data structures will be provided.
- We already published a paper on Logic Java, a combination of logic and object oriented programming languages that uses our SJVM [8]. This research will be continued.
- The constraint solver will be optimized. A diploma student is supporting us in enabling it to treat constraints disjunctly, i.e. to process parts of a constraint

in different solvers. Moreover, he will try to track down remaining bugs in the solver.

- We will continue general work on Muggl. Testing additional programs reveals bugs and invites to creatively solve emerging problems. In particular, further experimentation and its analysis is to be published.
- A formal description of the symbolic JVM (SJVM) will be released. It is meant to be a documentation and also a reference for other researchers.
- Once the number of executable programs has been increased, we have to address the execution of larger programs. On this account, novel techniques to keep the state space small have to be found. At the same time, the SJVM can be extended for parallel execution. A sophisticated strategy has to be found that processes multiple paths of the search tree at once without generating much overhead and memory usage.
- Since the method behind the IHK project was found to be feasible, we will try to attract funding for similar projects in other fields of software development. Moreover, we will try to attract funding for further industry supported projects on software testing and software quality.
- We will continue the collaboration on the research of e-assessment and try to improve the current solution.
- As a general aim, we will identify other areas of research that can be combined with our work on software quality. This could create interdisciplinary projects worth consideration.

Besides the above stated tasks, future work on Muggl *might* comprise additional tasks. While test case elimination *after* execution is feasible, execution speed could be increased by eliminating redundant test cases *on the fly*. Furthermore, we could search for a heuristic that detects uncovered paths in the execution tree that will not lead to (interesting) test cases. This would reduce the number of states that need to be discovered. In order to include more programs, a *native class loader* could be implemented that provides access to all kinds of third party libraries.

A long term goal is to support test case generation for other programming languages compiled to Java bytecode, and—eventually—for other programming languages in general. This would in particular include languages compiling to the CLI (.NET languages). Another long term goal is to enhance the search algorithm. Instead of using simple backtracking, *forward checking* and *look ahead* techniques [9] could be applied to avoid searching in paths that will not lead to solutions. In combination, advanced *constraint propagation* techniques [10, 11] could be used.

References

1. Slaughter, S.A., Harter, D.E., Krishnan, M.S.: Evaluating the cost of software quality. Commun. ACM **41**(8), 67–73 (1998). http://doi.acm.org/10.1145/280324.280335
2. Liggesmeyer, P.: Software-Qualität: Testen. Analysieren und Verifizieren von Software. Spektrum-Akademischer Verlag, Berlin (2002)

3. Liggesmeyer, P.: Software-Qualität: Testen, Analysieren und Verifizieren von Software, 2nd edn. Spektrum-Akademischer Verlag, Berlin (2009)
4. Fewster, M., Graham, D.: Software Test Automation: Effective Use of Test Execution Tools. ACM Press, New York (1999)
5. Wallmüller, E.: Software-Qualitätsmanagement in der Praxis, 2nd edn. Hanser, München (2001)
6. http://portal.acm.org/
7. http://scholar.google.com/
8. Majchrzak, T.A., Kuchen, H.: Logic Java: combining object-oriented and logic programming. In: Proceedings of the 20th International Workshop on Functional and (Constraint) Logic Programming (WFLP), no. 6816. Lecture Notes in Computer Science. Springer (2011)
9. http://ktiml.mff.cuni.cz/~bartak/constraints/propagation
10. Bartak, R.: Constraint programming—what is behind? In: Proceedings of the Workshop on Constraint Programming for Decision and Control (CPDC), pp. 7–15 (1999)
11. Barták, R.: Theory and practice of constraint propagation. In: Proceedings of the 3rd Workshop on Constraint Programming in Decision and Control (CPDC), pp. 7–14 (2001)

Glossary

Acceptance Test This → testing phase is part of most development projects. A program thats implementation has been finished is tested against its specification by customers.

Ajax The term Ajax (asynchronous JavaScript and XML) describes a number of methods for asynchronous client-side processing of Web pages. Instead of requesting Web pages from the server for every action performed. the client evaluates actions and asynchronously loads additional content from the Web server. This improves usability. Complex Web applications using Ajax are capable of (almost) resembling a rich client GUI. In General, using Ajax is attributed to Web 2.0 applications.

Aliasing Aliasing occurs if one memory address is described by more than one variable (or another kind of identifier) in a program. It poses a problem in program analyses and optimization. Aliasing is possible on high and low levels of abstraction, e.g. regarding variables in source code or pointers in machine code.

All Def-Use-Paths Synonym for → def-use chain.

All-Pairs Testing Synonym for → pairwise testing.

All-Pair Table An all-pair table can be used to reduce the number of → test cases when using → equivalence partitioning. Literature tip: [1, Chap. 18]

Anti Pattern Identifying anti patterns typically is combined with → code reviews. Anti patterns describe how *not* to implement a program. They are inspired by → design patterns. Literature tip: [2]

Audit See → code review.

Automatization Synonymously used for → test automatization.

T. A. Majchrzak, *Improving Software Testing*, SpringerBriefs in Information Systems,   141
DOI: 10.1007/978-3-642-27464-0, © The Author(s) 2012

Back-to-Back Test Back-to-back tests are used for critical systems. n prototypes are built with the same specification and iteratively tested until defects have been eliminated. Back-to-back tests are a → diversifying technique. Literature tip: [3, p. 376ff.]

Backtracking Backtracking describes a technique in that processing a → search tree is reversed to an earlier node. If applicable, the state connected to this node is recovered. Literature tip: [4, p. 90]

Benchmark Benchmarks measure a program's performance and try to generate key figures about it. They are particular useful for comparisons. Benchmarks relate to → load tests and similar tools can be used, but they are not a → testing technique. Literature tip: [5, p. 131ff.]

Best Practice Best practices are established and well proven methods to solve problems (usually within organizations).

Beta Test Beta tests extend the idea of → pilot tests to a larger number of testers. They can be conducted in a closed community or public.

Black-Box Test Tests that distance from the source code (whether it is known or not) and for that the actual implementation of a module or system has no meaning are called black-box tests.

Bottleneck A performance bottleneck describes a part of a program that significantly degrades its overall performance.

Bounce Test A bounce test is a special form of → stress test that varies between nominal and extraordinary loads to check whether a program adapts its resource usage. Literature tip: [6, p. 175]

Boundary Values Analysis A test based on → equivalence partitioning using numeric values (in particular intervals) is called boundary values analysis. Literature tip: [1, p. 144ff.]

Branch Test This simple → structure oriented technique creates as many test cases as are needed to cover each branch in the code at least once. Literature tip: [6, Chap. 5]

Bug Subsumes → defects and unexpected behavior of programs which does not violate the specification. Literature tip: [7, p. 19f.]

Bytecode Bytecode is a form of intermediate code. It is usually compiled from source code and either interpreted or run in a → virtual machine.

Capture and Replay A kind of → test tool that records user interaction with a program and automatically repeats it at a later point. Replay can be parametrized to add variety.

Certification Certifications for personnel attests humans a certain level of knowledge or skill in an IT related field. Testing is particular popular for certification. Literature tip: [8]

Code Review Code reviews manually assess source code. Not only defects are searched for but also the overall quality is checked. Review strategies greatly vary in complexity. Reviews are a → static analysis technique. Literature tip: [9, Chap. 9]

Code Smell See → anti pattern.

Component Test The earliest → testing phase in which developers test their own code is called component test.

Condition Test This simple → structure oriented technique creates as many test cases as are needed to cover each atomic conditions in the code at least once. Literature tip: [6, Chap. 5]

Control Flow Analysis Control flow analysis checks the code for anomalies with regard to the order of its execution. For example, *dead code* is detected. CF analysis is a → static analysis technique. Literature tip: [6, p. 118ff.]

Control Flow Graph A CFG is build from source, intermediate, or machine code. It illustrates possible paths trough a program. Each statement forms a node whereas transition between statements form edges. Literature tip: [9, p. 85]

Control Flow Test This test is based on a → control flow graph. Each transition is tried to be covered at least once while keeping the number of → test cases low. Control flow testing is a → structure oriented technique. Literature tip: [6. p. 92f.]

Dangling Pointer Synonym for → wild pointer.

Data Flow Analysis Code can be checked for a variety of anomalies with regard to variables. For example, redefining variables without reading them, defining and immediately dereferencing them, or dereferencing and then trying to read a variable can be detected. Data flow analysis is a → static analysis technique. Literature tip: [9, p. 292ff.]

Data Flow Test Data flow testing uses information on how data is processed by a program by checking when variables are read and written. An effective technique is to check → def-use chains. Data flow testing is a → structure oriented technique. Literature tip: [9, p. 142]

Deadlock A deadlock describes a state of a program in which execution is not continued because threads are waiting for resource access that can never be fulfilled since required resources are crosswise locked.

Debugging Debugging describes the systematic attempt to find and to remove → defects from a program. While testing detects failures and might reveal defects, debugging deals with finding their origin. Debugging is typically tool supported by a so called *debugger*. Literature tip: [7]

Decision Tables Decision tables arrange conditions and actions in a table. Tests are created that cover each combination of condition and action at least once. In most cases, the number of required → test cases can be reduced. Literature tip: [1, p. 174ff.]

Defect A defect is the absence of a guaranteed property of a software. It is statically bound to the code. Defects are caused by → errors and manifest as → failures. Literature tip: [1, p. 10ff.]

Def-Use Chain Full definition-usage chains (DU chains) describe paths between code statements that write and read a variable without the variable being modified on the path between them. A formal definition is given in Sect. 2.2.2.1. Literature tip: [11]

Design Pattern Design patterns describe best practices in designing software. Patterns are most commonly applied to object oriented programming languages. A pattern describes a typical structure of e.g. classes to solve a programming problem. Literature tip: [12]

Diversifying Diversifying techniques try to overcome the fuzziness bound to other → dynamic testing techniques. Literature tip: [3, p. 375]

Domain Testing Domain testing checks the boundaries of classes created by → equivalence partitioning. It reduce the number of → test cases required to test all (remaining) classes. Literature tip: [1, Chap. 16]

Dynamic Analysis These → dynamic testing techniques check executed programs for resource and performance problems. Literature tip: [6, p. 128ff.]

Dynamic Binding Invocation of a method does not necessarily need to be determined statically at compile time. It can also be bound dynamically in alignment with an affected object. It is used by many object oriented programming languages.

Dynamic Symbolic Execution If → symbolic tests are extended for dynamic execution, results are more precise. Information that are only available dynamically can be taken into consideration.

Dynamic Testing Dynamic testing techniques rely on the execution of a program. They usually identify → failures. Only some of them help to find corresponding → defects. Literature tip: [9, p. 43ff.]

Eclipse Eclipse is the arguably most popular → Integrated Development Environment for Java. Web tip: [13]

Efficiency Test Synonym for → performance test.

Equivalence Partitioning Equivalence partitioning partitions input value for a program into classes. For each class, only one → test case is created. Literature tip: [6, p. 35ff.]

Error Errors are mistakes in the life cycle of a software that lead to an incorrect result. They usually result from human mistakes. Errors cause → defects. Literature tip: [6, p. 354ff.]

Error Guessing Synonym for → intuitive testing.

Exhaustive Testing The complete enumeration of possible inputs for a program can be used for exhaustive testing. It is impractical even for smallest programs. Instead, → static testing and → dynamic testing techniques are used. Literature tip: [10, p. 54]

Experience Based Testing → Testing techniques that only rely on a tester's experience and skill are called experience based. In general, such tests are unstructured. Since testers *work* with the program under consideration, it is a → dynamic testing technique. Literature tip: [10, p. 169f.]

Explorative Testing If testers do not know a program they test, they can explore it. While doing so, → failures may be detected. Literature tip: [6, p. 108f.]

Failure Failures are the observable consequences from → defects. They occur dynamically when using a program. From a user's view, failures are malfunctions. Literature tip: [10, p. 6f.]

Fault Synonym for → defect.

Field In object orientation, fields are variables that are bound to classes. They can be static (one variable of a name per program instantiation) or non-static (one variable of a name per object).

Floyd Hoare Logic Synonym for → Hoare Logic.

Formal Technique Formal techniques are applied to prove that a program is consistent with its specification. They are a → verification techniques. Literature tip: [3, p. 285]

Functional Coverage Trying to cover each function with one → test case is the most simple → function oriented testing technique. Literature tip: [6, p. 334ff.]

Functional Testing Functional testing checks whether a program adheres to its specification. It must not be confused with → function oriented testing. Literature tip: [6, Chap. 10]

Function Orientation Function oriented → dynamic testing techniques focus on tests that align with a program's functions. Literature tip: [6, p. 31]

Garbage Collection Garbage collection automatically frees memory and deallocates data structures not used anymore. It is e.g. used in most programming languages that are executed in a → virtual machine. Literature tip: [14]

Generator Generator as a term used in this book describes a concept for the → test tool Muggl. A generator is utilized to generate data structures that are used as input data for → test case generation. Generators are specifically useful if input data structures are complex. This example applies to trees and other multi-object structures. See also: → validator.

Graceful Degradation Graceful degradation describes an emergency shutdown in a situation where a program crash would be unavoidable. It is desired as a last resort e.g. when conducting a → stress test. Literature tip: [6, p.174]

Glass-Box Test A test that is done with explicit knowledge of the source code of the tested module or system.

Gray-Box Test If testers that implement black-box test cases have at least partial knowledge of the source code and utilize this knowledge, this can be called gray-box testing. Literature tip: [5, p. 119f.]

German Testing Board The GT is a German committee for testing → certification and associated with the → ISTQB. Web tip: [15]

Hoare Logic Hoare logic is a formal system with a set of axioms that allow to reason about the correctness of programs. It can be used for → formal techniques. Literature tip: [3, p. 287ff.]

Incident Subsumes → failures and external effects, i.e. apparent violations of a program's specification that are caused by ill-conducted testing. Literature tip: [10, p. 10]

Inspection See → software inspection.

Integrated Development Environment An IDE is a tool used in software development. It offers source code editing along with a great number of other functions that integrate it into the development process. IDEs greatly aid implementation. Modern IDEs can be enhanced by loading plug-ins.

Integration Test Integration testing is a → testing phase in which single components are integrated and their interaction is tested.

Intuitive Testing With this → experience based testing technique, testers conduct tests for whichever functions they think should be tested. Literature tip: [10, p. 170ff.]

International Software Testing Qualifications Board The ISTQB is a not-for-profit association that promotes testing → certification and offers corresponding degrees. Web tip: [16]

Java Bytecode Java bytecode is the → bytecode compiled for the → Java Virtual Machine. It is stored in `class` files. Java source code is compiled to this bytecode but other programming languages that run on the JVM are also compiled to Java bytecode. Literature tip: [17]

Java Virtual Machine The JVM is the → virtual machine that executes → Java bytecode. Literature tip: [17]

Lockset Analysis A → dynamic analysis technique that aims at finding → race conditions. Literature tip: [18, p. 409]

Load Test Load tests assess a program's behavior under load. Thus, they are → performance tests. The workload used should be typical for that program. Literature tip: [6, p. 172ff.]

Make-or-Buy Make-or-buy is a business decision frequently faced with regard to software and thereby when planing to introduce → test tools. Choices are make, i.e. implement the tool, or buy—and probably customize—it.

Member Synonym for → field.

Memory Leak Memory leaks are → defects in programs that lead to the allocation of more memory than is afterwards released. They can be avoided by using → garbage collection. Literature tip: [19, p. 254]

Memory Leak Detection This → dynamic analysis technique is used to detect → memory leaks. It is usually supported by → test tools. Literature tip: [6, p. 131]

Metric Metrics describe key figures that are generated from code or by systems that manage testing related data. They allow to draw conclusions about a program's status or the effectiveness of → testing techniques. Generating metrics is accounted to → static analysis. Literature tip: [20, Chap. 11]

Mock Object A mock objects simulates the behaviors of components. It goes beyond the functionality of a → test stub by that it is more complex. Whereas test stubs are kept very simple, mock objects might contain functionality of their own. Literature tip: [21]

Model Checking Model checking is a technique for the automated → verification of software. A model that describes a software system is checked against its specification. Model checking is supported by so called *model checkers*, which have to deal with problems such as the → state space explosion. Literature tip: [22]

Model-View-Controller The MVC is a → design pattern used for Web applications. It roughly divides a program into layers for view, control, and model that are used to separate concerns in programming. Web tip: [23]

Module Test Synonym for → component test.

Mutation Test Mutation tests are used to *test* the tests written for a program. Mutants, i.e. altered copies of a program, are generated. The quality of → test cases is reflected by their ability to identify mutants. Literature tip: [3, p. 384ff.]

Oracle A test oracle is used to check the results of test execution and to classify the test as *passed* or *failed*. A common technique is to compare the actual result with an expected result. Literature tip: [18, p. 372ff.]

Orthogonal Arrays Orthogonal arrays are a technique to reduce the number of → test cases when using → equivalence partitioning. Literature tip: [24]

Pair-Wise Testing An optimization technique for → equivalence partitioning. Literature tip: [18, p. 215ff.]

Partition Analysis Partition analysis combines → verification and testing. → test cases are created if verification fails. Literature tip: [9, p. 206ff.]

Performance Bottleneck Detection This → dynamic analysis tries to detect → bottlenecks. Literature tip: [6, p. 135]

Performance Test Performance tests assess the runtime behavior of a program with regard to resource utilization and response times. This is only possible when executing a program. Thus, it is a → dynamic testing technique. Moreover, performance testing is a → testing phase. Literature tip: [6, p. 171f.]

Pilot Test Pilot tests can be a → testing phase of their own in which an almost finished program is tested by key customers under realistic conditions.

Portlet Portlets are distinct configurable components that are combined to form an user interface. They are typically managed by a portal server which is provided by an application server. Portlets are used in Web development. They are particularly useful for modularized Web sites that are customizable by their users. Literature tip: [25]

Race Condition When multiple threads of a program access shared variables, race conditions can occur. They might lead to a → deadlock.

Recommendation In this book, the term *recommendation* is used to describe suggestions of successful testing actions (if no other meaning can be derived from the context).

Regression Test Regression testing is not a technique of its own. It describes the repetition of tests after the tested program has been modified. Regression aims at keeping defects from entering already tested components. Literature tip: [9, p. 192f.]

Resource Monitor Resource monitors graphically depict resource utilization and system performance. They can e.g. be used to find → bottlenecks.

Rich Client A rich client is part of a client-server infrastructure. It does not only facilitate functionality to render content but has additional components. A rich client might be capable of pursuing complex tasks. In the most extreme form, the server is degraded to merely providing data which is processed completely by the client. Its opposite is a *thin client*.

Scaffolding Scaffolding is a term related to the early phases of testing. A scaffold comprises of elements required to test a program before it is finished. Typical elements are → test cases, → test stubs, and → mock object. Additionally, a → test harness can be attributed to the scaffold. Literature tip: [18, p. 369ff.]

Search Tree A search tree is an abstract data structure based on trees. It allows efficient access of a total ordered set.

Security Test Security tests subsume techniques that assess a program's security. Both common → testing techniques and distinct security tests can be used. Literature tip: [26, Chap. 24]

Slicing Slicing is used to automatically discover interrelations within programs, for example with regard to the influence of statements on variables. Besides static slicing, dynamic slicing strategies exist. It is a → static analysis technique. Literature tip: [9, p. 285ff.]

Smoke Test A smoke test typically is a → system test. It tries to find out whether a system can be considered to be *finished*. Literature tip: [27, Chap. 17]

Specification Orientation Synonym for → function orientation.

Software Crisis A term coined in 1972 by Edsger W. DIJKSTRA. It originally described that software costs exceeded hardware costs. Additionally, it can be used to describe the phenomenon that software becomes more complex steadily and cannot fully utilize hardwares' capabilities. Literature tip: [28]

Software Inspection Synonym for → code review.

Staging Describes the separation of testing activities into → testing phases.

Standard Standards summarize rules, norms, and conventions. They can be general guidelines or mandatory ruling. Literature tip: [20, Chap. 13]

State Oriented Testing Without knowing a program's code its possible states are figured out. The aim of testing is to cover each transition between states at least once. This technique is not applicable if the number of states is unknown or if a very high number of transitions has to be covered. Literature tip: [18, p. 129f.]

State Space Explosion Computational problems that are solved by discovering states, which might connect to further states, commonly face the problem of state space explosion. An example is an → search tree built from program code. A linear increment in search depth leads to an exponential growth in discoverable states. In general, algorithmic means to counter state space explosion have to be found. Even with vast computational power and parallel algorithms, techniques that rely on checking states cannot be applied to software that is too complex if they do not adequately reduce the number of states to check. Literature tip: [22, p. 78f.]

Static Analysis Static analysis analyzes and interprets code to gain conclusions. It belongs to → static testing. Literature tip: [29, p. 6]

Static Testing For static testing, a program is considered at a given point. It is not executed but structurally analyzed. In general, → defects are found directly. Literature tip: [9, p. 43ff.]

Statement Test This simple → structure oriented technique creates as many → test cases as are needed to cover each code statement at least once. Literature tip: [6, Chap. 5]

Statistic State Oriented Testing A → state oriented testing technique that takes into account the probability that a function is used. Literature tip: [3, p. 363ff.]

Statistic Testing With this technique → test cases are generated based on probability distributions of the usage of classes, methods, or other program components. It is a → dynamic testing techniques. Literature tip: [3, p. 368]

Stress Test Stress tests belong to → performance test techniques. They test a program with loads that are beyond the expected workload and try to fathom its response. Literature tip: [6, p. 174]

Structure Orientation Structure oriented → dynamic testing techniques test a program against its own code. Literature tip: [6, p. 94ff.]

Style Analysis Style analysis checks source code for compliance with predefined conventions. It is a → static analysis technique. Literature tip: [9, p. 271ff.]

Symbolic Execution Symbolic execution assumes input parameters to be logic variables instead of constant values. Execution is done based on these variables; the output of operations on logic variables are terms that can contain logic variables, operation symbols, and constants.

Symbolic Model Checking This is a → model checking technique that can be attributed to testing. It extends → formal techniques by using automata theory. Literature tip: [9, p. 45]

Symbolic Test Symbolic tests treat variables as logic variables instead of parameterizing them with constant values. It is a → verification technique but might include execution of the code. Literature tip: [3, p. 309f.]

Syntax Testing Syntax testing bases on → equivalence partitioning with alphanumerical values. Literature tip: [30, p. 85]

System Test This advanced → testing phase is an → integration test of the whole system. → Test stubs and → mock objects are successively removed

Test Automatization The process of delegating more or less steps of testing to be executed by systems that do not require human interaction. In general, automatization only means that → test tools relieve humans from repetitive tasks. True automatization describes (almost) completely automatic testing. Literature tip: [31]

Test Case A test case is the description of an atomic test. It consists of input parameters, execution conditions, and the expected result. The tern does not imply whether this is done in form of code or a textual description. Literature tip: [18, p. 171]

Test Case Generation → Test case generation (usually abbreviated as TCG) describes the process of creating a → test suit of test cases for a given program. The term is commonly used in the context of → test automatization.

Test Center Test centers are corporate divisions that provide central testing services. They can fulfill staffing tasks, provide advice and guidelines, and support the technical infrastructure for testing. Literature tip: [32, p. 47ff.]

Test Concept Companies can chose to create a test concept which defines overall aims, general approaches and activities, and the assignment of → test plans.

Test Driven Development TDD describes an approach of first writing → test cases and then implementing the functionality to successfully execute them. Literature tip: [33]

Test Driver Synonym for the code representation of a → test case.

Test Harness A test harness simulates the environment a program is embedded to. It is used for testing before a software is finished. It has to be distinguished from → test stubs and → mock objects in that it is not part of the tested program. Broader definitions also attribute software to run test cases and test data to the harness.

Testing Environment A testing environment comprises of hardware and software components and is used to execute tests. It should be similar to the target environment for the program to be tested but allow efficient testing. In particular, it should ensure that individual test runs can be done under equal conditions (i.e. the environment can be set to defined states) and that productive systems are not endangered by testing. Literature tip: [34, 27]

Testing Phase Testing usually is divided into several phases. Phases differ by techniques used, by the technical level, and by responsibility.

Testing Technique There is a great number of different ways to test software. Distinct approaches toward conducting tests can be called testing methods or testing techniques. Techniques can be categorized by their main characteristics (see Sect. 2.1.3). Literature tip: [9, p. 37f.]

Test Lab Synonym for → test center.

Test Method Synonym for → testing technique.

Test Plan A test plan describes detailed testing activities, scheduled times and durations, and the intended interaction with development activities. It can be part of a → test concept.

Test Stub Test stubs simulate the behaviors of components that are required for testing modules of an unfinished program. Literature tip: [35, p. 180f.]

Test Suit A test suit comprises a number of → test cases, usually compiled for testing a distinct program or parts of it. They can also be used hierarchically, i.e. small test suits are included in more comprehensive ones.

Test Tool Test tools are programs that support testing. They serve a variety of purposes and range from small low level tools to sophisticated solutions integrating functionality for the whole test process. Literature tip: [26, Chap. 5]

Unit Test Synonym for → component test.

Use Case A use case depicts a scenario in which a program is actually used. The Unified Modeling Language (UML) provides so called *use case diagrams* for visualization. Literature tip: [6, p. 59]

Use Case Testing Based on → use cases it is tried to cover each possible path through a program denoted by these use cases. Literature tip: [6, p. 59f.]

Validator Validator as a term used in this book describes a concept for the tool Muggl. A validator is used to analyze data structures that are used as input data for → test case generation. See also: → generator.

Verification Verification techniques formally check a program against its specification. They belong to → static testing. Literature tip: [10, p. 56]

Virtual Invocation Virtual invocation is a commonly used technique in → virtual machines of object oriented programming languages. The method to invoke is not statically set but determined dynamically. It can e.g. rely on an object passed to the virtual invocation instruction.

Virtual Machine A virtual machine is a virtual computer system (i.e. a programmable machine) capable of executing programs written for it. Virtual machines may run on a number of hardware platforms and dynamically optimize execution. Most virtual machines are stack based. A prominent example is the → Java Virtual Machine. Virtual machines can replace an operation system, which e.g. applies to hypervisors, or run on top of it (such as the JVM).

Volume Test Synonym for → load test.

White-Box Test Synonym for → glass-box test.

Wild Pointer A wild pointer is a program statement that incorrectly uses pointers. Thus, execution is prone to jump to illegal memory addresses or access data in an undesired way. Literature tip: [6, p. 132ff.]

Wirth's Law Wirth's Law states that software is getting slower more rapidly than hardware becomes faster. Literature tip: [36]

Y Unfortunately, there is no noteworthy testing term beginning with Y... the same applies to X and Z.

References

1. Black, R.: Pragmatic Software Testing. Wiley, Indianapolis (2007)
2. Brown, W.H., Malveau, R.C., McCormick, H.W., Mowbray, T.J.: Anti-Patterns: Refactoring Software, Architectures, and Projects in Crisis. Wiley, New York (1998)
3. Roitzsch, E.H.P.: Analytische Softwarequalitätssicherung in Theorie und Praxis: Der Weg zur Software mit hoher Qualität durch statisches Prüfen, dynamisches Testen, formales Beweisen. Monsenstein und Vannerdat (2005)
4. Hofstedt, P., Wolf, A.: Einführung in die Constraint-Programmierung. Grundlagen, Methoden, Sprachen, Anwendungen. Springer, Heidelberg (2007)
5. Thaller, G.E.: Software—Test, 2nd edn. Heise, Hannover (2002)
6. Bath, G., McKay, J.: Praxiswissen Softwaretest—Test Analyst and Technical Test Analyst. Dpunkt, Heidelberg (2010)
7. Zeller, A.: Why Programs Fail: A Guide to Systematic Debugging. Morgan Kaufmann, San Francisco (2006)
8. Graham, D., Veenendaal, E.V., Evans, I., Black, R.: Foundations of software testing: ISTQB certification. Intl Thomson Bus Pr (2008). http://www.amazon.com/Foundations-Software-Testing-ISTQB-Certification/dp/1844803554
9. Liggesmeyer, P.: Software-Qualität: Testen, Analysieren und Verifizieren von Software, 2nd edn. Spektrum-Akademischer Verlag, Berlin (2009)
10. Cleff, T.: Basiswissen Testen von Software. W3L GmbH, Witten (2010)
11. Majchrzak, T.A., Kuchen, H.: Automated Test Case Generation based on Coverage Analysis. In: TASE '09: Proceedings of the 2009 3nd IEEE International Symposium on Theoretical Aspects of Software Engineering, pp. 259–266. IEEE Computer Society, Washington (2009)
12. Gamma, E., Helm, R., Johnson, R., Johnson, R., Johnson, R.: Design Patterns. Elements of Reusable Object-Oriented Software. Addision-Wesley, Munchen (1995)
13. http://www.eclipse.org/
14. Jones, R., Lins, R.: Garbage Collection: Algorithms for Automatic Dynamic Memory Management. Wiley, New York (1996)
15. http://www.german-testing-board.info/
16. http://www.istqb.org/
17. Lindholm, T., Yellin, F.: The Java Virtual Machine Specification, 2nd edn. New Jersey, Prentice Hall (1999)
18. Pezze, M., Young, M.: Software Testing and Analysis: Process, Principles and Techniques. Wiley, New York (2007)
19. Mayr, H.: Projekt Engineering: Ingenieurmäßige Softwareentwicklung in Projektgruppen, 2nd edn. Hanser, München (2005)
20. Spillner, A., Roßner, T., Winter, M., Linz, T.: Praxiswissen Softwaretest—Testmanagement. Dpunkt, Heidelberg (2008)
21. Thomas, D., Hunt, A.: Mock objects. IEEE Softw **19**(3), 22–24 (2002)
22. Baier, C., Katoen, J.P.: Principles of Model Checking (Representation and Mind Series). MIT Press, Cambridge (2008)
23. http://heim.ifi.uio.no/trygver/themes/mvc/mvc-index.html

24. Lazic, L., Mastorakis N.: Orthogonal array application for optimal combination of software defect detection techniques choices. WSEAS. Trans. Comp. **7**(8), 1319–1336 (2008)
25. Linwood, J., Minter, D.: Building Portals with the Java Portlet API (Expert's Voice). Apress, Berkely (2004)
26. Perry, W.E.: Software Testen. Mitp-Verlag, Bonn (2003)
27. Grood, D.: TestGoal: Result-Driven Testing. Springer, Heidelberg (2008)
28. Dijkstra, E.W.: The humble programmer. Commun ACM **15**, 859–866 (1972)
29. Sneed, H.M., Winter, M.: Testen objektorientierter Software. Munchen, Hanser (2002)
30. Alper, M.: Professionelle Softwaretests: Praxis der Qualitätsoptimierung kommerzieller Software. Vieweg (1994)
31. Fewster, M., Graham, D.: Software Test Automation: Effective Use of Test Execution Tools. ACM Press/Addison-Wesley, New York (1999)
32. Beck K.: Test-Driven Development by Example. Addison-Wesley, Boston (2002)
33. Majchrzak, T.A., Kuchen, H.: IHK-Projekt Softwaretests: Auswertung. In: Working Papers, no. 2 in Working Papers. Förderkreis der Angewandten Informatik an derWestfälischen Wilhelms-Universität Münster e.V. (2010)
34. Pol, M., Koomen, T., Spillner, A.: Management und Optimierung des Testprozesses: Ein praktischer Leitfaden für erfolgreiches Testen von Software mit TPI und TMap, 2nd edn. dpunkt, Heidelberg (2002)
35. Vigenschow, U.: Objektorientiertes Testen und Testautomatisierung in der Praxis. Konzepte, Techniken und Verfahren. Dpunkt, Heidelberg (2005)
36. Wirth, N.: A plea for lean software. Computer **28**(2):64–68. http://doi.ieeecomputersociety.org/10.1109/2.348001 (1995)

Index